Data Communications

Data Communications

CONCEPTS AND APPLICATIONS

Tom McGovern

Northern Alberta Institute of Technology

Prentice-Hall Canada Inc., Scarborough, Ont.

Canadian Cataloguing in Publication Data

McGovern, Tom
  Data communications

Includes index.
ISBN 0-13-197385-1

1. Computer networks. 2. Computer networks –
Problems, exercises, etc. 3. Data transmission
systems. 4. Data transmissions systems – Problems,
exercises, etc. 5 Business – Data processing.
I. Title.

TK5105.5.M34 1988   004.6   C87-094680-3

Prentice-Hall, Inc., Englewood Cliffs, New Jersey
Prentice-Hall International, Inc., London
Prentice-Hall of Australia, Pty., Ltd., Sydney
Prentice-Hall of India Pvt., Ltd., New Delhi
Prentice-Hall of Japan, Inc., Tokyo
Prentice-Hall of Southeast Asia (Pte.) Ltd., Singapore
Editora Prentice-Hall do Brasil Ltda., Rio de Janeiro
Prentice-Hall Hispanoamericana, S.A., Mexico

ISBN 0-13-197385-1

Production editor: Edward O'Connor
Text and cover design: Brian Lehen
Manufacturing buyer: Matt Lumsdon
Composition: Computer Composition of Canada
Cover: A computer-generated image depicting packets — sets of bits packaged as
single units — travelling through a network (see The Network Control Level in
chapter 6, Protocol). Reproduced with the kind permission of Bell-Northern
Research Ltd.

Printed and bound in Canada by John Deyell Company

1 2 3 4 5   92 91 90 89 88

To Gill, my sweetheart of the roses

TABLE OF CONTENTS

PREFACE

The aim of this book is to provide an introduction to networks and their application both for business students and technologists, but especially for those students who plan to work as programmers, analysts, or end-users in a network environment.

Most computer installations make use of remote terminals and many computers access other computers via wide area networks. Public data networks are playing a larger role in the information needs of organizations that are geographically dispersed or that have need of external data from national and international sources. Within local centers, organizations are making more and more use of local area networks for sharing data and equipment. It is important that programmers, analysts, and users be familiar with the terminology and the applications of networks of all types.

The book is divided into three parts. The first part deals with the fundamentals of data communication and with the physical and functional characteristics of networks. Compared with an electronics text for technologists, the hardware coverage is relatively superficial. The emphasis is on software that is more appropriate to programmers, analysts, and users. The style is mainly descriptive, the content focuses on the ISO-OSI seven-level protocol model. Emphasis is placed on communications protocol, which lies at the heart of an understanding of networks, as well as on public and local area networks.

The second part of the book deals with the application of networks to data processing, from simple remote access to distributed processing applications. Distributed data processing and distributed database are still in their infancy as far as practical applications are concerned, with the possible exception of the concept of a local area network as a distributed system. The major network applications today are in micro/mainframe links and computer manufacturers' network architectures. This section includes examples of an academic network, an inter-city government network, and a national/international network.

The difficulty in teaching this material to programmers, analysts, and business students lies in the descriptive nature and the hardware content of the subject. In order to make the material more interesting, palatable, and comprehensible to non-technologists, I have developed simple practical exercises, demonstrations, and laboratories for use in my own course. The third part of the book consists of a series of sessions of varying degrees of difficulty that illustrate and reinforce the concepts of the first two parts of the book and that give the student a more practical grasp of data communications.

Throughout the book, I have used flowcharting wherever possible to explain network processes since this is a familiar technique to anyone who has programmed. I have also chosen to place the material in the context of the standards of the Consultative Committee for International Telephony and Telegraphy and of the International Standards Organization. As well as a glossary of the technical terms used in the book, I have included an acronym index, which perhaps reinforces the view that the data communications world is buried even more deeply than the computer world in acronyms.

ACKNOWLEDGMENTS

I want to thank my office mate, Jeff, for the development of the USART material and for the technical discussions that have at times verged on argument. I want to thank Rick not only for his painstaking editing but also for his pedagogical perception. I want to thank Terry, who developed the emulation lab, as well as Randy and Jim, all of whom taught the course with me and provided valuable criticism.

I am grateful to Kym and the rest of the N.A.I.T. data center staff for information on the NAIT network, to David Evans of the Alberta Government Network Management branch for several valuable discussions and help with the description of the AGN network, and to Myron Kupnowicki of Interprovincial Pipe Line Limited for information and editorial comment on the IPL network. These valuable contributions give the book a sense of reality.

I wish to thank my reviewers for their detailed and constructive criticism. It took some adjustment on my part, but the criticism no doubt contributes to the quality of the book and to its usefulness to students. My reviewers were R.G. Bell, Durham College; Neil Robb, Sheridan College; William Beesley, Seneca College; Patricia Jones, Mohawk College; and Clive Simmons, British Columbia Institute of Technology.

The process of producing a book is interesting and complex. I was fortunate to have Ed O'Connor of Prentice-Hall Canada as my editor. I would like to thank him not only for giving the book form and consistency but also for making the experience of the publishing process a mostly pleasant one. I'd also like to thank Monica Schwalbe for, among other things, assistance with the *Instructor's Manual.*

Finally I would like to thank my students over the last eight years who have continued to surprise and delight me with their insights and make my work so much fun. I would also like to thank Janet and Ruth, two special students, who put up with a part-time Dad for a while.

INTRODUCTION

When starting to study a new subject, it is helpful to consider a broad overview of the material. This provides the student with a framework that can be used to associate the details, concepts, and relationships of the subject. This broad overview, by its nature, is an oversimplification of reality, but it provides a basis for the gradual accumulation of the subject matter in the student's mind. It may even be important, initially, to avoid those questions which can lead to a deeper understanding of one aspect of the subject, in order to build a basic structure. If education is "a process of diminishing deception," the corollary may be that you must understand the broad relationships before you can appreciate the subtleties. With this in mind, I have created a model that describes the layout of this book and provides a framework for data communications networks. It deals with hardware and software, with physical and functional characteristics, and with layers of relationships (fig. I).

Fundamentals

At the center of the model lie the fundamentals: definitions, terminology, basic concepts. They provide the foundation on which to build understanding.

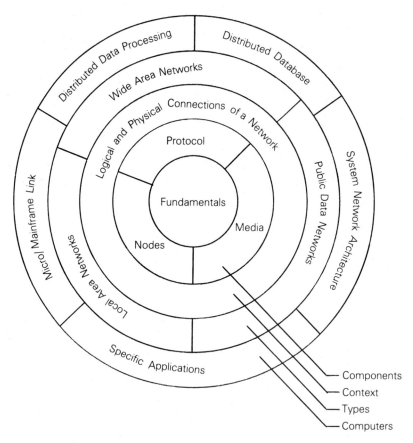

Inner circle: Fundamentals

Middle ring: Protocol, Nodes, Media

Ring: Logical and Physical Connections of a Network, Specific Applications

Outer ring labels: Distributed Data Processing, Wide Area Networks, Distributed Database, System Network Architecture, Public Data Networks, Micro/ Mainframe Link, Local Area Networks

Legend:
— Components
— Context
— Types
— Computers

Figure I Topic relation diagram for data communications systems

Components

The component layer of the model has three parts: the *nodes* are centers of activity, the *media* link the nodes, and *protocol* controls the transactions.

Nodes can be end points in the network, in which case they use the network to transmit and receive information. Nodes within the network provide routes and services to the end points with the requisite speed, accuracy, and reliability.

There are a variety of media that connect network nodes and play a major role in network performance. An important provider of connectivity in networks is the telephone system.

Perhaps the most interesting part of a network is where hardware becomes software and vice versa. This occurs within a network's protocol, which provides the means and control of the information movement in the network. Network protocol is of such complexity that it is implemented as a series of levels, each having a specific responsibility and each communicating with the level below and the level above.

Context

The next layer on the diagram represents the context of the network. The most obvious context is that of geography. As well as the physical location of nodes, the population centers will govern major routing junctions in a national network.

The choice of path between two end points is another important contextual consideration. The path between two telephone subscribers is a temporary combination of specific portions of the line which may change every time the end points are connected. Another kind of path common to data communications networks is the logical path, which is traced by means of identification imbedded in the information as it moves through the network.

Types

The major network types include the wide area or distance networks which may span cities, countries, or continents. Local area networks are confined to contiguous buildings and are used as much for resource sharing as for communications. Public data networks, supplied by independent network organizations and telephone companies, provide an important way of sharing distance communications costs as well as a focus for standardization strategies on a global basis.

Computers

The final layer of data communications systems refers to the purpose of these systems, which is the exchange of information processed by computers. Distributed data processing and distributed database are conceptual ways of sharing computer resources effectively. These ideas are partially realized in local area networks, in connecting microcomputers to mainframe computers, and in the integration of a specific manufacturer's computer systems under a common architecture. The description of specific real data communications networks provides insight into the nature of networks.

If all of this seems a trifle heavy for an introduction, it may be that this description of the contents of the book and this model of the constituents of networks will be more useful as you progress through the text. You may wish to return to this section from time to time to clarify specifics that you find in the remainder of the book.

SECTION A
NETWORKS

Telecommunications can be defined as the process of sending and receiving information. The principal sources of the information may be people, computers, or cameras. The telephone system was created for the transmission of voice, but because of the cost of building communication links on a national and international scale, the telephone system has been adapted for data communication between computers and terminals. Although voice is now the major form of communication between business organizations, there is a growing need for data communication within and between organizations. Data processing has become a central controlling function within business organizations. The distribution of this information, both locally and to remote places, is of primary importance for the efficient functioning of any business. In most organizations, data processing leads to a requirement for data transmission. The future of information communication lies in the integration of facilities for voice, data, and pictures for facsimile transmission, freeze-frame television, and video conferencing.

DATA COMMUNICATIONS NETWORKS

The word *network* is a broad term similar in meaning to system. Both terms are used to describe organized complexity. A data communications network can be defined as a collection of computers, terminals, and related devices connected by communications facilities. Data communications networks are concerned principally with the transfer of information between computers and terminals. As the number of terminals and computers in a network increases, problems concerned with the design, efficiency, cost, and control of such networks become paramount.

To begin with, a network can be described as a group of *nodes* connected by *media*. These nodes can be either *terminations* or *junctions*. Terminations are devices, including computers and computer terminals, that are connected to the network for the purpose of sending or receiving information. Junctions are devices that perform such functions as completing a link between two terminals (switching), deciding in which order the various information transfers should take place (scheduling), and allocating temporary storage of information along the route of its travel (buffering). The connecting medium may come in the form of an electrical conductor, a light-beam channel, or

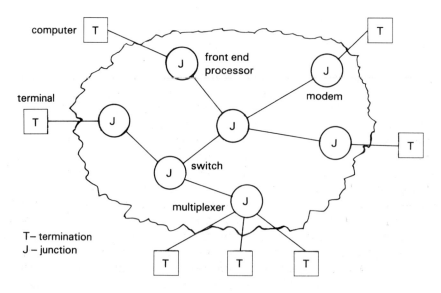

Figure A-1   Network Nodes

even free space. Figure A-1 illustrates the basic components of a network and the interrelationship of the nodes.

Before we can study data communications networks we must establish a common background in terms of vocabulary and concept. As in the computer industry, network technology is changing rapidly, and this is naturally accompanied by a vocabulary that is constantly being expanded, redefined, and abused by an industry whose members are all seeking a competitive edge in the marketplace. Nevertheless it is possible to define the basic terms and explain the fundamental concepts of data communication, and this is the intent of chapter 1. (For the sake of easy reference, the reader will also find a glossary of terms and an acronym index at the end of the book.) We can console ourselves with the notion that this is the price we must pay for participating in an exciting and quickly developing field.

Networks can be described in many different ways, for example:

in terms of the medium (the physical path between components):

    twisted pair
    coaxial cable
    optical fibers
    air (radio transmission)

in terms of their components:

    terminations: terminals
                    personal computers
                    mainframe computers

    junctions: multiplexers
                  front-end processors
                  switches

in terms of their topology (layout):

    irregular
    bus
    tree
    ring
    star

in terms of the network's protocol (how it functions):

    BISYNC
    X.25
    CSMA/CD
    Token passing

These terms may be unfamiliar to you now but by the end of Section A we will have covered:

fundamentals		(chapter 1)
media		(chapter 2)
components:	terminations	(chapter 3)
	junctions	(chapter 4)
connections		(chapter 5)
protocol		(chapter 6)

In addition, we will have considered the major network types to which we can apply these dimensions, namely:

public networks	(chapter 7)
local area networks	(chapter 8).

Section A begins with a pretest (fig. A-2), a good way of finding out a group's data communication background, and of promoting a discussion on the goals and objectives of a course.

DATA COMMUNICATION CONCEPTS

PRETEST

Match the terms below with the definitions following:

a. baud
b. DDP
c. serial
d. asynchronous
e. Baudot
f. modem
g. half-duplex
h. modulation
i. DTE
j. USART

k. PACX
l. data link control
m. protocol
n. F.E.P.
o. B.E.P.
p. self reconfiguring
q. multiplexing
r. routing
s. LAN
t. SNA

DEFINITIONS

1. A private automatic computer exchange.
2. A set of rules.
3. Processing applications in a remotely connected installation.
4. Bits are sent over a channel one by one.
5. A data communication term for a network node called data termination equipment.
6. A universal synchronous/asynchronous receiver transmitter.
7. A unit of transmission speed, usually one bit per second.
8. A five-bit code used in telegraphy.
9. A device for modulating and demodulating signals.
10. Transmission between terminals that do not operate in synchronism.
11. A network restricted to a few buildings located adjacent to each other in a local area.
12. A processor used to handle data base requests.
13. A processor to handle terminal requests.
14. Communication in one direction at a time.
15. A terminal that can simulate other terminals.
16. A technique used to send information over long distances.
17. The division of a communication facility into separate channels.
18. IBM's network architecture.
19. The second level of ISO-OSI.
20. The paths information takes in a network.

Figure A-2   Pretest

Chapter

1

FUNDAMENTALS

INTRODUCTION

There are several reasons for establishing a common vocabulary. First, it is as important to establish good communication between people as it is between machines. Data processors have to converse with technical personnel, to read and evaluate performance specifications for new hardware, to use communications software ranging from simple terminal emulation to sophisticated multilevel protocols. They are also called upon to employ a variety of unfamiliar databases using unfamiliar networks. For these reasons, it is essential for them to become familiar with the basic terms and concepts associated with data communications, not from a mathematical or electrical viewpoint but from a descriptive and functional viewpoint.

Data transmission involves the production, movement, and delivery of information over a transmission medium between a transmitter and a receiver (fig. 1-1) and includes consideration of:

- — the type of signal or information to be sent,
- — conversion of the data to a form suitable for the medium,
- — the quality of information received,
- — the number of users, and
- — the cost of transmission.

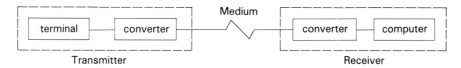

Figure 1-1   Data Transmission

TERMINOLOGY

Information is produced, moved, and delivered as electrical signals. These signals have two forms: analog and digital. *Analog* signals are continuous and can be thought of as electrical voltages that vary continuously with time (fig. 1-2). For example, the voltage in a battery, which is related to its power, starts out constant then gradually decreases with use. Historically, analog signals are associated with sound and the telephone system, but since this system is so widely available, it has also been adapted as a medium for transmitting computer data.

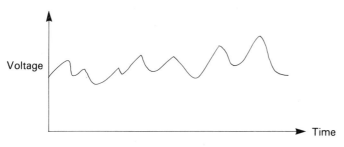

Figure 1-2   Analog Signal

Digital signals are discrete signals that have two stable states. For example, five volts can be thought of as a true condition or a logic "one" state and zero volts can be considered a false condition or a logic "zero" state (fig. 1-3). This is how information is stored in a computer. These patterns of ones and zeros are grouped together in codes that can represent alphabetic characters, numbers, special characters (like the asterisk), and control information. Data transmission is primarily concerned with the transmission of computer codes (digital signals) over what has traditionally been a medium designed for voice (analog signals) and thus requires conversion facilities. Researchers have gradually been implementing a digital transmission medium in the telephone system to support the demand for a way of transmitting digital signals from the computer directly.

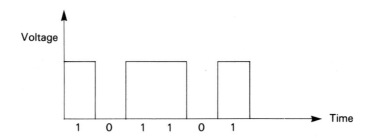

Voltage

Time

1   0   1   1   0   1

Figure 1-3   Digital Signal

   Analog transmission is more complex than digital transmission because it involves modification of the original signal. This is performed by a second signal that supports or carries the information signal. This second signal is called a *carrier*. The information signal is said to modulate the carrier. *Modulation* is the process of converting an information signal into a form suitable for analog transmission. The carrier is a special type of analog signal known as a sinusoidal waveform or sine wave and has attributes that can be altered to facilitate analog transmission. The attributes that can be altered are amplitude, frequency, and phase. Figure 1-4 shows one cycle of a carrier waveform. The *amplitude* of the signal is a measure of its size and can be thought of as the maximum voltage reached. Since this signal is continuous, the sine wave is repeated for the duration of the transmission. The *frequency* is

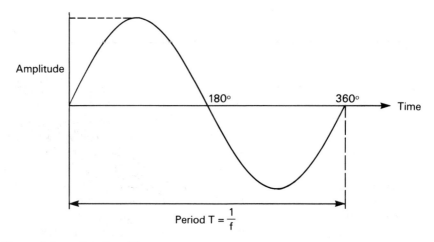

Amplitude

180°   360°   Time

$$\text{Period } T = \frac{1}{f}$$

Figure 1-4   The Sine Wave

the number of complete waveforms or cycles per unit time measured in cycles per seconds (cps) or hertz (hz). The *period* of the waveform is the inverse of the frequency and is a measure of the time taken to generate one cycle. Two carriers with the same amplitude and frequency can be displaced horizontally from each other. This means that they are out of phase. One cycle of a sinusoidal wave is considered to be three hundred and sixty degrees. *Phase* angle is the displacement between two sine waves of equal amplitude and equal frequency (fig. 1-5).

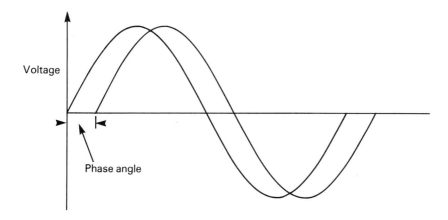

Figure 1-5   The Phase Angle

Bandwidth is the range of frequencies present in a particular signal or the capacity of a path or channel used to transmit signals. The bandwidth of a voice signal is 3 khz (300 to 3300 hz). The capacity or bandwidth of a telephone line is much greater than this. The full use of the line can be realised by modulating several voice signals at different carrier frequencies and transmitting them all simultaneously. For example if we allocate 4 khz per voice signal (one khz to avoid interference) and we have a channel capacity of 48 khz, then we can transmit 12 voice signals at the same time all with different carrier frequencies (fig. 1-6). This process is known as *broadband* transmission. If we send the one voice signal at its original frequency without modulation the process is known as *baseband* transmission. Although in this example baseband is much less efficient than broadband, there are applications for which baseband has the advantage, but more of that in chapter 8, which discusses the distinction between baseband and broadband local area networks.

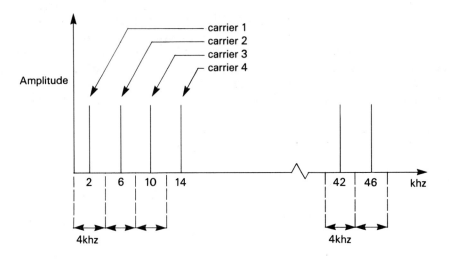

Figure 1-6   Allocation of Carriers over 48khz Bandwidth

TRANSMISSION

Analog Transmission

Computer information signals are usually digital in nature, but to be transmitted over telephone lines they must be converted to analog signals. The process of conversion is called modulation. The device that performs the conversion is called the *Modem* (MOdulator-DEModulator) or data communication equipment (DCE). The device sending or receiving the information is called data terminal equipment (DTE), and it may be either a terminal or a computer. In order to transmit data over the telephone system, modems are used to convert the digital information signal into an analog form for transmission and then reconvert it to its original form (fig. 1-7).

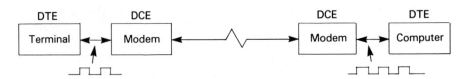

Figure 1-7   A Modem Link

Modems operate in one of three modes: simplex, half-duplex, or full-duplex. In North America the terms have the following meanings.

Simplex operation indicates transmission in one direction only. The modems either receive or transmit. Examples of this mode include the ticker tape system of the stock exchange, and the arrival/departure monitors at airports.

Half-duplex lines can transmit in either direction, but only in one direction at any particular time. Modems are switched back and forth between transmit and receive, resulting in some loss of transmission time due to this process. In many applications integrity of the data is more important than speed. There are a number of microcomputer packages on the market, highly regarded for their reliability, that operate in half-duplex.

Full-duplex lines can transmit in both directions simultaneously. Obviously more efficient than half-duplex, full-duplex requires both the terminal and the computer to be able to send and receive simultaneously. This means a more sophisticated software package associated with high-speed communication (fig. 1-8).

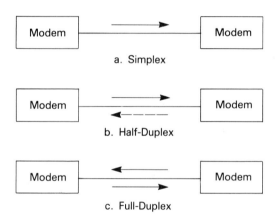

Figure 1-8   Modem Operation

Modem Modulation Techniques

Three basic types of modulation schemes are used to convert digital data into a suitable analog signal.

Amplitude modulation, in which the digital signal (information), often referred to as a series of pulses or "pulse train," is used to select one of two amplitudes associated with the analog signal (carrier).

Frequency modulation, in which the digital data is used to select one of two frequencies associated with the carrier.

Phase modulation, in which the digital data is used to change the phase of the carrier.

In each case the transmitted signal is demodulated (returned to its original form) by the receiving modem. These modulation schemes are illustrated in figure 1-9.

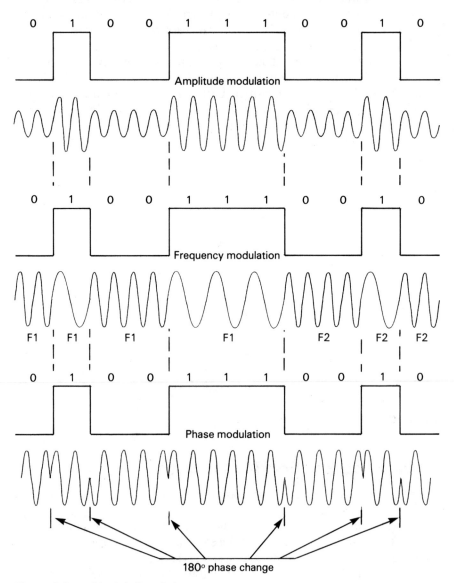

Figure 1-9   Modulation Schemes

Bits and Bauds

The term *baud* is used to indicate the rate at which changes occur in a signal over a given period of time. It is the unit of signaling speed or modulation rate, and is found by taking the reciprocal of the time taken up by one signal event. In the past, the digital signal was transmitted as a two-level signal, so that the number of bits-per-second, the bit rate, was the same as the baud rate. Now that digital signals can be transmitted as four-, or eight-level signals, the bit rate is correspondingly twice or three times the baud rate. To avoid confusion, we will always refer to the rate at which data is transmitted as the bit rate and measure this in bits-per-second (bps).

Digital Transmission

Digital transmission occurs when the information is transmitted in its original form. Although conversion, in the form of modulation, is not required, energy loss in the signal can be a problem over long distances.

Although our emphasis in data transmission is on digital information, it is worth noting that the transmission of voice over a digital medium is becoming increasingly popular. In this case the voice signals are converted into digital signals using a *codec* (COder-DECoder), which accomplishes what the modem does but in reverse: analog-to-digital conversion for transmission and back to analog at the receiver (fig. 1-10).

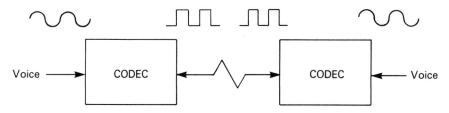

Figure 1-10   The Coder/Decoder

The method used to convert the analog signal to digital form for transmission is called pulse modulation. The most common form of pulse modulation is pulse amplitude modulation (PAM), which generates a digital pulse of different height for each different height of the analog signal. When each digital pulse is further encoded to a two-level pulse train for transmission, the process is referred to as pulse code modulation (PCM).

CODES

Information is converted by terminals and computers into digital pulses. Codes are used to give meaning to a group of pulses (ones and zeros); for example, in one code the letter A is represented by 1000001.

There have been two streams of development of codes, one for telecommunications and one for computers. First, in telecommunications the *Morse* code and the *Baudot* code preceded the now internationally accepted American Standard Code for the Interchange of Information (ASCII).

Secondly, in the early days of computers, each manufacturer developed his own code, but it soon became apparent that this was contrary to the best interests of the manufacturer, the user, and the computer industry as a whole. Because of the predominance of IBM, the Extended Binary Coded Decimal Information Code (EBCDIC) emerged as the standard for the computer industry.

The Baudot Code

The Baudot code (fig. 1-11) is a five-bit code used mainly for telegraphy and for some keyboards, printers, and readers. Although five bits can accommodate only thirty-two unique codes, two of the codes, "figures" (FIGS) and "letters" (LTRS), extend the capacity of the Baudot code. Preceding the other bit combinations by either FIGS or LTRS permits dual definition of the remaining codes. In other words, each bit combination could represent either a particular letter, or a particular number or special character, depending on whether a LTRS character or a FIGS character comes before it. A substantial amount of international data communications traffic uses the Baudot code.

The ASCII Code

The ASCII code (fig. 1-12) is a seven-bit-plus-parity code. Most communication terminals on the market today are designed to conform to ASCII format. Some manufacturers, however, use minor variations of the ASCII code to make it more applicable to special-purpose terminals. For example, a card reader/line printer terminal that communicates using asynchronous transmission might use the SYN code (normally used for establishing synchronization during synchronous transmission) as a control character to indicate that the printer is out of paper. The parity bit is another change that many manufacturers make. Figure 1-13 identifies the purpose of the control characters. There are three categories of control character: communication control (CC), format effector (FE), and information separator (IS). We shall be primarily interested in the communication control characters.

CHARACTER		BIT POSITION				
LOWER CASE	UPPER CASE	1	2	3	4	5
A	.	•	•			
B	?	•			•	•
C	:		•	•	•	
D	S	•			•	
E	3	•				
F	!	•		•	•	
G	8		•		•	•
H	#			•		•
I	8		•	•		
J	'	•	•		•	
K	(	•	•	•	•	
L	)		•			•
M	.			•	•	•
N	,			•	•	
O	9				•	•
P	0		•	•		•
Q	1	•	•	•		•
R	4		•		•	
S	BELL	•		•		
T	5					•
U	7	•	•	•		
V	;		•	•	•	•
W	2	•	•			•
X	/	•		•	•	•
Y	6	•		•		•
Z	"	•				•
LETTERS (SHIFT TO LOWER CASE)		•	•	•	•	•
FIGURES (SHIFT TO UPPER CASE)		•	•		•	•
SPACE				•		
CARRIAGE RETURN					•	
LINE FEED			•			
BLANK						
PRESENCE OF • INDICATES MARK BIT ABSENCE OF • INDICATES SPACE BIT						

Figure 1-11 The Baudot Code

MOST SIGNIFICANT DIGIT (HEX)

LEAST SIGNIFICANT DIGIT (HEX)	0	1	2	3	4	5	6	7
0	NUL	DLE	SP	0	@	P	`	p
1	SOX	DC1	!	1	A	Q	a	q
2	STX	DC2	"	2	B	R	b	r
3	ETX	DC3	#	3	C	S	c	s
4	EOT	DC4	$	4	D	T	d	t
5	ENQ	NAK	%	5	E	U	e	u
6	ACK	SYN	&	6	F	V	f	v
7	BEL	ETB	'	7	G	W	g	w
8	BS	CAN	(	8	H	X	h	x
9	HT	EM	)	9	I	Y	i	y
A	LF	SUB	*	:	J	Z	j	z
B	VT	ESC	+	;	K	[	k	{
C	FF	FS	,	<	L	\	l		
D	CR	GS	-	=	M	]	m	}
E	SO	RS	.	>	N	^	n	~
F	SI	US	/	?	O	—	o	DEL

Figure 1-12 The ASCII Code

code	mnemonic	meaning	category
0	NUL	null character	
1	SOH	start of header	CC
2	STX	start of text	CC
3	ETX	end of text	CC
4	EOT	end of transmission	CC
5	ENQ	enquiry	CC
6	ACK	acknowledge	CC
7	BEL	bell	
8	BS	backspace	FE
9	HT	horizontal tabulation	FE
10	LF	line feed	FE
11	VT	vertical tabulation	FE
12	FF	form feed	FE
13	CR	carriage return	FE
14	SO	shift out	
15	SI	shift in	
16	DLE	data link escape	CC
17	DC1	device control 1 (XON)	CC
18	DC2	device control 2	
19	DC3	device control 3 (XOFF)	CC
20	DC4	device control 4	
21	NAK	negative acknowledge	CC
22	SYN	synchronization character	CC
23	ETB	end of transmission block	CC
24	CAN	cancel	
25	EM	end of medium	
26	SUB	substitute	
27	ESC	escape	
28	FS	file separator	IS
29	GS	group separator	IS
30	RS	record separator	IS
31	US	unit separator	IS
127	DEL	delete	

Figure 1-13   The Control Characters

The EBCDIC Code

IBM's EBCDIC code (fig. 1-14) has its roots in data processing. Its origins can be traced to 1884, when Herman Hollerith created the twelve-bit Hollerith code for punched cards, long before computers were invented. The computer version of this was the binary coded decimal (BCD) code, a six-bit compression of the Hollerith code. The EBCDIC code is the BCD code extended to eight bits. The extra capacity is used for additional control codes as well as for providing spare capacity for future expansion. The main problem with this code for communications purposes is the lack of a parity bit for error checking. The solutions are to convert back and forth between ASCII and EBCDIC, and, in the IBM world, to incorporate other forms of error checking.

LEAST SIGNIFICANT DIGIT (HEX)

	0	1	2	3	4	5	6	7	8	9	A	B	C	D	E	F
0	NUL	SOH	STX	ETX	PF	HT	LC	DEL			SMM	VT	FF	CR	SO	SI
1	DLE	DC_1	DC_2	DC_3	RES	NL	BS	IL	CAN	EM	CC		IFS	IGS	IRS	IUS
2	DS	SOS	FS		BYP	LF	EOB	PRE			SM			ENQ	ACK	BEL
3			SYN		PN	RS	UC	EOT					DC_4	NAK		SUB
4	SP										¢	.	<	(	+	|
5	&										!	$	*	)	;	¬
6	-	/										,	%	–	>	?
7											:	#	@	'	=	''
8		a	b	c	d	e	f	g	h	i						
9		j	k	l	m	n	o	p	q	r						
A			s	t	u	v	w	x	y	z						
B																
C		A	B	C	D	E	F	G	H	I						
D		J	K	L	M	N	O	P	Q	R						
E			S	T	U	V	W	X	Y	Z						
F	0	1	2	3	4	5	6	7	8	9						

(MOST SIGNIFICANT DIGIT (HEX))

Figure 1-14   The EBCDIC Code

INTERFACE

PARALLEL TRANSMISSION

To transmit a code character, the bits can be transmitted either in parallel or serial fashion. In parallel data transmission, all code elements are transmitted simultaneously. That means that for the five-level Baudot code, five pairs of lines must interconnect the receiver and transmitter (fig. 1-15). Parallel transmission is only used over short distances and is therefore restricted to communication between devices in the computer center, for example between the processor and the printer.

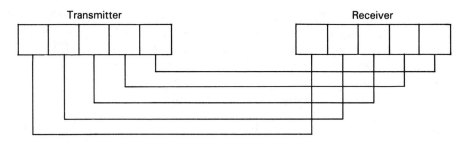

Figure 1-15   Parallel Data Transmission

SERIAL TRANSMISSION

In serial data transmission each code element is sent sequentially (fig. 1-16). This requires only one pair of wire conductors for interconnecting the receiver to the transmitter. Serial transmission forms the basis of network communication. Whether the network nodes are geographically remote as in wide area networks or quite close together in local area networks, serial communication is obviously more economical, although slower, than parallel transmission.

Figure 1-16   Serial Data Transmission

PARALLEL/SERIAL TRANSMISSION

If we can visualize characters moving around the computer on an eight-lane highway that must be reduced to a single-lane bridge to reach another computer or a terminal, then we can see the need for a device that acts as a traffic policeman. This device must convert the parallel traffic to serial for external transmission and convert the incoming serial traffic to parallel for computer processing. Such a device is the Universal Synchronous/Asynchronous Receiver/Transmitter (USART) (fig. 1-17). The USART is available as an integrated circuit or "chip" that permits the selection of a number of parameters, including baud rate and modem control. Since this device is found in all terminals and in all computers, even for communication between the computer and local terminals, we will examine it in detail.

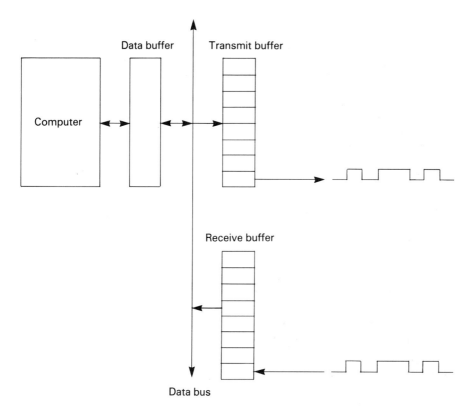

Figure 1-17   The USART

Synchronous and Asynchronous Serial Communication

All remote communication is serial. There are two ways of implementing this serial communication: synchronously and asynchronously.

Asynchronous communication is the simpler of the two in that each character is transmitted independently of all other characters. In order to separate the characters and synchronize transmission, a start bit precedes the character and a stop bit follows it. Information can be transmitted at typewriter speed or, in the case of micro to mainframe communication, at speeds up to 56 000 bits per second (56 kbps). As an example of asynchronous serial transmission, consider the transmission of the letter E in the ASCII code (fig. 1-18). The data bits of each character are preceded by a start bit which is always a zero and followed by an optional parity bit and one or more stop bits.

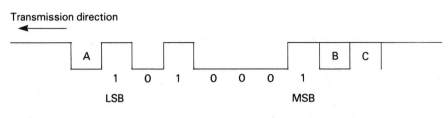

A = start bit
B = optional parity bit
C = stop bit
$1000101_2 = 45_{16}$ = E(ASCII)

Figure 1-18   Asynchronous Transmission of an "E"

In the idle condition, the transmission remains in the one state. As soon as a zero is detected, the receiver begins to detect the incoming character. After seven bits (or eight bits if there is a parity bit), a stop bit should be detected and the receiver is ready for the next character. Because the start and stop bits take up a significant amount of time, the information throughput is less than for the case where they are not present.

Synchronous transmission (fig. 1-19) is used for the high-speed transmission of a block of characters. Synchronization is established by preceding the data block with SYN control characters. The sending modem clock controls the timing of each bit in the block of characters sent, including the SYN characters. The receiving modem clock uses the SYN characters to establish clock timing for the rest of the block. This process occurs for each block transmitted and received. Each block is also terminated by SYN characters.

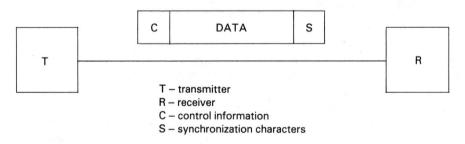

T – transmitter
R – receiver
C – control information
S – synchronization characters

Figure 1-19   Synchronous Transmission

Interface Standards

Early in the history of planning data communications networks, the Electronic Industries Association (EIA) accepted a set of standards for the interconnection of DTEs and DCEs known as the EIA RS-232-C specification. This standard contains:

1. the electrical signal characteristics,
2. the interface mechanical characteristics, and
3. a minimal amount of control information.

New standards continue to appear as both computer and telecommunications technology advance. Any attempt to upgrade operational equipment to a new standard is seriously undermined by the costs involved. For this reason, and because it has been so successful, the RS-232-C specification will continue to be a major communication standard.

SUMMARY

Data transmission is concerned primarily with the transmission of computer data over the telephone system. Computer data is digital in nature, but the transmission process is analog in nature. The digital signal must be converted to analog for transmission, a process that is called modulation. There are three forms of modulation: amplitude, frequency, and phase.

The serial communication taking place between two nodes of a computer network is most often simultaneous in both directions (full-duplex), and may be synchronous or asynchronous. The meaning of the information transferred is often conveyed using the ASCII code.

In this chapter we have attempted to introduce the terminology and ideas that are at the heart of data communications without burying the reader in a morass of jargon and detail. The first part of Section C is aimed at reinforcing these fundamentals in an interesting, problem-solving manner.

Review Questions for Chapter 1

1. Calculate the transmission time for a 10-page report with an average of 50 lines per page, 10 words per line, 6 characters per word transmitted over a 4800 bps line (excluding control considerations) using 7-level ASCII plus parity.

2. Match the following terms with their definitions.

    a. speed   _____   f. parallel   _____
    b. asynchronous   _____   g. bandwidth   _____
    c. simplex   _____   h. modem   _____
    d. analog signal   _____   i. channels   _____
    e. full-duplex   _____

    i. A remote terminal that can send and receive would be attached to this line.

    ii. Transmission of data by character.

    iii. The radio broadcast of the news.

    iv. The difference between the upper and lower frequency of a channel.

    v. Transmission between computer and printer where printer has no control.

    vi. Transmission of data bit by bit.

    vii. Device that converts signals between digital and analog.

    viii. Control information is provided with each character.

    ix. A line carrying information both ways at the same time.

    x. 0 to 300 hz.

    xi. A path for transmission between stations.

3. How many unique information codes can the BAUDOT code accommodate?

4. What is the computer industry standard code?

5. Identify the main classes of code within the ASCII code.

6. Are asynchronous transmissions clocked?

7. On what kind of circuit would turnaround time be a factor?

8. Add the even parity bit for 1011010 __ .

9. List two major advantages for both synchronous and asynchronous communication.

Advantage	synchronous	asynchronous
1		
2		

10. Describe the main function of a USART.

11. Why is alternating current more useful for transmission than direct current?

12. Draw the asynchronous pulse train for the ASCII character "8", including odd parity.

Chapter

MEDIA

INTRODUCTION

The public telephone system has been a major factor in the development of
networks that have been able to take advantage of a connection system
already in place. Computers in the same building, the same campus, the same
city, the same province or state, and so on, already have the means of
communicating via the telephone. Unfortunately, the public telephone system was not designed for data communication but was intended for voice
communication. This has caused problems for data communications since
the transmission requirements are more stringent, particularly with respect to
noise interference and transmission speed. A variety of measures can be taken
to make the public telephone voice-grade lines more suitable for data
transmission.

The telephone systems of the world are managed by common carrier
organizations (usually telephone companies), and once the need to adapt and
upgrade their services became apparent, the common carrier became a key
component in the development of data transmission services. In virtually
every country of the world there is a regulatory agency that controls communication services.

In Canada, the federal government regulates communication services
through the Canadian Radio, Television and Telecommunication Commission (CRTC). Data communication services are provided by Telecom Canada, an association of the nine major telephone companies in the country.

In the United States, the Federal Communications Commission (FCC) is a federal government agency that regulates interstate and international communications. Since the deregulation of the American Telephone and Telegraph Company (AT&T), data communications services are provided by a variety of local and long distance carriers that include former AT&T operating companies.

Since our discussion includes small networks confined to a few buildings, called local area networks, it is important to note at this point that these small networks are privately owned and not subject to government regulations. Only wide area networks using facilities supplied by common carriers are subject to government regulations.

All computer networks have as a common element the medium of transmission. The form of the medium is dependent on a number of factors, including the volume of data, the distance involved, the rate of transmission and, most importantly, the cost of communication. Some of the media described in this chapter are used in wide area networks, some in local area networks, and some in both.

THE TELEPHONE SYSTEM

Facilities

The public telephone system provides two basic services, the normal dial-up connection that is provided to most homes, and a permanent connection between two subscriber points. Dial-up lines are often referred to as switched lines because the connection between two telephones requires a series of intermediate switches to be activated. One important characteristic of this service is that each time the connection is made a different path can be traced through the telephone network. This makes it impossible to control the quality of the connection between the two subscriber points.

The permanent connection or private line is leased from the telephone company, and since there is a single traceable line between the two subscriber points, the opportunity exists to improve the quality of the line. Private lines are generally less prone to noise than dial-up lines, are always available, and more expensive than dial-ups.

There are three categories of data transmission facilities available either directly from the telephone company or indirectly from private organizations, depending on which country you are in.

1.   The existing telephone network provides both dial-up and leased line facilities. Dial-up connections tend to be noisy and useful only for low-speed asynchronous and synchronous data transmission up to 2400 bps. Leased

lines operate up to 2400 bps on asynchronous connections, and 9600 bps on synchronous lines.

2. Data networks provide digital transmission facilities (no modulation involved) for high-speed, high-volume transmission over long distances. In Canada, there are three data networks available from Telecom Canada.

a) Datalink, a switched digital data transmission service, in which the cost is based on use of the service, in the same way that the long-distance telephone call is charged on the basis of connection time.

b) Dataroute provides dedicated routes between major Canadian centres and is similar to the leased-line analog facility. Costs are based on the distance between the points of communication.

c) Datapac uses packet-switching, a store-and-forward process that divides data into packets that are transmitted independently and reassembled at the destination. Charges are based on the volume of data transmitted rather than the time or distance involved. Datapac is referred to as a packet-switched data network or PSDN. CN/CP Telecommunications provide similar facilities.

   In the United States similar facilities are available. Measured-use services include the wide area telecommunication service (WATS). There are digital private line services for both point-to-point and multipoint lines (a one-to-many form of communication often used between a computer and a group of terminals). PSDNs are provided by private companies such as Telenet and Tymnet and often categorized as value added networks (VAN). VANs lease telephone lines from a carrier, add hardware to improve the speed and quality of transmission, and provide other data transmission services.

3. Other services include message-switching services used for electronic mail, commercial and governmental database enquiry, word processor and electronic typewriter intercommunication systems, and satellite-based systems.

CONNECTIONS

Telephones are connected to each other via a hierarchy of switching centers. The lowest-level switching center is called the *end office* or *central office*. The central office can service up to 10 000 subscribers per exchange code within its local exchange area. This area is one in which subscribers can reach each other without paying toll charges. An exchange area can be serviced by one central office rurally or several central offices in a city. The last four digits of a telephone number can be thought of as the address of a telephone relative to a particular central office. The preceding three digits of the telephone number, the exchange code, identify the address of the central office. This means that there can be up to 1000 central offices per toll office, the next level up. Remember, subscribers can only access other subscribers connected to other central offices toll free within the local exchange area (fig. 2-1). The connection between the subscriber and the central office is called a *local loop*. Central offices within a local exchange area are connected by inter-office trunk lines.

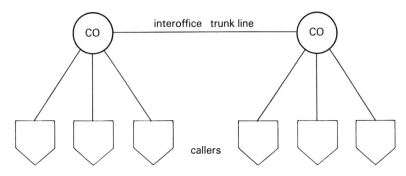

Note: CO = Central Office

Figure 2-1   Local Exchange Area

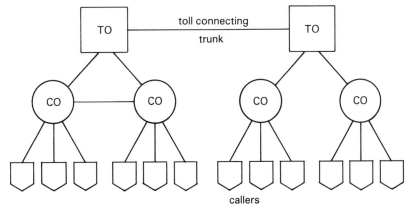

Note: CO = Central Office
      TO = Toll Office

Figure 2-2   Toll Office

An area code, the three digits that come before the seven-digit telephone number, is used to identify a large geographical area and the address of the toll office. Two types of long distance calls may be made.

1.   Outside the local exchange area but within the area code requires a '1' + central office address (3 digits) + subscriber address (4 digits).

2.   Outside the area code requires a '1' + toll office address (3 digits) + central office address (3 digits) + subscriber address (4 digits).

All long distance calls are routed through the toll office (fig. 2-2).

The hierarchical system continues upward with the primary office, the sectional office, and finally the regional office. There are ten regional offices in the USA and two in Canada that manage operations in the most populated areas and provide network control functions for the rest of the hierarchy (fig. 2-3).

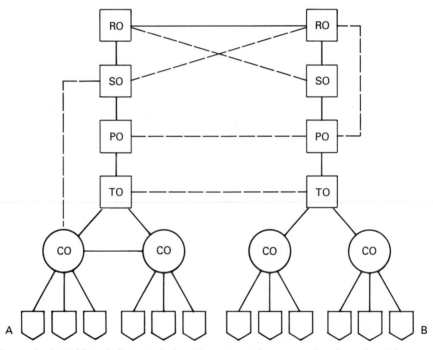

Note: the dotted lines indicate typical routing patterns between subscribers A and B.

CO = Central Office   TO = Toll Office
PO = Primary Office   SO = Sectional Office
RO = Regional Office

Figure 2-3   The Hierarchy

TRANSMISSION MEDIA

The transmission medium is the physical path between nodes of a network. In wide area networks, the physical path can be wires, cables, fibers, microwave guides, or the atmosphere via radio transmitters or satellites. In local area networks the choice is limited to wires, cables, fibers, and radio transmission.

Open-wire Pairs

Open-wire pairs consist of copper or copper-sheathed steel wires hung from poles. The major advantage of the open wire system was its ability to carry voice-grade communication over long distances without amplification, an important factor in the pre-vacuum tube, pre-transistor, pre-integrated circuit days. From today's perspective, it may appear primitive and full of problems such as severe crosstalk (signals interfering with each other), cable resistance, and physical bulk. Nevertheless, it was the earliest practical form of a communication medium.

Twisted Pair

A twisted pair consists of two insulated wires wound round each other to minimize interference from other pairs in a multiwire cable. This is a traditional form of wiring in telephone systems and for that reason is readily available and inexpensive. Twisted pair cabling is also easy to install. The main disadvantage is that it is susceptible to electrical interference that can cause the transmitted information to be garbled. One solution to this problem is shielding the twisted pair with a metallic alloy that reduces the vulnerability of the wires and increases the cost. Twisted pair can support data transmission speeds up to 10 Mbps (mega bits per second) over several hundred meters. The use of active repeaters, which reshape the signal to its original form, increases the distance a signal can travel.

Coaxial Cable

Coaxial cable (coax) is the most widely used medium in the field of local area networks. It consists of a central insulated wire that carries the signal, surrounded by a fine copper mesh and an outer insulated shield. Depending on the quality of the conductor used, it can operate at several hundred Mbps. This means that high-grade coax can be used on lower-speed links that span larger distances than twisted pair cabling without the need for regeneration.

There are two signaling techniques used with coax that have been mis-leadingly applied to describe the electrical and physical characteristics of the cable. Baseband coax is erroneously defined as 50 ohm (3/8inch) cable and broadband coax is erroneously defined as 75 ohm (1/2inch). In fact both kinds of cable can be used in both baseband and broadband applications.

Coax used in baseband applications is easy to install, moderately expensive, and used to transmit a single digital signal at speeds up to 10 Mbps.

Broadband network components must be tuned carefully to handle specific ranges of frequencies. Both the hardware and the connecting cable are sensitive to changes in temperature and humidity. For this reason they require careful installation and maintenance. Coax is also used in cable television and for networks transmitting voice and video as well as data signals.

Radio Transmission

Microwaves are high-frequency radio waves with a capacity of between 3 and 20 Gbps (giga bits per second). Energy forms in this range cannot be transmitted through solid objects. This limits microwave signals to line-of-sight transmission because of the earth's curvature. Microwave relay antennae are typically located on top of high towers to maximize the line-of-sight distance between them. Repeater stations must be installed approximately every fifty kilometers along a route. Radio transmission can provide high-volume, high-speed, high-quality communication for computer data over long distance.

Satellites

Unlike low-frequency radio waves, microwaves can penetrate the upper layers of the earth's atmosphere. This means satellites can be used in micro-wave transmission. Satellites provide a broad bandwidth for long distance transmission (over one thousand kilometers) at competitive prices. In addition, satellites can reduce the complexity of networks by eliminating inter-mediate nodes and the need for complex algorithms to calculate the best route between nodes. Satellites are reliable because they are simple, like a mirror that reflects computer messages. They consist of repeater circuits that amplify received signals and retransmit them back to earth. Satellites decrease the number of microwave relay towers between two nodes and dramatically increase the scope of networks. The major problems associated with satellites are the costs for the terrestrial station, the central office facilities, and the satellite itself, as well as the propagation delay incurred in transmitting a signal 36 000 kilometers into space. A typical signal propagation time is approximately 0.5 seconds for the delay in both directions.

A limited number of communications satellites in synchronous earth orbits cover specific geographic areas within a pair of radio frequencies. The oldest satellite transponder frequency band is the 4/6 Ghz (C-band), which has the advantage of having thousands of earth stations in existence. The newer 12/14 Ghz (ku-band) offers high power, minimal terrestrial interference from microwaves, flexibility, and smaller, less expensive earth stations. Other frequency assignments are the 20/30 Ghz and the 30/40 Ghz bands.

Submarine Cables

Before satellites, submarine cables were the only means of transmission across large bodies of water. Their main disadvantage has been the use of relatively low frequencies compared to land cable due to the extra distance between repeater stations (points on the cable where the signal is regenerated). By increasing the distance between repeater stations, the total number of these stations is reduced. This, in turn, means that the costs of installing and maintaining deep-sea cable are reduced, since these costs are mainly incurred by the repeater stations. Submarine cables are still used extensively and provide a viable backup for satellite systems.

Fiber Optics

Optical fiber is made of plastic or glass and serves as an extremely high-performance transmission medium. Its characteristics are impressive: extremely wide bandwidths (in the gigahertz range), speeds of 1 Gbps, and immunity to electrical interference. It is also extremely compact and lightweight. The transmission characteristics of fiber optic cables make them well suited for both local area networks and for additional trunk lines on telephone systems. The cost of light sources and detectors needed for the complete transmission system has also fallen to a level that makes this type of system competitive.

A fiber optic transmission link consists of:

1. The transmitter that accepts analog or digital input and projects it along the cable in the form of light pulses; and

2. The receiver or detector that accepts the light input and converts it back to analog or digital form.

A pair of fiber optic modems, one at each end of a fiber optic link (consisting of a two-fiber cable for two-way full-duplex communication) can be used to connect a computer to a terminal. The modem usually provides a standard RS-232-C connection for the terminal. A pair of fiber optic multiplexers can be used in place of modems for multi-terminal connection.

A permanent connection between two fiber optic lines requires alignment of the central axes of the fibers. Without proper alignment, critical losses are introduced at the splice point. The connection is made using a splicing jig and a microscope, and it is moulded with a rapidly setting plastic compound for protection.

The major problem associated with fiber optics across the communications industry has been its incompatibility with all previous development. As experience with the medium grows, this problem diminishes.

MEDIA IN THE TELEPHONE NETWORK

Multipair cable consists of individually insulated twisted pairs of conductors enclosed in a common protective sheath. It is used extensively in the telephone network for wiring within buildings, between the customer's premises and the central office, and between central offices. It will therefore have a major influence on the performance of the telephone network and on the development of digital services built on the existing telephone network.

Coaxial cable, because of its wide bandwidth and noise immunity is used in high-traffic-density portions of the long-haul toll network and where radio-frequency congestion precludes the use of microwave systems. It is also used within communications subsystems, for example, to connect a radio transmitter to an antenna.

Radio transmission systems are used for telephone transmission over water and mountains, or for mobile communications. The received signal power depends on transmitter power, antenna patterns, path length, physical obstructions, and meteorological effects. This makes it very difficult to predict performance on the basis of transmission theory. A wide variety of communications applications use radio transmission. These are classified by band in figure 2-4. The most significant of these for data transmission is the SHF used for terrestrial and satellite links.

Optical fiber systems are used extensively in telephone networks for metropolitan-area interoffice trunk applications as well as for long-haul intercity systems. They are also being used at the central office level of the telephone hierarchy but to a lesser extent.

FREQUENCY BAND	FREQUENCY RANGE	APPLICATION
VLF	3 – 30 khz	navigation
LF	30 – 300 khz	time signals
MF	300 khz – 3 Mhz	a.m. radio
HF	3 – 30 Mhz	ship-to-shore
VHF	30 – 300 Mhz	television
UHF	300 Mhz – 3 Ghz	land mobile radio
SHF	3 – 30 Ghz	terrestrial and satellite links
EHF	30 – 300 Ghz	military

Figure 2-4   Applications of Radio Transmission

SUMMARY

The main factors in a comparison of communication media are the band-width or operating frequency range, the number of voice channels per line (if the medium has multi-line capability), and the distance between repeaters. A voice channel may be defined as the capacity required for two voice-grade circuits of approximately four kilohertz each, in other words, approximately eight kilohertz of bandwidth (fig. 2-5).

A telephone-switching office level is known as the class of the office; for example, the toll office is a class three office. The relationship between the medium used for office interconnection and the office class is based on customer demand but can be summarized thus: as the class decreases, the volume and the transfer rate of data increases as does the need for high performance media (fig. 2-6).

In local area networks, the popularity of twisted pair cable will continue because of its low cost and availability and because IBM's local area network uses twisted pair. Coax cable is widely used in baseband LANs because of its speed and noise immunity. The use of coax in broadband LANs may become important in the future, particularly for those companies planning an integration of voice, video, and data transmission. The inability to tap a fiber optics signal, a major advantage in terms of security, is a disadvantage for LANs in terms of future changes and expansion of the network. As the speeds demanded by users of LANs increase, optical fibers are likely to be one of the main transmission media in use. They are now frequently used in new LAN designs (fig. 2-7).

Transmission Media	Construction	Distance Between Repeaters	No. of Channels on a Single Line or Carrier	Operating Frequency Range	Notes
Open Wire	25 cm ≈ 3.25 mm Diameter	40 km	12	Up to 160 kHz	Bulky and Unsightly. Affected by Weather Conditions, i.e. Large Leakage with Wet Insulators. Severe Crosstalk. High Radiation Losses at the Higher Frequencies. Resistance Increases with Frequency Due to Skin Effect. Large Distance Between Amplifiers.
Twisted Wire Pair Cable	Polyethylene	3 to 6.5 km	12–120	Up to 1 MHz	Subject to Severe Crosstalk Because of Nearness of Conductors. Resistance Increases with Frequency Due to Skin Effect.
Coaxial (Tube)		3 to 65 km	L5 Carrier 10,800 per Tube 108,000 per Cable	3 to 60 MHz	No Radiation Losses. Negligible Crosstalk. Large Number of Channels can be Sent Over a Single Tube.
Microwave	Parabolic Dish (1° Beamwidth) Feed Horn	30–50 km	TD-2 Carrier 600–1200 per Radio Channel 10,800 per Route	3.7 to 4.2 GHz 5.925 to 6.425 GHz etc.	Fewer Amplifiers Required than Coaxial System. Affected by Rain when Frequency Exceeds 10 GHz. Large Number of Channels can be Sent Over a Single Antenna. High Velocity of Propagation, Minimizing Delay Times. Can Cause Radio Interference.

Transmission Media	Construction	Distance Between Repeaters	No. of Channels on a Single Line or Carrier	Operating Frequency Range	Notes
Geosynchronous Satellite	Satellite / Earth	Direct	600 per Transponder (12 Transponders per Satellite)	Intel Sat IV Uplink 5.925 to 6.425 GHz Downlink 3.7 to 4.2 GHz	Subject to Interference from Terrestial Link and to Interfere with Terrestial Link Long Delay Times — Up to 270 ms Large and Thus Costly Earth Transmitting Antennas Required Large Distance and Large Area Coverage. Economical Receive Only Earth Stations. Much Lower Cost per Channel than Submarine Cable for Transatlantic Communications.
Submarine Cable	Copper (Inner Conductor) / Steel Strength Member / Copper (Outer Conductor) / Polyethylene	18 km	4000	28 MHz max. Frequency	Employ Time Assignment. Speech Interpolation (TASI) While a User is Silent, Even Between Words, the Channel is Transferred to Another Talker.
Optical Fibre	Protective Coat / Core / Cladding / Graded Index Fibre	4 to 30 km	Several Hundred Voice Channels	1 micron Wavelength 1 Ghz–km	Difficult to Splice in the Field. Cannot be Used to Carry DC Power. Not Subject to Interference or Tapping.

Figure 2-5   Media Summary

LEVEL	CLASS	MEDIUM
Local Loop	-	2-wire twisted pair
Central Office	5	4-wire twisted pair
Toll Office Primary Office Sectional Office Regional Office	4 3 2 1	some coax, mainly microwave (including satellite) with increasing use of fiber optics

Note: the five levels of switching center are often referred to by class.

Figure 2-6   Media in the Telephone System

Medium	Cost of LAN	Speed	Application
twisted pair	low	10 Mbps	data
baseband coax	low	10 Mbps	data
broadband coax	high	20 channels at 5 Mbps	data voice video
fiber optics	very high	1 Gbps	data voice video

Figure 2-7   Comparison of LAN Media

Review Questions for Chapter 2

1. Complete the following table:

Facility	Application
telephone system VANs message switching PSDNs	

2. Draw the telephone switching hierarchy for the following calls.

    a) 465-1234 to 465-5678

b) 471-3847 to 922-6162
c) 403-469-3421 to 604-325-8684

3. What is the main difference between a local loop connection and a trunk line?

4. State the maximum frequency response for:

twisted pair   _____
coaxial cable   _____
submarine cable   _____

5. Complete the following table:

Medium	Advantage	Disadvantage
twisted pair		
baseband coax		
broadband coax		
fiber-optics		

6. Identify the main difference between baseband and broadband coax applications.

7. Compare and contrast radio and satellite transmission.

8. What factors limit the development of fiber optics as the most widely used medium?

9. Match the medium with its transmission rate for LANs.

Medium	Transmission Rate
coax (broadband)	10 Mbps
fiber optics	10 Mbps
twisted pair	1 Gbps
coax (baseband)	20 x 5 Mbps

10. Which media are used by distance networks but not by LANs?

Chapter

3

TERMINATIONS

INTRODUCTION

Terminations are user network nodes. They include terminals, personal computers (PCs), minicomputers, and mainframes. They can be classified by their degree of intelligence. The primary interface between a termination and the rest of the network requires special consideration. Networks can be constructed privately for a particular user, but most often a large number of users share a public network. The most common of these is the packet-switching network. Some terminations require an extra interface for use on packet-switching networks. PCs are converted to terminals by software or by a combination of hardware and software. This process is referred to as terminal emulation.

CLASSIFICATION

Network nodes can be either terminations or junctions. A junction provides the facility for communication, while a termination provides the user access to the network. It is useful to divide the network into two parts: the computer network that interprets the meaning of the information transferred and the communication network, which is concerned with the speed, accuracy, and reliability of the transmission process (fig. 3-1). A goal of the network designer

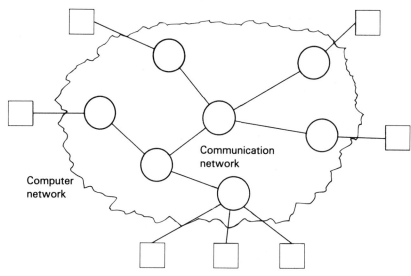

Figure 3-1   Network Parts

is to make the communication network transparent to the user. This means that neither the route, the distance travelled, nor the method of handling the data affect the user's ability to process the data. The computer network contains the terminations.

A termination is a node with one connection to one network though it may be used to access other networks at different times. A termination can be:

— a terminal used to transmit instructions or data to a remote computer;
— a terminal that receives output from a remote computer;
— a PC operating as a terminal; or
— a microcomputer, a minicomputer, or a mainframe computer.

Major factors that influence the selection of terminations are: the method of data collection and the form and quality of output, processing power, transmission rates, and price. Terminations can be classified in different ways. The approach that has the maximum implication for the network is the processing power or "degree of intelligence." This determines the level of sophistication of equipment used to connect the termination to the network. Another equally important consideration is the relationship between the intelligence of the terminal and the trade-off between processing costs and communication costs. Terminations can be classified as simple, pre-programmed terminals, self-reconfiguring terminals, user-programmable terminals, and computer.

Simple Terminations

Prior to the advent of microprocessors, the majority of user terminals would have been thought of as simple, general-purpose electromechanical devices. Simple terminals are usually inexpensive and best defined by what's missing. They have no local memory for buffering, no local editing facility, and no data processing capability. In addition, most simple terminals operate at low transmission rates. Simple terminals may be connected to packet-switched networks through special-purpose devices called packet assembly/disassembly modules (PAD).

1. *Keyboard terminals* are used for inputting alphanumeric information to the network. They normally contain the standard character set of a typewriter plus control characters for network communication. Keyboard terminals are usually coupled with printer terminals or display terminals often referred to as CRTs (cathode-ray tube) or VDTs (video display terminal).

Figure 3-2   The LA120 Decwriter

2. *Printer terminals* are used to obtain local hard copy of instructions or data input to a computer, to provide a record of the terminal/computer dialogue, or to provide reports generated by the computer if the volume of data is low. Printer terminals are sometimes used on their own for a local paper copy or in conjunction with a keyboard. A typical keyboard/printer terminal is the Digital Equipment Corporation's LA120 DECwriter which accepts and prints characters at speeds up to 30 characters per second (fig. 3-2). Keyboard/printer terminals can be operated in a stand-alone mode as a simple typewriter. This is called local mode. When they are connected to the computer (on-line) we can understand that they are two separate peripheral devices connected via the computer. It is quite surprising to consider that a struck key can travel over half the country and back again before it is printed on the paper (fig. 3-3). This phenomenon will become even more significant when we discuss network interaction.

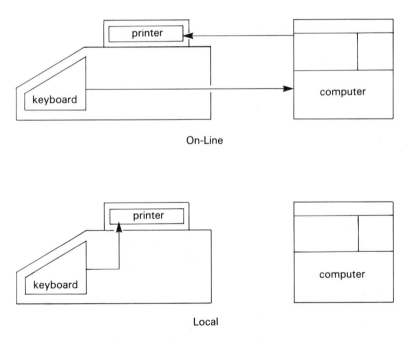

Figure 3-3   Local versus On-Line

3. *Display terminals* have come to dominate the simple terminal market. They too can operate in local or in on-line mode although local mode is of limited use. A significant addition to the simple terminal is the use of buffers

to temporarily store keyboard data and, more importantly, to refresh the screen and keep the picture flicker free (fig.3-4). Advantages over printer terminals include savings in paper costs and much higher transmission speeds. They are more expensive than printer terminals but are more reliable and perform better. DEC's VT100 operates at speeds of up to 19.2 kbps.

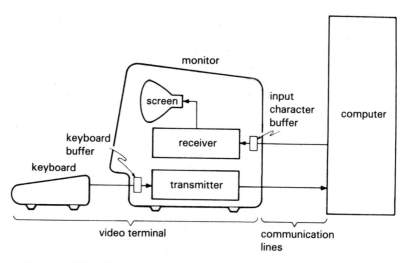

Figure 3-4   Video Terminal

4. *Remote-batch terminals* provide a remote input and output facility for batch mode operation. This generally means high-volume data input, large reports, and jobs that do not require immediate execution. For example, a payroll program can produce reports for a chain of retail stores each with their own remote-batch terminal connected to a central computer system at head office. A typical remote-batch terminal would consist of a magnetic tape reader for high-speed/high-volume input and a line printer for high-speed/high-volume output. The price of intelligence is such that it is now more feasible to provide the tape reader/line printer combination with its own microcomputer, thus creating a local stand-alone facility as well as a remote batch terminal.

5. *Special-purpose terminals* come in a wide variety. Those that fall into the "simple" category include: the touch telephone used by travelling salesmen to input the day's orders, factory data-collection terminals used to keep track of the production progress in manufacturing plants, and some versions of point-of-sale terminals (cash registers) and banking terminals.

Simple terminals are generally less expensive, low-performance devices that transfer network costs to the lines and communication nodes of a network.

Pre-programmed Terminals

The pre-programmed terminal contains several attributes that are not available in a simple terminal. There is data buffering capacity to allow data to be accumulated prior to transmission. This type of terminal also has a local editing facility for correction, insertion, and deletion of information prior to transmission. The main distinction that categorizes the pre-programmed terminal is its program execution capability. This means that anticipated functions have been stored as programs in a hardwired read-only memory and that although the intelligence to execute these programs is available, the user has no way of modifying or adding to the terminal's capability. The increased capability of the pre-programmed terminal over the simple terminal makes it more expensive but more appropriate for a variety of network applications. A typical example of the pre-programmed terminal is the VUCOM 1 (fig.3-5).

Figure 3-5   VUCOM 1

Self-reconfiguring Terminals

A relatively new feature in terminal development, the self-reconfiguring terminal makes use of memory technology. Electronically-erasable-programmable-read-only-memory (EEPROM) provides a means of storing a selection of programs required for a particular terminal use and a way of replacing these programs with another set of programs for a different application. This feature allows the terminal to behave like an entirely different device, that is, it reconfigures itself. For example, the Radio Shack DT-1 can emulate the ADDS 25, the Esprit 1410, the Lear Siegler ADM-5, and the CIT-101e (fig. 3-6). The CIT-101e, in turn, emulates the VT100 and VT52 terminals.

Figure 3-6   CIT-101e Video Terminal

User-Programmable Terminals

These are computers that range from simple microcomputers with dual diskettes, keyboard/CRT, and local 300-character-per-second printers, to powerful systems with hard disk and high-quality, high-volume laser printers.

Such small computer systems would normally be used in a stand-alone capacity, but for jobs requiring greater resources or interaction with other systems, the small computer system would operate as a user-programmable terminal connected to a network. The user-programmable terminal provides the user with the maximum flexibility for communications requirements, that is, open self-reconfiguration, as well as a wide range of options within the associated network. The user-programmable terminal may act as a node in a dispersed (unconnected) processing system or it may provide partial processing and local file handling for a distributed processing system.

The distinction between a user-programmable terminal and a computer termination (see below) may, in some applications, be one in which the degree of control, the type of processing, and the significance of data files, may be local rather than global.

Computer Terminations

We have discussed termination nodes in terms of the variety of terminals available. The resource termination nodes in a network are computers. They supply the major portion of the data, the processing power, the storage space, and the special-purpose hardware facilities (database access, laser printing, plotting) used in network applications. In a network of reasonable complexity, the computer terminations would have separate processors (front-end processors) to handle network communication. The computer termination may be a minicomputer or a mainframe computer. In today's market, there is little or nothing to distinguish minicomputers from mainframe computers in terms of performance. The main distinction is one of power, and therefore price. Minicomputers are less powerful and less expensive than mainframe computers.

DATA TERMINAL EQUIPMENT (DTE)

A major network interface occurs at the boundary between the computer network and the communications network. This is described as the interface between the termination or DTE and the modem or data communication equipment (DCE). The modem is a special node in the network that handles the physical conversion of the data for transmission (modulation). The RS-232-C specification is an example of this interface. It should be noted here that the DTE/DCE interface is also found within the communication network between modems and other junctions. This will be discussed in detail in chapter 4.

PACKET ASSEMBLY/DISASSEMBLY MODULES

Networks must be controlled. Control requires the establishment of a set of rules or protocol. A variety of wide-area networks have been developed in recent years with a variety of protocols. There has been a slow but discernible movement towards an international standard for protocol, based on a recommendation by the Consultative Committee for International Telephony and Telegraphy (CCITT), called X.25 protocol. X.25 provides a set of guidelines that describe the physical interface and logical interface between the DTE and the DCE as well as the movement of data through the network. The X.25 specification requires that the terminal use point-to-point synchronous circuits. It is not difficult to meet this requirement, since most terminal manufacturers now include it as a standard feature or as an option.

Terminations not capable of directly interfacing to a network using X.25, such as the simple and preprogrammed terminals, can be connected to a network through a packet assembly/disassembly module (PAD). A PAD is a shared communications controller that enables non-user-programmable terminals access through synchronous or asynchronous connection. X.3 and X.29 are recommendations defined by the CCITT that specify the standards for PADs.

TERMINAL EMULATION

Self-reconfiguring terminals have the ability to behave as a variety of different terminals. They do this by means of programs stored in EEPROMs. This feature could be termed "hardware emulation." User-programmable terminals are microcomputers that can be made to behave like a variety of different terminals. They accomplish this by means of a program called a terminal emulator package. This feature could be termed "software emulation." Software emulators provide many additional features including the ability to upload and down-load files to and from a mainframe computer.

DEVELOPMENTS

Ever since the appearance on the data processing scene of the microcomputer, observers have been predicting the demise of the terminal. Since the price of microcomputers has been falling rapidly while their performance has been improving dramatically, including their ability to emulate any popular terminal on the market, it is not surprising that users who need personal computers for their workplace also appreciate their potential as terminals. In reaction to this, terminal manufacturers have begun to compete by incorporating micro-processors in their terminals. This allows them to decrease prices while at the same time increasing flexibility and functionality. Our classification of termi-nals as simple, preprogrammed, and self-reconfiguring, is being obscured by the incorporation of features from sophisticated terminals into simple termi-nals. Developments include:

— special graphics;
— multinational character sets;
— standard sophisticated editing facilities including:
  • character and line insertion and deletion,
  • smooth and incremental scroll,
  • paging modes,
  • protected fields,
  • tab functions, and
  • split screens (windows);
— low profile, detachable keyboards;
— non-glare screen;
— tilt/swivel monitors;
— 60 hz refresh rates;
— CRT saver function; and
— user-friendly, menu-driven, set-up procedures.

A comparison of specific display, edit, and communication parameters for current, typical, self-reconfiguring terminals provides a clear indication of the power and versatility of these machines (fig.3-7).

The competition for market share between terminals and microcomputers is not over. As usual, success will depend not only on price and performance but also on market strategy.

SUMMARY

The most important kinds of terminations, apart from the computers that supply the hardware, software, and database resources to the remote user, are the self-reconfiguring terminals and the PCs. Their competition is based on the ergonomic design and user-friendly features of the terminal versus the dual functioning ability of the PC. To be able to download a portion of the database and use it in a local spreadsheet application as well as emulate a remote terminal computer gives the PC a powerful advantage. For less

Parameters	CIT-101e	DT-1	WY-75	VC4604
DISPLAY				
screen diagonal (in)	12	12	14	12
tilt/swivel	x	x	x	x
24 lines x 80 columns	x	x	x	x
24 lines x 132 columns	x	x	x	x
matrix	7 x 9	-	7 x 13	7 x 10
ASCII characters	96	96	128	128
EDITING				
autorepeat	x	x	x	x
scroll/page	x	x	x	x
split screen	x	x	x	x
cursor control	x	x	x	x
blink	x	x	x	x
half/full intensity	x	x	x	x
reverse video	x	x	x	x
underscore	x	x	x	x
character/line insert/delete	-	x	x	x
protected fields	-	x	x	-
COMMUNICATIONS				
max. speed	19.2 kbps	s	s	s
half-duplex	x	x	x	x
full-duplex	x	x	x	x
variable parity	x	-	-	x
variable stop bits	-	-	x	-
RS-232-C	x	x	x	x

x available   - unavailable   s same

Figure 3-7   Comparison of Performance Characteristics

sophisticated applications the versatility, ease of use, and lower cost of the terminal is more attractive.

The need for a standard interface between terminations and networks will become more apparent when we discuss the protocol of networks. It is obvious that networks connect together a variety of devices from a variety of manufacturers. The problems of incompatibility are more severe in data networks than they ever were within the computer center.

Packet-switched networks require terminations to be synchronous in nature. Simpler terminals need to be made compatible to packet-switched networks by connecting them to the network via a PAD.

Review Questions for Chapter 3

1. As well as classifying terminals by degree of intelligence and power, one can also classify them by application, for example:

   a. transaction terminal
   b. batch terminal
   c. retrieval terminal (enquiry/update)
   d. time sharing terminal
   e. message switching terminal

   Which of the terminals listed above would be used for:

   1) an airline reservation
   2) remote program computation
   3) administrative correspondence
   4) banking system
   5) processing order entry transactions daily

2. Complete the following table:

Terminal	Strength	Weakness
1. simple 2. pre-programmed 3. self-reconfiguring 4. user-programmable		

3. With reference to figure 3-7, Comparison of performance characteristics, answer the following questions:

   a) Which terminal has the clearest character set?
   b) Which terminals have more control capability?
   c) Which terminal has the poorest editing capability?
   d) Which terminals have flexible error-checking capability?
   e) Which terminal has flexible asynchronous character length?

4. Rate the following terminal characteristics in order of priority.

   multinational character sets
   windows
   detachable keyboards
   CRT saver function
   user friendly set-up procedures
   tilt swivel moniters

Chapter

JUNCTIONS

INTRODUCTION

This chapter classifies communication network nodes (junctions) and examines the function of each as it relates to its position in the network. Network junctions provide an interface between network terminations, usually between terminals and computers but often between computers and computers. There are two kinds of junction that will be discussed here: modems and control nodes.

The *modem* is used by data networks to transmit data over long distances across the telephone system. It provides the terminal with its initial connection to the network, modulates and demodulates the data signals going to and coming from the network, and supplies the appropriate control signals to effect data transmission.

Control nodes are responsible for line control, message buffering, and error detection, as well as for optimizing the efficiency of the network. Each node has its own function related to its position in the network. This category of junction includes multiplexers, concentrators, front-end processors, and switches.

Multiplexers and *concentrators* are used by groups of remote terminals to provide a cost-effective way of transmitting and receiving data via a shared high-speed line.

Front-end processors are used to off-load the communications handling chores from a mainframe computer. The function of the mainframe computer is to run applications programs that help to solve a wide variety of business problems. Direct interaction with a network could downgrade the mainframe's ability to handle its application workload.

Switches act as traffic police in networks by providing a variety of routes between terminations. They have the intelligence to schedule transfers and optimize routings.

Because of the impact of IBM on computers, dataprocessing, and data networks, and because of IBM's unique terminology, a section on IBM junctions is included later in this chapter. The principal junctions are: the communications controller, the cluster controller, and the protocol converter.

Public networks require monitoring and control of the complete network, which is often being shared by many unrelated users. This overall supervision of the network is performed by the network control center (NCC).

Like terminals, junctions can be classified in terms of their level of sophistication. They range from simple physical switches to full-fledged computer systems with specialized instruction sets dedicated to communications handling.

MODEMS

There are a number of ways of connecting a DTE to a DCE or modem. The standard for this connection is the Electronic Industries Association (EIA) RS-232-C cable, which specifies the interchange circuits or signals for a DTE to DCE connection. The most common plug and socket associated with the RS-232-C standard is a DB-25 (a D-type 25-pin connector) that specifies the pin assignments (fig.4-1). Neither the pin assignments nor the names given to the signals associated with these pins are part of the RS-232-C standard but have become de facto standards through general usage.

Over shorter distances there are alternatives to the use of modems. Over longer distances there are different classes of modems.

Direct Connection

The reason for modulating a data signal is to transmit that signal over a longer distance than would otherwise be possible on telephone lines. Data signals quickly lose amplitude and shape when transmitted directly over telephone lines. Nevertheless there are occasions when a direct connection between DTEs is implemented using the standard RS-232-C cable. Since the cable is

Signal Type	Description	Mnemonic	Pin No.
Ground	protective ground	PG	1
	signal ground/		
	common return	SG	7
Data	transmitted data	TD	2
	received data	RD	3
Control	request to send	RTS	4
	clear to send	~~CLS~~ CTS	5
	data set ready	DSR	6
	data terminal ready	DTR	20
	ring indicator	RI	22
	received line		
	signal detector	DCD	8
	signal quality detector	SQ	21
	data signal rate		
	selector (DTE)		23
	data signal rate		
	selector (DCE)		23

Note: Timing, secondary, and test signals have been omitted.

Figure 4-1   The RS-232-C Interface

designed for DTE to DCE connection, modifications must be made to account for the fact that the DCE signals will not be available. Specifically, the transmit and receive connections must be reversed, and the responding signals from the DCE end must be tied to DTE signals to simulate operation (fig.4-2). The modified RS-232-C cable is usually referred to as a null modem or modem eliminator. The EIA has prescribed a maximum cable length of 15m (50ft) and a maximum transmission rate of 20 kbps. There will be more about this in Section C.

Line Drivers

Another way of connecting a DTE to a DTE without using modems is to use a line driver. This is a relatively inexpensive way of replacing modems with devices that operate at speeds that are inversely related to the distance involved. For example, a speed of 1200 bps is possible for up to 8km (5mi); at 9600 bps the maximum distance is 2km (1.25mi); and at 56 kbps the limit is 600m (2000ft).

Limited Distance Modems (LDMs)

LDMs are available in both full- and half-duplex models and in both synchronous and asynchronous models. They use modulation for transmission

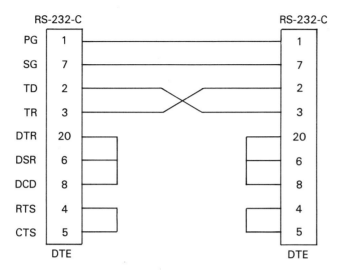

Figure 4-2   DTE to DTE Connection

but do not have the sophisticated equalizing and filtering capability of long-distance modems. A major restriction of LDMs is that they can only communicate over a metallic wire circuit. These limitations account for their relatively low cost. A typical example is the Gandalf LDS 125 Asynchronous Data Set, which operates over 4-wire dedicated lines at distances up to 8km (5mi) and at speeds up to 9600 baud. Newer LDMs have extended the distance capability to 30km (18mi).

Types of Standard Modem

There are many modem manufacturers and each has its own design criteria. Modems may be classified by cost, by type (whether synchronous or asynchronous), or by speed. We will classify them in terms of speed as follows:

low-speed modems	300 bps
medium-speed modems	1200/2400/4800 bps
high-speed modems	9600 bps/19.2 kbps
wide-band modems	above 19.2 kbps

LOW-SPEED MODEMS

As soon as you require transmission through the telephone system, a standard modem must be used. The low-speed modem generally operates asynchronously at 300 baud and employs frequency modulation.

Modems operate in one of two modes: the originate mode and the answer mode. A modem goes into the originate mode when a call is initiated through it, for example, when it is directly connected to a terminal that is communicating with a computer. A modem goes into an answering mode if it initially answers a call, for example, when it is connected to a computer. Remember that two modems are required to connect a terminal to a computer.

Frequency-modulated modems are restricted to low speeds because the bandwidth required for higher frequencies exceeds the bandwidth available on a standard voice channel. The AT&T Bell 103 is the industry standard for low-speed modems. It is capable of full-duplex operation over a two-wire channel and can be employed on both dial-up and leased lines, and it can also operate in originate or answer modes.

MEDIUM-SPEED MODEMS

The 1200 bps modem is the most common of the medium-speed modems and is used in asynchronous dial-up applications. It uses a variation of phase-shift modulation called differential-phase-shift modulation. The phase angle of the incoming signal is compared to the phase angle of the previously received signal.

The SwitchCom 212A modem is a typical example of one that can auto-originate or auto-answer at both 300 bps (frequency modulation) or 1200 bps (differential-phase-shift modulation). It will automatically adjust to the speed of an incoming call and has a built-in directory for storing telephone numbers that can be autodialed.

The 2400 bps and 4800 bps modems are most often used in synchronous applications on leased lines. The Gandalf SAM 24V synchronous/asynchronous dial-up modem can operate at 300 bps using frequency modulation, 1200 bps using phase shift modulation, and 2400 bps using quadrature amplitude modulation (a combination of amplitude and phase modulation).

HIGH-SPEED MODEMS

By employing quadrature amplitude modulation (QAM), speeds of 19.2 kbps can be achieved in full-duplex over private four-wire voice-grade lines. The Bell 209A is a synchronous modem that uses QAM to provide up to four channels at 2400 bps, sharing a high-speed line of 9600 bps.

WIDEBAND MODEMS

These are modems that operate at speeds in excess of 19.2 kbps in synchronous mode. The high-speed serial data from the computer is divided into a number of individual bit streams that are modulated and transmitted over multiple wideband voice-grade channels such as AT&T's Series 8000 channels, where a 56 kbps pulse train is divided into two 28 kbps signals for transmission and then recombined at the other end.

Modem characteristics are summarized in figure 4-3.

Connection	Distance	Speed
Direct	15 m	19.2 kbps
Line driver	8/2/0.6 km	1.2/9.6/56 kbps
Limited distance modem	8 km	9600 bps
Low-speed modem	unlimited	up to 300 bps
Medium-speed modem	unlimited	1200/2400/4800 bps
High-speed modem	unlimited	9.6/19.2 kbps
Wideband modem	unlimited	above 19.2 kbps

Figure 4-3 Modem Summary

MULTIPLEXERS

Multiplexers combine data input from a number of low-speed channels and transmit the data over one high-speed communications line. Their main purpose is to make communications efficient and therefore cost effective. It is cheaper to lease one high-speed line than several low-speed lines. Multiplexers can be used in different ways. First, where remote users are at a distance from each other, the multiplexer can be located near the mainframe. Second, the multiplexer is more commonly located near a group of remote terminals and used to transmit their data on a high-speed line into one computer channel. Finally, two multiplexers must be used first to combine a number of channels together and then to separate or "demultiplex" them at the computer (fig.4-4). There are two categories of multiplexer: frequency division multiplexers and time division multiplexers.

Figure 4-4 Multiplexer/Demultiplexer

Frequency Division Multiplexer (FDM)

FDMs operate over high-speed analog lines and do not require modems to modulate the data signals. Each terminal connected to the multiplexer is assigned a unique frequency within the capacity of the line. The transfer of information from each terminal at a different frequency can occur simultaneously on a single line. The demultiplexer operates like a series of filters that extract a single frequency from the range of frequencies transmitted. This function is similar to the tuner on a radio, which selects (and amplifies) a single frequency transmitted by a particular radio station, extracts the information from it and converts it to sound. The information extracted from a particular terminal's frequency is input to the computer (fig.4-5). FDMs divide the allocated bandwidth into independent, permanently assigned, lower-speed subchannels. The amount of bandwidth assigned to each channel depends on the speed at which the channel operates. The slower the transmission rate, the more subchannels can be assigned within the bandwidth. FDMs are the oldest type of multiplexer available. They are slow and physically bulky and have mostly been replaced by the less expensive, higher-speed

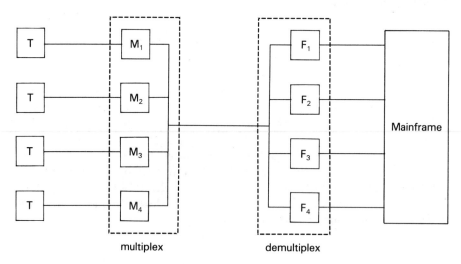

Note: M_1-M_4 modulators
F_1-F_4 filters
Diagram shows multiplexing in one direction.

Figure 4-5 Frequency Division Multiplexing

devices. They are still used in combination with time division multiplexers (see below) to cut costs by reducing the need for modems.

Time Division Multiplexer (TDM)

TDMs are digital devices. Rather than dividing bandwidth into separate channels as in FDMs, they divide the bandwidth into time slots (fig.4-6). The TDM works on the basis of accepting data from many terminals in succession.

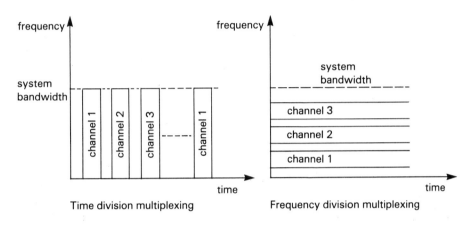

Figure 4-6   Time versus Frequency

This process is known as interleaving. If digital information from a low-speed terminal is transmitted on a high-speed line, then much of the time no information is being transferred. The TDM uses the spaces between the information to add more information from other low-speed terminals. The concept of time division multiplexing can best be understood by considering the TDM as a switch that samples each terminal so fast that no terminal is aware of any interruption (fig.4-7). The interleaved information is transmitted on a high-speed line and demultiplexed using a second switch that routes the information from the individual user terminals via a series of input/output channels to the computer. Transferring from the computer to a user terminal uses the same principle. TDMs can be bit-interleaved, that is, one bit of each terminal's message is sampled at a time, or character-interleaved, when one character of each terminal's message is sampled at a time or block interleaved. TDM's support aggregate line speeds of between 9600 baud and 1544 Mbps.

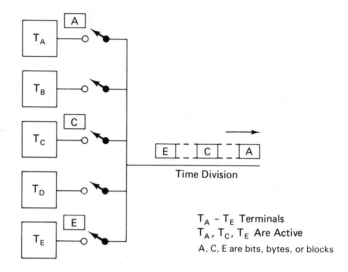

Figure 4-7   Time Division Multiplexing

Statistical Time Division Multiplexer (STDM)

The STDM is an intelligent TDM (thanks to a microprocessor) that increases line utilization by allocating time slots on the basis of a line activity algorithm. The TDM multiplexes n asynchronous channels at m bps into one synchronous channel operating at nm bps. This is true when all terminals are active. As soon as a user signs off, the transmitted information contains gaps. Since terminals are inactive a large part of the time, TDMs normally operate well below capacity. STDMs increase line usage by transmitting only from active terminals. The microprocessor in the STDM manages the data flow and provides memory for data buffering. The STDM provides variable-length, rather than fixed-length, time slots so that more than one byte of data can be accepted from a given terminal before the STDM moves on to the next active terminal. STDMs are loaded beyond the capacity of TDMs with the same number of channels so there will be times when all terminals are active and the input data rates exceed the line capacity. The buffer area in the microcomputer is used to temporarily store the overflow. Another problem that may occur is with line errors causing retransmission and perhaps an overload condition. Again, excess data are stored in the microprocessor until the traffic overload subsides. STDMs operate at a lower line maximum than TDMs, normally between 9600 baud and 19.2 kbaud. Since they make more efficient use of a channel, they can achieve the same throughput using a low-speed line (fig.4-8). At present STDMs constitute the largest segment of units sold in the data communications market.

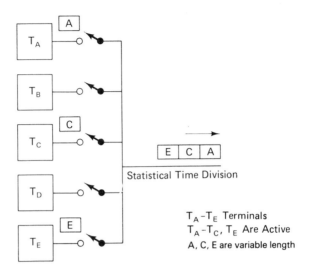

Figure 4-8   *Statistical Time Division Multiplexing*

CONCENTRATORS

A concentrator performs many of the same functions as a multiplexer. The main distinction is in the way it uses its intelligence. Just as the STDM uses intelligence to make the line sharing more efficient, so the concentrator uses its intelligence to manage contention. A concentrator is a switch that allocates one of a number of inputs to one of a number of outputs. In its simplest form, the concentrator has a single output. Although it looks like a multiplexer (many inputs, one output), it operates quite differently. The multiplexer combines the inputs on a high-speed line; the concentrator allocates a particular input to the line for the duration of its information transfer. The allocation of the output line to a specific input depends on when the request is made, the speed of the input line, and the class or importance of the request. This is what is meant when it is said that the concentrator "manages contention."

The concentrator may be used in a number of different ways. It can be used, for instance, for modem sharing, when several terminals contend for one modem (fig.4-9). The advantage in this configuration is the saving in modems, lines, and computer ports. A *computer port* is the input/output channel through which informaton is transferred between the computer and its own peripherals (disks, printers), or between the computer and other computers or terminals.

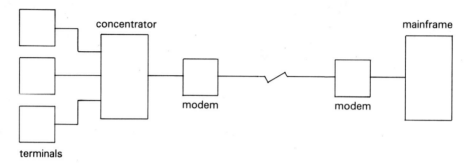

Figure 4-9   Modem-sharing Concentrator

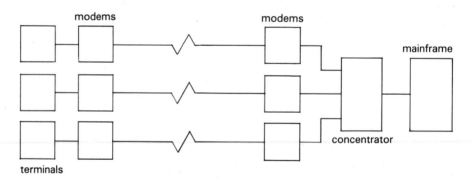

Figure 4-10   Port-sharing Concentrator

The concentrator can be used as a port sharer. Again, the computer polls the remote terminals and the concentrator connects one to the computer port (fig.4-10). This is a common application for limited distance modems. Large scale M-to-N concentrators (M-inputs, N-outputs) require more sophisticated hardware. They continuously check all the input lines till a request is made then search for a free computer port and make the connection (fig.4-11). Most M-to-N concentrators have a provision for forming subcontention groups on the basis of speed or user class.

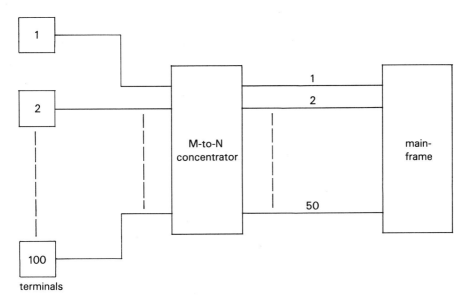

Figure 4-11 M-to-N Concentrator

Data Switch

The data switch is a simplified version of the M-to-N concentrator. Its primary function is to share a number of computer ports with a number of terminals. Often these terminals are in remote locations and can communicate with the host computer by dual multiplexers, by remote concentrators for modem sharing purposes, or by using modems independently. The data switch provides an interface between all of these possibilities and the host computer. Since the data switch is digital in nature it contains modulation/demodulation capability on the terminal side of the interface.

The Gandalf Private Automatic Computer eXchange (PACX) system is an example of a data switch. It is designed to connect a number of terminals to a number of computer ports (fig.4-12). The PACXIV is microprocessor-controlled and includes the following features:

— accommodation for 512 terminals and 256 ports,
— asynchronous channels up to 9600 baud,
— synchronous channels up to 19.2 kbaud,
— up to 128 different user classes,
— restriction of services to authorized users, and
— full statistics and port monitoring capability.

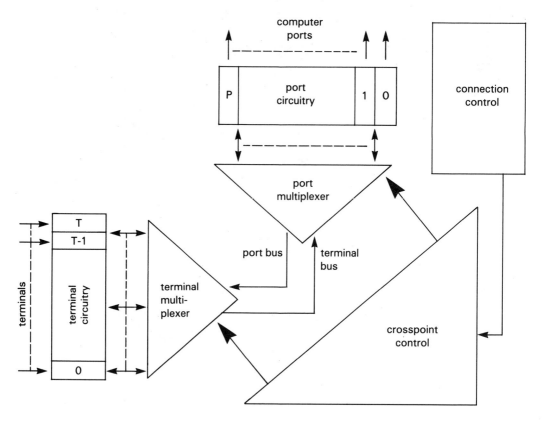

Figure 4-12   PACX Control and Multiplexing

FRONT-END PROCESSORS

The purpose of the front-end processor is to handle the communication functions for a mainframe computer. The primary function of the mainframe is to process applications, whether it be an enquiry to a database, the printing of a monthly report, updating a master file, or building a prototype using a fourth-generation language. The aim of the front-end processor is to provide an interface between the mainframe computer and the network such that data is passed to and from the mainframe efficiently. The front-end processor is responsible for supervision of the input/output controllers or channels attached to the network, for providing buffering and partial processing of incoming and outgoing data, for the assembly and disassembly of messages, and for error handling.

Message Switch

A message switch participates in the management and control of a network by scheduling, routing, and forwarding messages in the network. It also provides temporary storage facilities to help smooth network flow during peak demands. This store and forward device performs no data manipulaton. The message switch is often incorporated into nodes with other responsibilities such as front-end processing and concentration. A communication network node that performs this function alone is becoming rare.

THE IBM WORLD

The IBM 3725 is a modular, programmable communications controller. It can function either as a front-end processor or as a remote concentrator. The 3725 allows for the attachment of up to 256 lines. The lines can be either half- or full-duplex, using synchronous or asynchronous transfer, at speeds of up to 256 kbps.

The IBM 3274 cluster controller is a concentrator that can be used locally or remotely to connect multiple synchronous terminals to an IBM host. Up to 32 terminals can be attached, operating at speeds of up to 56 kbps.

Protocol converters connect incompatible terminals to a mainframe. They communicate with the terminals in a simple protocol, for example, in ASCII (or TTY) protocol with little error checking. They communicate with the mainframe in more complex protocols that incorporate error checking and retransmission capability. The protocol converter changes the protocol by extracting the data from the old protocol and enclosing it in the new one. In addition to this task, the protocol converter acts as a concentrator by providing access to the network and can include a facility for preprocessing, for example, code conversion. The protocol converter is sometimes known as a terminal controller. The IBM 7171 is a protocol converter that provides the ability to attach a variety of full-duplex asynchronous terminals directly to IBM host processors via a multiplexer. Up to 64 asynchronous terminals can be connected via RS-232-C interfaces at speeds of up to 19.2 kbps.

NETWORK MANAGEMENT

Managing a network means monitoring and controlling it. These functions are performed by the network control center (NCC) for public networks and by a dedicated computer in private networks. The distinction between the two is that on public networks many independent users share the facilities provided by the telephone companies (or public network organizations in the United States), whereas on private networks an organization can lease facilities that are shared only by its constituent parts. The functions of the network management system include:

— the monitoring of the network's components;
— the provision of alternate routes through the network;
— the provision of standby facilities; and
— maintenance of information relating to network status, configuration, inventory, and performance history.

Figure 4-13 shows how these network junctions can be interconnected.

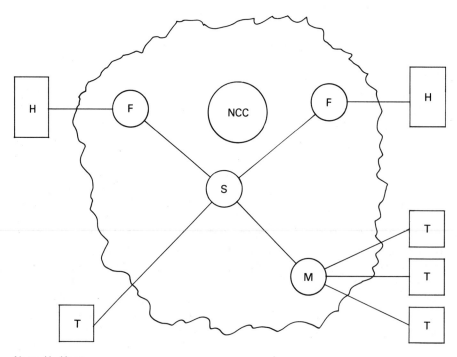

Note: H - Host
      T - Terminal
      F - Front-end Processor
      M - Multiplexer/Concentrator
      S - Switch
      NCC - Network Control Center

Figure 4-13   Network Junctions

SUMMARY

Network junctions connect computers and terminals efficiently. Modems transmit data accurately and efficiently. The multiplexer, the concentrator, and the switch improve efficiency by providing line sharing. The front-end processor permits the host processor to focus on data processing. The network control center is responsible for the overall performance of the network.

Perhaps the most significant development in communication network nodes parallels that of terminal development, namely, that the functional demarcation lines of different kinds of equipment are becoming less well defined. A communications processor is a general-purpose computer adapted to perform as a front-end processor, a multiplexer, a concentrator, or an intelligent switch. The adaptation consists of configuring the input/output capability and modifying the software to specific purposes. We have already seen that many of the software functions are standard, for example, transmission and reception of data, buffering, message assembly and disassembly, error handling, routing, and scheduling. It may be that in the future the function of a communications processor will depend solely on its position in the network.

Review Questions for Chapter 4

1. Match the junction with a characteristic of the junction.

JUNCTION	FUNCTION
multiplexer	ASCII ---> BISYNC
FEP	frequency or time sharing
NEC	contention management
modem	communications controller
concentrator	traffic cop
protocol converter	DCE
intelligent switch	monitor

2. Identify the key characteristic of the following connection methods:

line drivers _____   LDMs _____
acoustic couplers _____   direct connection _____
standard modems _____

3. Match the speed of the standard modem with the modulation technique.

speed (bps)	modulation
300 1200 9600	phase shift QAM frequency

4. Identify the multiplexer associated with each of the following characteristics:

intelligence   _____

no output modem   _____

character interleaved   _____

filter   _____

overloading   _____

digital service   _____

slow   _____

most popular   _____

5. List three functions of an NCC.

6. Identify the junction types in the following diagram.

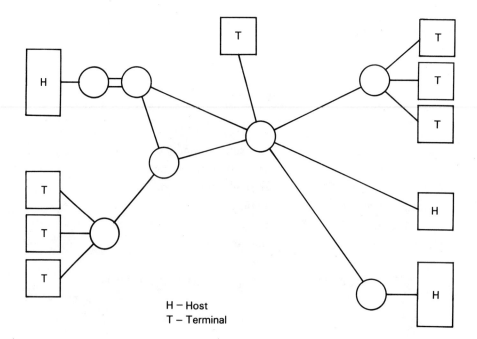

H − Host
T − Terminal

CONNECTIONS

INTRODUCTION

Computer networks (terminations) and communication networks (junctions) are connected together to form data networks. Because the physical shape of wide area networks is dictated by geography, we can consider their development in terms of how they are interconnected to optimize performance (logical connection) and how their irregular shape has placed an emphasis on routing (physical connection). Local area networks are characterized by simple physical shapes such as the ring network in which each node is connected to the next node in line until a ring is formed. Since their logical interconnection is governed by these simple physical shapes we need only consider their physical connections.

The concept of logical connection deals with ways of connecting the nodes of a network to optimize termination interaction. As the number of terminations increases, so does the need to maximize throughput, minimize network overhead and costs, maintain flexibility of routing, ensure data integrity and security. Methods of logical connection of network nodes have developed from simple physical switching, through polling and interrupt systems, to a sophisticated multilayer protocol environment employing virtual circuit connections.

Topology is defined as the physical description of a network. Examination of the simple shapes a network may take helps us to understand the nature of the information flow in the network. For example, a fundamental approach to problem solving is the use of hierarchies to break the problem up into manageable pieces. So, too, a hierarchical network design lends itself to levels of control, general at the top, detailed and specific at the bottom.

Wide area networks are shaped by geography and tend to be highly irregular. The need for intermediate nodes depends on the number of users, the volume of data transmitted, and the flexibility of network routing.

Local area networks are confined to one or more contiguous buildings and have simple topologies with a high degree of symmetry.

LOGICAL CONNECTIONS

The need for sophistication in protocols developed as networks grew in complexity. The first connections between terminations were made point-to-point (fig.5-1). In point-to-point connection, each termination is connected to another termination by an individual and permanent line. The obvious disadvantages of this system include cost and underutilization of lines; that is, the user pays for the line whether it is being used or not.

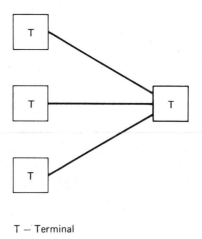

T — Terminal

Figure 5-1   Point-to-Point Connection

Circuit and Multipoint Switching

One solution found to the drawbacks of point-of-point switching was circuit switching (fig.5-2). In this system, a switching center is created to provide a

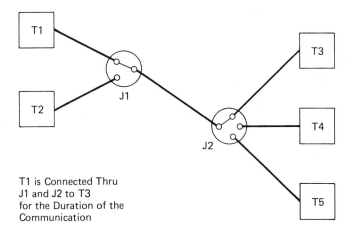

T1 is Connected Thru
J1 and J2 to T3
for the Duration of the
Communication

Figure 5-2   Circuit Switching

path between two terminations for the duration of the communication. The user pays only for the time connected and for sharing the lines and switching centers with other users.

An alternative improvement over point-to-point connection is a multipoint, or multidrop, network that facilitates a one-to-and-from-many termination connection (fig.5-3). One termination controls the data transfer between itself and all other terminations by means of polling. *Polling* describes the process by which the controlling node checks, in a predefined sequence, whether any of the other nodes need to establish a communication dialogue. The other nodes in the network must wait for the completion of this dialogue before they in turn are polled.

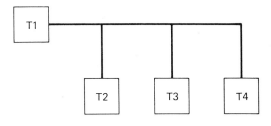

T1 is the Controlling Terminal

Figure 5-3   Multipoint Network

Both circuit switching and multipoint networks have their drawbacks. Circuit switching times can be lengthy and therefore present a problem for interactive systems. Most users of a remote enquiry system would expect an almost immediate response, for example, in checking customer credit ratings. Even a delay of a few seconds, when experienced on a regular basis, becomes intolerable.

In multipoint systems, polling implies a programming overhead, that is, time must be spent checking each terminal to find out if there is a requirement for data transfer from a particular terminal. This is accomplished by the execution of a program in the controlling termination. The cost of polling is normally distributed among the terminal users. Another problem of multipoint systems is underutilization of terminals due to the fact that there is only one connecting line.

Packets

Two factors in computer communication systems that were fundamental to the development of data networks are the creation of international standards and the idea of packet switching.

The establishment of standards within countries and across continents is essential to the development of such data processing applications as electronic funds transfer. The network of the future must be accessible to a wide variety of users, and it must perform its own housekeeping functions, that is, it must be intelligent and use its resources efficiently.

Packet switching is a refinement of message switching. Message switching involves transferring messages between terminations as units of information (fig.5-4). The message travels through the network with a header that precedes the message and identifies the destination. Subsequent messages can take entirely different routes.

In packet switching, information is transferred between terminations in discrete, fixed-length units called packets. Figure 5-5 shows that each packet consists of:

a) a header that contains control information and the destination address, and

b) the message or data field that is transparent to the network.

A frame check sequence (FCS) is attached to the packet for error control at the local level.

Transparency is a term frequently used on computer systems to describe a lack of awareness. For example, the user is often unaware of how much the operating system does to satisfy a request made in a high-level language. It can be said that the operating system is "transparent" to the user. In this regard, it

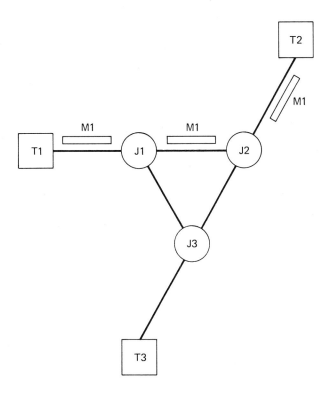

Message M1 is Transmitted from Terminal T1
to Terminal T2 via Junctions J1 and J2

Figure 5-4   Message Switching

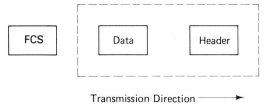

Transmission Direction ⟶

Figure 5-5   The Packet

can be claimed that the network and the software that drives the network have no interest in the actual information being transmitted. The network is concerned about the source, the destination, the quantity, and the accuracy of the information, but the information itself is transparent to the network.

Packets are transmitted via specialized computers that interpret header information, check for accuracy, and route the data. Circuit switching describes the physical linking of two terminations for the period of the communication. In packet-switched networks, the physical interconnections are permanently in place (fig.5-6). Logical switching occurs at each node of the network by means of the destination address (part of the header). A routing decision is made by the node on the basis of the destination address.

Packet-switched network facilities are charged primarily on the basis of the quantity of information rather than connection time. Packet-switching systems are becoming less sensitive to distance with respect to charging than they were in the past.

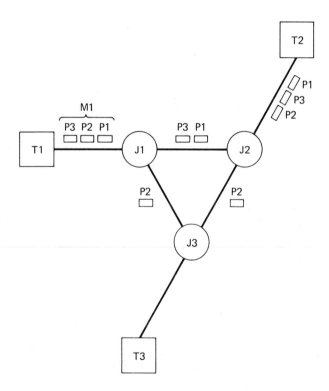

Message M1 Becomes Packets P1, P2, P3
P1 and P3 are Transmitted from T1 to T2 via J1, J2
P2 is Transmitted from T1 to T2 via J1, J3, J2
The Packets are Returned to their Original Sequence
at Terminal T2

Figure 5-6   Packet Switching

PHYSICAL CONNECTIONS

Topology describes the pattern of connection for network nodes. It determines the layout of communication links between terminations and junctions. Topological design algorithms must select links and link capacities on the basis of message transmission delay, cost, network traffic, and, perhaps most importantly, future expandability.

Wide Area Network Topologies

A fully connected mesh network (fig.5-7) is one in which each junction has a direct link to every other junction and has a routing table defining the unique link to be used to reach each destination. The routing algorithm consists of a simple table search. A more realistic mesh network is called the irregular mesh (fig.5-8). Junction node location is governed by user requirements. Node interconnection depends on route availability, line bandwidths and costs. Route selection is much more sophisticated than in the fully connected mesh. The public telephone system is the largest irregular mesh in the world.

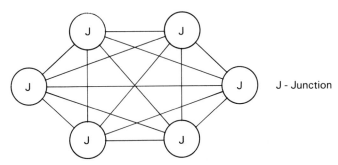

Figure 5-7   Fully Connected Mesh

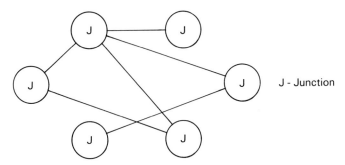

Figure 5-8   Irregular Mesh

ROUTE SELECTION

In a circuit-switched network the routing algorithm operates during call set-up, while the route is being selected. In the packet-switched network the algorithm can either determine individually the routing of each data packet or else set up a route for a sequence of packets. For an irregular mesh-connected, packet-switching network it may not be possible to apply a routing algorithm because the topology at specific nodes can be unknown or can be subject to change. In this case, packets can be transmitted by flooding, where multiple copies of each packet are transmitted to all connecting nodes. An alternative is to use random routing in which single copies of a packet are transmitted to a connecting node chosen at random. In modern packet networks directory routing is used. The destination address obtained from the packet header provides access to a routing table to determine the best route. Simple schemes choose on the basis of the shortest path, while more sophisticated schemes take network loading into account.

Local Area Network Topologies

Local area networks (LANs) were created to share resources within an organization's local environment. As personal computer usage grew in organizations, both for management applications and for office automation, it became clear that dramatic savings in disk storage, printing facilities, and software purchases could be made by connecting these personal computers together. The result was the creation of networks, within and between buildings, called local area networks.

LAN topologies are principally known for their simplicity and their symmetry. These factors, together with their restricted physical boundaries, account for their low operating system overhead and high performance.

STAR

In the star topology each node is connected via a point-to-point link to a central control node (fig.5-9). All routing of network traffic, from the central node to outlying nodes and between outlying nodes, is performed by the central node. Getting the routing algorithm is a simple matter of looking up a table.

The star formation works best when the bulk of communication is between the central node and outlying nodes. When the message volume is high among outlying nodes, the central switching feature may cause delays.

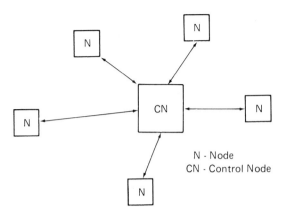

Figure 5-9   Star Topology

The central control is the most complex of the nodes and governs the success, size, and capacity of the network. Star networks require a greater emphasis on reliability for this reason.

RING

Each node is connected to two other nodes by point-to-point links in a closed loop (fig.5-10). Transmitted messages travel from node to node around the ring in one direction. Each node must be able to recognise its own address as well as retransmit messages addressed to other nodes. Since the message route is determined by the topology, no routing algorithm is required, messages automatically travel to the next node on the ring. This is achieved by circulating a bit pattern, called a token, to facilitate sharing the communications channel. A node gains exclusive use of the channel by "grabbing" the token. It passes the right to access the channel on to the other nodes when it has finished transmitting. This is the basic protocol used in ring topologies. When control is distributed, each node can communicate directly with all other nodes under its own initiative.

Ring networks with centralized control are often referred to as loops (fig.5-11). The control node permits the other nodes to transmit messages and acts like the central control node of a star network.

Since ring communication is unidirectional, failure of one node brings the network down. However, simple bypass mechanisms can be employed to minimize downtime.

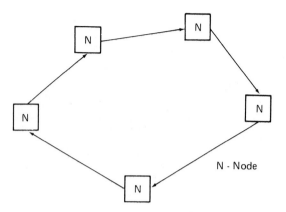

Figure 5-10 Ring Topology

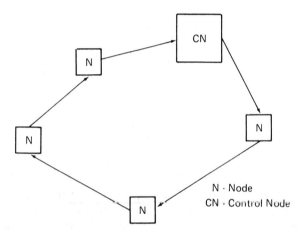

Figure 5-11 Loop Topology

BUS

In bus topology, unlike the star topology, there is no switching required, and no repeating messages as they are passed round the ring. The bus is simply the cable that connects the nodes (fig.5-12). As with the ring, the message is "broadcast" by one node to all other nodes and recognized by means of an address by the receiving node. This broadcast of the message propagates throughout the length of the medium. One advantage the bus has over the ring is that the delays due to repeating and forwarding the message are eliminated. Since the nodes are passive, the system is failsafe. A faulty node will not affect the other nodes. Bus networks are also easily installed and expanded.

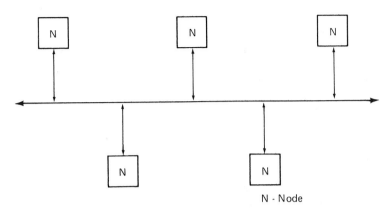

N - Node

Figure 5-12   Bus Topology

A tree is a generalization of bus topology in which the cable branches at either or both ends, but which offers only one transmission path between any two nodes (fig.5-13). As with the bus, any node "broadcasts" its message, which can be picked up by any other node in the network.

In the past, the LAN market in North America was dominated by bus and tree topologies. With the entry of an IBM ring-based LAN, this is expected to change.

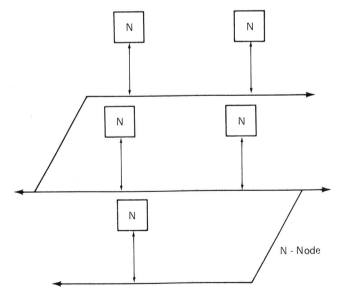

N - Node

Figure 5-13   Tree Topology

SUMMARY

Wide area networks are usually irregular mesh topologies that are subject to frequent change based on user demand. Private networks are often implemented with leased and dial-up lines. Public networks often use packet switching. It is not surprising, given the degree of complexity involved, that an emphasis in the development of these large networks is being placed on dynamic routing algorithms.

Local area network topology is relatively simple and easily expandable. Growth in this area is directed towards the interconnection of LANs to form simple mesh networks that are compounds of the LAN topologies discussed. These compound networks have been described as metropolitan area networks, networks linking LANs throughout a city or metropolitan area. Another way of extending the capability of LAN nodes is the gateway, which connects LANs to wide area networks. The *gateway* is a special node on the LAN that converts the LAN packet to the wide area network's format and vice versa.

Review Questions for Chapter 5

1. Complete the following table.

Logical Connection	Advantage	Disadvantage
point-to-point multipoint circuit switching message switching packet switching		

2. Give three examples of transparency in computer systems.

3. Identify the following topologies.

(a) 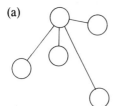 (b) 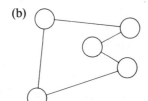 (c)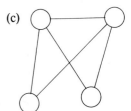

4. Define the following terms as they apply to packet-switching routing algorithms.

    a) directory
    b) random
    c) flooding

5. Describe the routing algorithm for each of the following LAN topologies:

ring, star, bus, tree, loop

Chapter

PROTOCOL

INTRODUCTION

As networks become more complex and wide-reaching and as the require-ments for interlinking grow, the need for international protocol standards grows proportionately.

A protocol is defined as a "set of rules." Most familiarly used in a military or diplomatic sense, the term is now applied to data communication systems. There are protocols for making connections, transferring messages, and per-forming enough other functions that they can be considered as a hierarchy of levels or layers. The establishment of a connection between two terminals would obey the lowest level of protocol. The transfer of a file of information to solve a specific problem would follow the protocol of a more advanced level on the hierarchy, and so on.

A protocol can be defined in terms of its level of "closeness" to the hardware in the same way that computer languages are categorized as high- or low-level. The International Standards Organization (ISO) has proposed a seven-level architecture called the Reference Model of Open Systems Interconnection, which can be remembered by the palindromic acronym ISO-OSI (fig.6-1). It should be remembered that the ISO-OSI is a set of guidelines, not a precisely defined standard.

Level	Function	Examples
1. Physical	physical transmission via a medium	RS-232-C RS-449 X.21
2. Data link control	reliable transmission of messages across a single data link	HDLC SDLC BISYNC ASYNC
3. Network control	packet handling, addressing, routing, call establishment, maintenance and clearing	X.25
4. Transport control	end-to-end control, transmission control and efficiency	
5. Session control	system-to-system control session monitoring and management	
6. Presentation control	library routines, encryption, compaction, code conversion	
7. Application	network management, network transparency	

Figure 6-1   ISO-OSI

THE PHYSICAL LEVEL (LEVEL 1)

Protocols at this level involve such parameters as the signal voltage swing and bit duration, the question of whether transmission is simplex, half-duplex, or full-duplex, whether it is synchronous or asynchronous, and how connections are established at each end. To interconnect data terminal equipment (DTE) such as a computer, terminal, word processor, or printer, to data communication equipment (DCE) commonly known as a modem or data set, an interface standard is required. The EIA RS-232-C, the EIA RS-449, and the CCITT X.21 are three prominent physical-level standards.

The EIA RS-232-C

This standard is used extensively in North America and contains detailed specification for a 25-pin connector in terms of:

— electrical signal characteristics,
— mechanical characteristics, and
— a functional description of the interchange circuit specifications for particular applications.

The most significant standards for establishing the protocol for communication between a terminal and a modem are the signals defined for the interchange circuits. The most important of these are:

Request to send (RTS):   an indication by the DTE to the DCE that it is ready to transmit.

Clear to send (CTS):   an indication by the DCE to the DTE that it is ready to receive and to retransmit the data.

Transmitted data: serial data is transmitted from the DTE to the DCE to be modulated.

Received data: demodulated data is received serially by the DTE from the DCE.

Data carrier detect (DCD): an indication by the remote DCE to the remote DTE that it is receiving a carrier signal.

Recall that the two main problems associated with serial transmission are the conversion between serial and parallel data and mutual synchronization. The solution to the synchronization problem leads to two major classes of communication systems: those that use asynchronous and those that use synchronous communication.

ASYNCHRONOUS COMMUNICATION

The proliferation of personal computers has increased the demand for a relatively low-speed, unsophisticated method of communication between the microcomputer and a mainframe installation. The most commonly used system to date is an asynchronous full-duplex link running at 300 – 1200 baud.

Figure 6-2 shows the signal sequence for a half-duplex communication at level 1. The RTS initiates the carrier, which turns on DCD and CTS, then the data is transmitted. When transmission is complete, RTS is turned off, which turns off the carrier and CTS. Turning off the carrier also automatically turns off DCD.

In full-duplex mode both DTEs are transmitting and receiving so that Transmitted Data and Received Data are active at the same time. This means RTS and DCD are always on.

We have assumed here that there is no dialing or switching involved. On a switched line, manual or autodialing would precede these steps. On a leased line, the modem power switch also initiates the communication sequence.

SYNCHRONOUS COMMUNICATION

For large volumes of data transmitted between mainframes, a higher transmission rate reduces line costs. Synchronous transmission is more efficient in

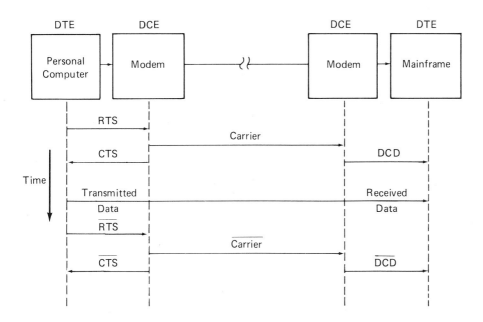

Figure 6-2   Level 1 Communication

this context, particularly in conjunction with a large number of remote sites.

At level 1, the protocol established between the DTE and the DCE is similar to that of the asynchronous system. The main difference is that the data is sent in synchronism with timing signals generated by a clock in the DCE. Synchronous modems communicate with one another to synchronize their clocks. Two additional signals on the RS-232-C are required, therefore, for:

transmit timing: a signal from the DCE to the DTE to "clock" the data being transmitted from the DTE to the DCE.

receive timing: a signal from the DCE to the DTE to enable the incoming data to be sampled at the correct speed. This clock is derived from the carrier by the DCE.

The EIA RS-449

An EIA upgrade of the RS-232-C, the RS-449 consists of a 37-pin connector containing additional functions such as diagnostic circuits and a 9-pin connector for secondary channel circuits. The RS-449 has been designed to accommodate a growing variety of communication needs including increased cable length and transmission speeds.

The X.21

X.21 is the level 1 standard for X.25, the CCITT's packet-switching protocol. Instead of each connector pin being assigned a specific function (RS-232-C and RS-449), each function is assigned a character stream. This approach has reduced the connector requirement to 15 pins but demands more intelligence of the DTE and the DCE. Because of the enormous investment in the RS-232-C interface, X.21 is not used in North America.

THE DATA-LINK CONTROL LEVEL (LEVEL 2)

At this level, outgoing messages are assembled into frames, and acknowledgments (if called for at higher levels) are awaited following each message transmission. Outgoing frames include a destination address at the link level and, if the higher levels require it, a source address as well, plus a trailer containing an error-detecting or error-correcting code. The data portion of the frame is whatever comes down to this level from level 3, without reference to its significance. Correct operation at this level assures reliable transmission of each message. Data link control is the most interesting level of protocol because it occurs at the interface between hardware and software. It is the most important level of control because it includes consideration of protocols ranging from the simple microcomputer/printer interface to the most sophisticated high-speed synchronous packet-switched networks. It is the most difficult level because of the number of different facets involved and their interrelationships. First, we need a map of the data link control world (fig.6-3). The major characteristics of data link control that must be considered are:

— whether the protocol is half- or full-duplex,
— how the units of information are laid out;
— how nodes establish and relinquish control of the line,
— how errors may be detected and corrected, and
— how continuous sending and receiving may be controlled.

Duplex

We have already established how simplex, half-duplex and full-duplex circuits work. It now turns out that there are two distinct categories of protocol called half-duplex protocols and full-duplex protocols that work on either half- or full-duplex lines, that is, these protocols are independent of circuit type.

Half-duplex protocols permit transmission between two nodes to occur in

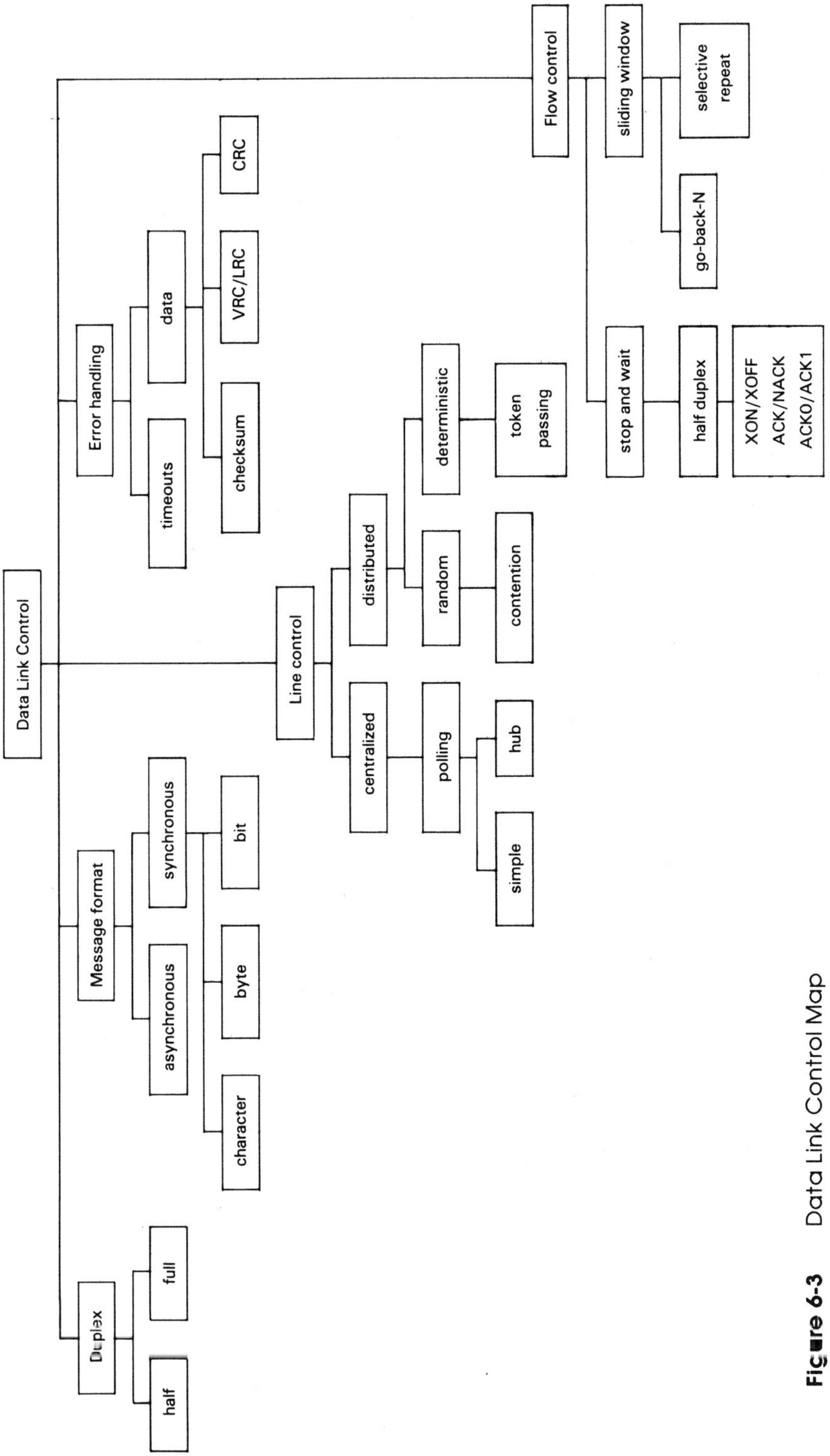

Figure 6-3   Data Link Control Map

one direction at a time. The relationship between the nodes is described as *master/slave*. The master node is responsible for the data transfers and the slave node for acknowledging receipt of data from its partner. Half-duplex protocols are most widely used for asynchronous transfer between microcomputers and mainframes at relatively low transmission rates, typically 1200 bps. Kermit is a popular asynchronous half-duplex protocol because there are versions available for almost every microcomputer on the market. IBM's BISYNC is a well-established widely used example of a synchronous half-duplex protocol.

Full-duplex protocols permit data transmission between two nodes to occur in both directions at the same time. In this case both nodes are responsible for their own information transfers as well as for acknowledging the receipt of data from their partner. All packet-switching networks use synchronous full-duplex protocol, typically at 9600 bps and above.

Since each protocol type can operate with each circuit type, there are four possibilities. Half-duplex protocols are used with half-duplex circuits (two-wire) on dial-up systems, since local loops have only two wires. Half-duplex protocols are used with full-duplex circuits (four-wire) on leased lines. Micro/mainframe file transfer is normally effected using half-duplex dial-ups for remote access and four-wire limited distance modem connections locally. Full-duplex protocols are used with full-duplex circuits in packet-switching networks. Full-duplex protocols are also used with half-duplex circuits on dial-up lines as a way of eliminating modem turnaround time (fig.6-4).

Circuit	Protocol	Process	Application
HD	HD	alternate	asynchronous file transfer on a dial-up line
FD	HD	alternate	asynchronous file transfer on a leased line
FD	FD	simultaneous	synchronous transfer
HD	FD	simultaneous	dial-up using a split channel modem

Figure 6-4   Circuit/Protocol Combinations

Message Format

The signals required for synchronous and asynchronous transmission are generated at level 1. The message format for synchronous and asynchronous communication is a level 2 consideration. The asynchronous message format has been traditionally a one-character format, start and stop bits providing a significant transmission overhead. File transmission between microcomputers and mainframes has sparked the development of asynchronous communication packages with error checking mechanisms that combine the individual character transmission of asynchronous transmission with the packet concept of synchronous transmission. This topic will be discussed in the chapter on micro/mainframe communications.

Synchronous communication formats are subdivided into three categories: character-, byte-count-, and bit-oriented. In character-oriented synchronous communication protocols the data is framed by specific control characters. The industry standard is IBM's Binary Synchronous Communications Protocol (BISYNC), which uses special characters for control of message transmission (fig.6-5).

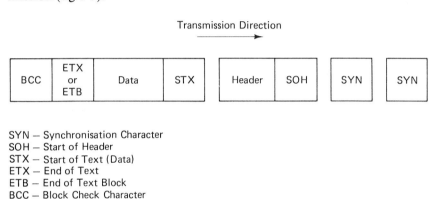

Transmission Direction

| BCC | ETX or ETB | Data | STX | | Header | SOH | | SYN | | SYN |

SYN — Synchronisation Character
SOH — Start of Header
STX — Start of Text (Data)
ETX — End of Text
ETB — End of Text Block
BCC — Block Check Character

Figure 6-5   BISYNC (IBM's Binary Synchronous Communications Protocol)

Byte-count-oriented protocols include a count of how many characters follow in the data portion of the message. An example of byte-count protocols is DEC's Digital Data Communication Message Protocol (DDCMP), which is a generalized method of data link control that includes message-numbering information and a field to keep track of the number of characters in the message (fig.6-6).

Bit-oriented protocols are by far the most popular and recently developed protocols for packet-switching networks. A standard with minor variations has emerged. The X.25 protocol was adopted by the Consultative Committee on International Telephony and Telegraphy (CCITT) to define the rules governing the use of a public packet-switching network. It was developed jointly by France, Japan, the United States, the United Kingdom, and Canada. In addition, all nine countries of the European Common Market adopted X.25 as the basis for the packet-switching Euronet network. This protocol is

Transmission Direction

CRC 2 (16)	Data	CRC 1 (16)	Address (8)	Sequencer (8)	Response (8)	Flag (2)	Count (14)	Class (8)	SYN (8)	SYN (8)

The Bracketed Numbers Show the Allocation
in Bits for Each Control Field for a Total of
12 Bytes (96 Bits) of Control Information.
The Maximum Number of Bytes in the Data
Field is 16,383

Figure 6-6   DDCMP (Digital Equipment Corporation's Digital Data
Communications Message Protocol)

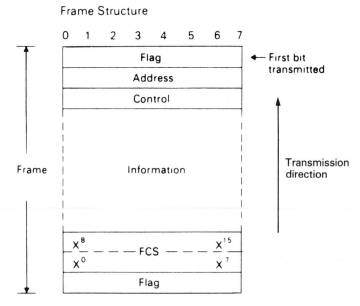

Figure 6-7   Frame Structure

compatible with the International Standards Organization's (ISO) High-level
Data Link Control (HDLC) protocol. IBM's Synchronous Data Link Control
(SDLC) protocol is a variant of HDLC. All transmissions between stations are
organized in blocks of information, or frames, with a standard basic structure
(fig.6-7).

Bit-oriented protocols are simpler, have superior error-handling mechanisms, and are independent of network structure.

Line Control

Line control determines which station is going to transmit and which is going to receive. It is of particular significance in cases of multipoint connections.

Centralized line control or polling is the basis for mainframe/terminal configurations with star or multipoint topologies. One variation is called hub polling, in which each terminal that does not desire to communicate with the mainframe passes the request on to the next terminal on a multidrop line. This eliminates the line turnaround time that occurs if each station has to receive a poll from the master.

In distributed line control, which is confined to local area networks, each node participates equally in controlling the network. There are two categories of distributed line control: random, in which each node competes for the line on a first-come, first-served basis (contention protocol), and deterministic, in which each node waits its turn (token passing).

Error Handling

Errors incurred in transmitting messages or frames or packets or blocks or any other unit of information transfer over noisy lines are usually handled by error check characters. These are calculated by the transmitter and appended to the message. The receiver repeats the calculation and compares check characters.

CHECKSUM

This error detection method adds together the numerical values of all the characters in the block and takes the least significant n bits of the result, where n is the number of bits in the checksum characters (fig.6-8). This is a relatively poor method of error detection used primarily with asynchronous half-duplex communication packages.

	Hex	ASCII Code
C	43	1000011
H	48	1001000
E	45	1000101
C	43	1000011
K	4B	1001011
ƀ	20	0100000
S	53	1010011
U	55	1010101
M	4D	1001101
SUM = 100		1110011
Checksum = 1110011		

Figure 6-8   Checksum

VRC/LRC

This error detection method is a combination of the traditional parity addition to each character transmitted (vertical redundancy check) and a horizontal parity bit generated from each row of the block (longitudinal redundancy check). VRC/LRC is used by IBM's BISYNC protocol (fig.6-9).

Bit position	Character V R C / L R C	Block check character
1	0 0 1 1 0 0 1	0
2	1 1 1 1 0 1 1	1
3	1 0 0 1 1 0 0	0
4	0 0 0 1 1 0 0	1
5	1 1 0 0 0 1 0	0
6	0 0 0 1 0 0 0	0
7	1 1 1 0 1 1 1	1
Odd parity	1 0 0 0 0 0 0	0

Figure 6-9   VRC/LRC (used to create BCC for BISYNC)

CRC

The cyclic redundancy check is a more accurate way of checking a block of characters than checksum or VRC/LRC. This method divides the data stream by a preset binary number. The transmitted data is the dividend, and the remainder is the check data appended to the block. CRC is used by bit-oriented protocols such as X.25. The CCITT recommended divisor is 10001000000100001, which produces 16 bits of check data. The derivation of the check data for CRC is illustrated in figure 6-10 using a five-bit divisor. The information, plus the number of bits in the FCS as zeros (in this example, four), is divided by the generator polynomial to produce the real FCS. At the receiving end, the division of information and FCS should produce a zero remainder, signifying no errors in transmission.

Flow Control

The heart of the data-link control level of protocol is flow control, which is concerned with controlling the rate of transmission of units of information on

```
                    10110  1101001 10000
                           10110xx x x x x x
                           011000
                          ⊕10110
                           011101
                          ⊕10110
                           010111
                          ⊕10110
                           000010
                          ⊕00000
                           000100
                          ⊕00000
                           001000
                          ⊕00000
                           010000
                          ⊕10110
 ⊕ Exclusive "or"          0110
 Information: 11010011
 Generator Polynomial: 10110
 Frame check sequence: 0110
```

Figure 6-10   CRC (illustrated using a five-bit polynomial)

a link so that the receiver always has sufficient buffer storage to accept the data transmitted to it. Inherent in the consideration of flow control is a method for correcting errors and smoothly incorporating the corrections back into the communication process. There are two main types of flow control: the stop-and-wait method, more appropriate to lower-speed asynchronous systems, and the sliding window approaches used in high-speed packet-switching networks.

STOP-AND-WAIT

The simplest flow control protocol incorporated into many data link protocols is also used as a printer control. The printer acknowledges the receipt of data with an XON (transmit on) signal. When the transmission rate exceeds the printer's capacity it sends an XOFF (transmit off) signal to halt transmission (fig. 6-11).

Another simple flow control technique is the ACK/NAK (acknowledge/ negate acknowledge) combination in which the receiver has the option of accepting the block of data or, after having checked it, rejecting it, and giving the transmitter the chance to send it again (fig. 6-12).

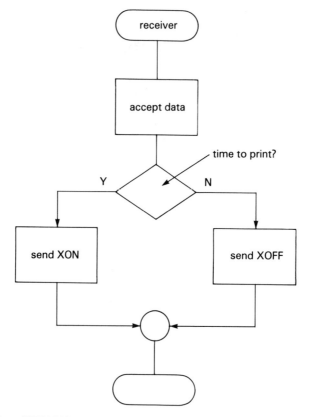

Figure 6-11   XON/XOFF

The inclusion of simple sequence control in the form of two signals ACK0 and ACK1 improves the ACK/NAK combination by permitting the detection of the same block being sent twice or the omission of a block (fig. 6-13).

SLIDING WINDOWS

In full-duplex protocols where two nodes are simultaneously sending blocks of data, the stop-and-wait technique does not work. Depending on the communication distance, each node may be several blocks ahead before detection of an error in a specific block occurs. The go-back-N signal from the receiver tells the transmitter to re-send the last N blocks (fig. 6-14).

A refinement of this technique is the selective-repeat approach that only requires those blocks with errors to be re-sent (fig. 6-15).

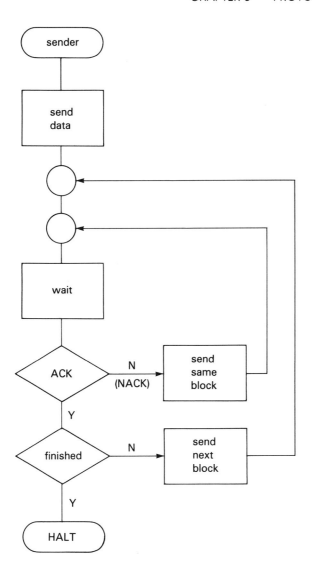

Figure 6-12   ACK/NACK

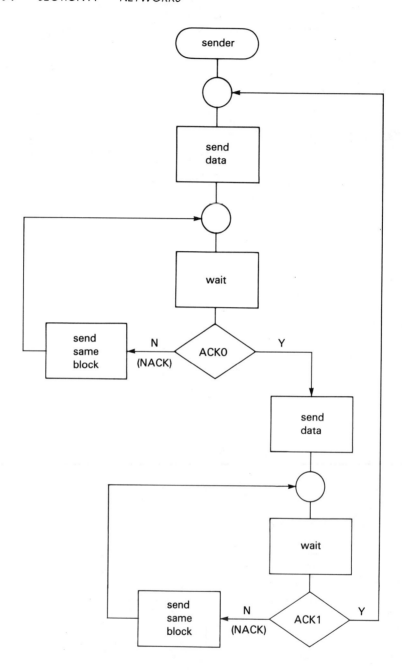

Figure 6-13   ACK0/ACK1

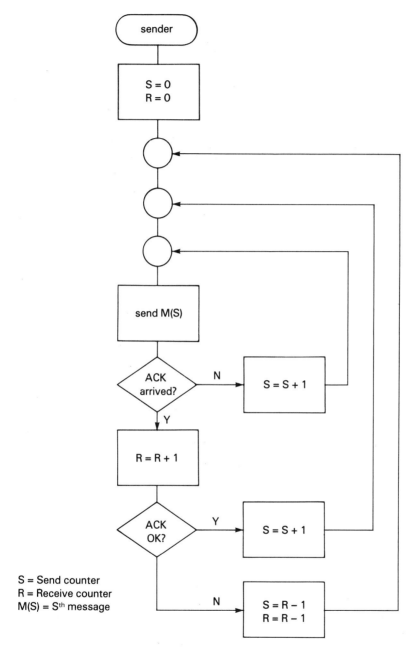

Figure 6-14   Go-back-N

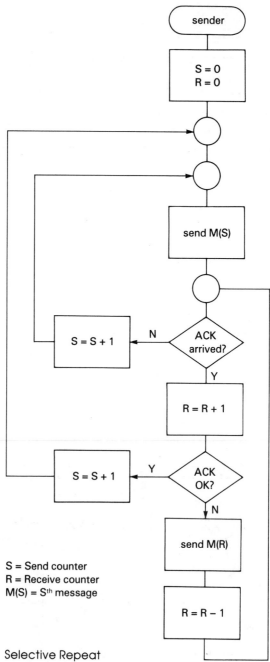

S = Send counter
R = Receive counter
M(S) = Sth message

Figure 6-15   Selective Repeat

Applications

Level 2 protocol can be subdivided into two categories: synchronous and asynchronous protocols. The synchronous protocols can be further classified, as we learned earlier, into character, block-count, and bit protocols. The asynchronous protocols can be subdivided into the simple character-at-a-time transfers that are used to transmit information via a keyboard, and asynchronous block transfer used by asynchronous communication packages for file transfer. Asynchronous block transfer is a combination of the start/stop character used for simple asynchronous operations and the header/data/trailer layout of synchronous protocols (fig. 6-16).

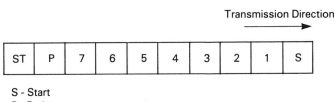

S - Start
P - Parity
ST - Stop

a) Typical 7-bit plus parity asynchronous protocol.

b) Asynchronous block transfer in which each character is transmitted with start and stop bits as in a) above.

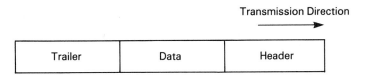

c) Synchronous transfer in which the data has no start/stop bits.

Figure 6-16   Synchronous and Asynchronous Protocols

ASYNCHRONOUS PROTOCOLS

In the context of personal computer communication with mainframes, a variety of software packages have been developed, with varying degrees of sophistication, that provide the level 2 requirements for:

(a) converting the personal computer to a simple (dumb) terminal (simple asynchronous operation).

(b) transmitting files by block in either direction (asynchronous block transfer).

(c) detecting errors and retransmitting blocks.

A copy of the package has to be available at each end. Typical examples include Kermit, ASYNC, and Zstem. These communication packages will be explained in Section C.

SYNCHRONOUS PROTOCOLS

(1) A character-oriented protocol: BISYNC

IBM's Binary Synchronous Communications, a more traditional approach to protocol, is still in common use. The format of a BISYNC message is shown in figure 6-5.

> SYN is a synchronization character that is used to keep the sending and receiving terminals in step. SYN is added by the sender and removed by the receiver.

> SOH (start of header) tells the receiver that the information following is control information that relates to addressing and sequencing of user data.

> STX (start of text) identifies the start of the user's information.

There are two kinds of information that can be transferred:

1. Characters from a standard character set, such as ASCII or EBCDIC. The user's information is then terminated by ETX (end of text) or ETB (end of text block) (fig. 6-17).

Transmission Direction ⟶

ETX or ETB	Data	STX

Figure 6-17   Standard Character Set

2. Data that may contain control characters, from an analog to digital converter, for example. To prevent user data from being "recognized" by the receiver as control characters, BISYNC uses DLE (data link escape) (fig. 6-18).

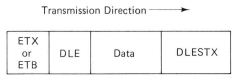

Figure 6-18   Non-Standard Text

When DLE is first encountered by the receiver, the data that follows is treated as user data; that is, it is not tested for control characters. Any control characters present on the data are "transparent" to the receiver. The only problem, of course, is that DLE is also used to signal termination of the user's data. If a pattern of bits occurs on the user's data that is equivalent to a DLE, the transmitter adds a second DLE to indicate that the first one is data. The receiver removes the second occurrence of all pairs of DLEs. The end of user's data is detected by means of DLE ETX or DLE ETB.

BCC (block check character), is used for detection of errors which have occurred during the transmission of the user's data. Since ASCII is a seven-bit code, BISYNC incorporates parity into its error-checking mechanism and uses a combination of LRC and VRC when transmitting in ASCII. The BCC is the LRC part of the combination. Because EBCDIC is an eight-bit code with no parity, BISYNC uses a CRC error-checking mechanism for its BCC when transmitting EBCDIC. The BISYNC sequence of operation is illustrated in the flowchart of figure 6-19.

The transmitter attempts to make contact with the receiver by sending an enquiry signal (ENQ). The receiver may respond with an ACK (acknowledgement) to say "you may send the data." The data to be sent is handled in blocks, and the transmitter keeps track of these by a numbering system. The transmitter initializes the block number to 1 and transmits the first block. The receiver acknowledges receipt (ACK). The transmitter checks to see if all blocks have been sent. If not, it sends the next block until all the blocks have been sent. Then the transmitter will terminate the communication by sending an end of transmission signal (EOT).

The flowchart in figure 6-19 is an oversimplification of the situation, but it does cover initiation, termination, and control of a two-way communication. It contains one obvious flaw. If the receiver sends an NAK signal back to the transmitter indicating an error in the message it received, the flowchart enters an endless loop. This problem can easily be solved by means of a retry counter which would limit the number of times a transmitter would send a particular block of data.

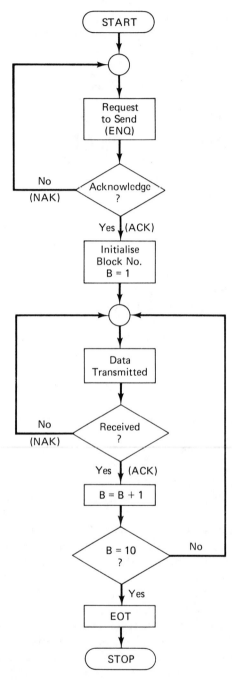

Figure 6-19   BISYNC Flowchart (Simple)

There are many other problems associated with accurate data transmission that have been solved in various ways. For example, to prevent a block of data from being lost completely, two forms of acknowledgement are used, ACK0 for even blocks and ACK1 for odd blocks.

There are contingencies associated with delays incurred in the system. Timeouts are used to create pauses before resending data and reseeking acknowledgement of accurate transfer.

Figure 6-20 is an improved version of the figure 6-19 flowchart. It explains the sequential operation of BISYNC protocol and incorporates the retry counter, busy receiver, and timeouts.

(2) A bit-oriented protocol: X.25

The prime function of level 2, the data link, is the transfer of data between the user (DTE) and the network (DCE). This transfer must include control transmissions for initiating, sequencing, checking, and terminating the exchange of user information. For this level of protocol, the CCITT X.25 recommends a procedure compatible with the High-level Data Link Control (HDLC) procedure standardized by the International Standards Organization (ISO). IBM's Synchronous Data Link Control (SDLC) is a variant of HDLC used within IBM's own networks.

The control procedures subscribe to the principles of a new ISO class of procedures for a point-to-point balanced system. (A balanced electrical circuit is more tolerant of electrical noise than an unbalanced circuit is. Because of this, the speed and distance characteristics of balanced circuits are superior to unbalanced circuits.) The link configuration is a point-to-point channel with two stations. Each station has two functions. The primary function is to manage its own information transfer and recovery. The secondary function is to respond to requests from the other stations. In essence, these functions are commands and responses respectively.

The data link procedures are defined in terms of commands and responses and can be thought of as two independent but complementary transmission paths that are superimposed on a single physical circuit. The DTE controls its transmissions to the DCE, and the DCE controls its transmissions to the DTE.

SYNCHRONIZATION

To transmit information across a link, the link must be synchronized. This is accomplished by enclosing each frame with unique bit patterns, called flags. Once the receiver recognizes the flag, it knows it is in step with the transmitter

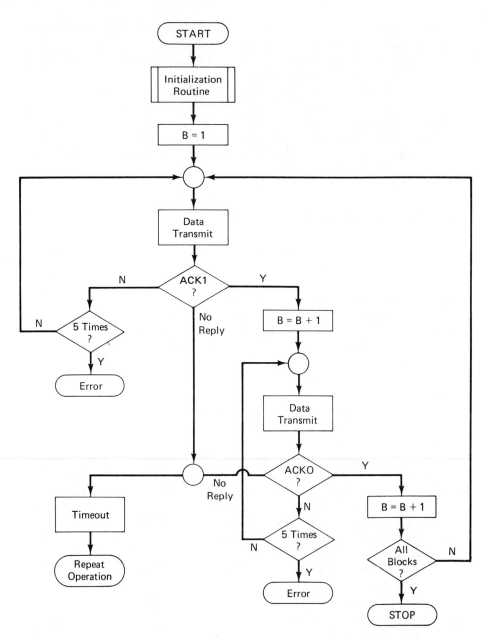

Figure 6-20   BISYNC Flowchart (Improved)

and in a position to accept the content of the frame. Similarly, when the receiver recognizes the second flag, it knows that all the information has been received. The receiver is now in a position to check the transmission and act upon the information it contains.

The potential occurrence of a flag bit pattern within the information is prevented by a mechanism similar to that described in the BISYNC protocol. The occurrence of a flag bit pattern in the information is made transparent to the receiving station. The transmitting station examines the frame content between the two flags, which includes the address, control, and FCS (frame control sequence) data, and inserts a 0 after all sequences of five contiguous 1 bits to ensure that a flag sequence is not simulated. The flag bit pattern is 01111110. The receiving station removes any 0 bit that directly follows five 1s.

COMMANDS AND RESPONSES

There are three variations on the frame structure of the X.25 data link control protocol:

1. Information frames, which are used to perform an information transfer, and may also be used to respond to a correctly transmitted information frame.

2. Supervisory frames, which are used to perform link control functions responding to received information frames.

3. Unnumbered frames, which provide additional link control functions.

Figure 6-21 provides a summary and a comparison of BISYNC and X.25 based on the facets of data-link control discussed at the beginning of this chapter.

Factor	BISYNC	X.25
Duplex	half-duplex	full-duplex
Message format	character	bit
Line control	centralized	centralized
Error handling	VRC/LRC	CRC
Flow control	ACKO/1	go-back-N

Figure 6-21   BISYNC versus X.25

THE NETWORK CONTROL LEVEL (LEVEL 3)

At this level, outgoing messages are divided into packets. Incoming packets are assembled into messages for the higher levels. Routing information, included in the packet, defines the destination of the packet and indicates the order of transmission. (The packets are not necessarily received in the same order in which they were sent when a packet network is used.) The header usually includes a source address.

This level of protocol specifies the way in which users establish, maintain, and clear calls in the network. It also specifies the way in which a user's data and control information are structured into packets. The relationship between the user data packet and the frame structure of the X.25 data link control protocol is shown in figure 6-22.

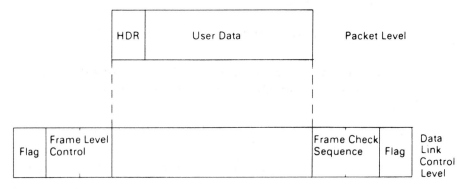

Figure 6-22   Frame/Packet Relationship

Source: Reproduced courtesy of Telecom Canada.

A fundamental concept of packet switching is that of the *virtual circuit.* Just as circuit switching permits a physical link between two stations, a virtual circuit permits a logical bi-directional association between two stations (DTEs). This logical link is assigned only when packets are being transferred. A permanent virtual circuit is a permanent association between two DTEs, much like a private line. A switched virtual circuit is a temporary association between two DTEs and is initiated when a DTE sends a call-request packet to the network.

At the packet level, DTEs can establish simultaneous communication with a number of other DTEs in the network. This is accomplished in a single physical circuit by means of asynchronous time-division multiplexing (ATDM). This type of multiplexing is similar to the straightforward time-division multiplexing concept of improving the efficiency of information transfer by interleaving messages into gaps of other messages. Dynamically allocating the bandwidth to active, virtual-circuit ATDM further improves the transfer rate and was referred to in chapter 4 as statistical multiplexing. The time previously allocated to non-active terminals is now used on a first-come, first-served basis.

The interleaved packets are transferred from the DTE to the DCE using the frame format of the data link control protocol. Each packet contains a logical channel identifier to relate the packet to a switched or permanent virtual circuit. Figure 6-23 illustrates a typical packet transfer between the DTE and the DCE.

The logical channel identifier (LCI) is used strictly at the local level of the network, or between a DTE and a DCE. The LCIs are selected at each DTE and are used independently of all other DTEs. The LCIs associated with permanent virtual circuits cannot be used for any other purpose. The LCIs used with switched virtual circuits are all free initially and can be used by the DTE to originate new calls or to receive incoming calls from the network.

Call Establishment and Clearing

There are several packets associated with setting up a communication link between two DTEs. These packets include:

1. A *call request packet* sent by the calling DTE to the network. This packet includes the logical channel identifier; the address of the DTE called; a facility field for reverse charging, priority, or user restrictions; and user data of 16 bytes.

2. A *call connected packet* sent to the calling DTE to confirm that the call has been accepted.

3. A *clear indication packet* sent to the calling DTE to indicate that the call was not established and to provide one of several reasons for this, such as number busy.

4. An *incoming packet* received by the called DTE in an available logical channel as a result of a call request packet (the formats are very similar).

5. A *call accepted packet* sent by the called DTE that indicates a positive response to a call request. The network uses the call accepted packet to generate a call connected packet for the calling DTE.

6. A *clear request packet* sent by either DTE to free the logical channel after data transfer is complete.

A sequence diagram showing the stimulus/response relationship required to establish a call between two DTEs is given in figure 6-24.

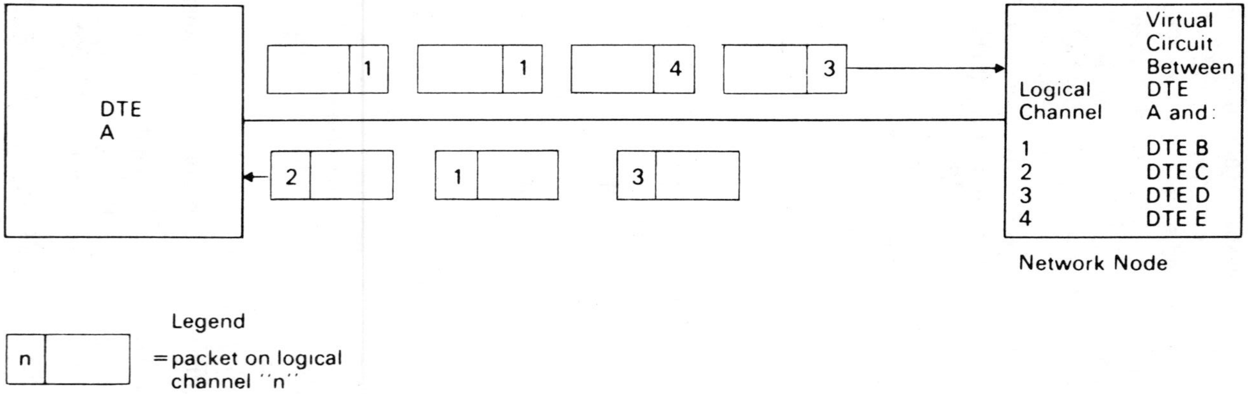
DTE
A
1
1
4
3
2
1
3
Logical
Channel
Virtual
Circuit
Between
DTE
A and:
1 DTE B
2 DTE C
3 DTE D
4 DTE E
Network Node
Legend
n
= packet on logical
channel "n"

Figure 6-23 Packet Flow

Source: Reproduced courtesy of Telecom Canada.

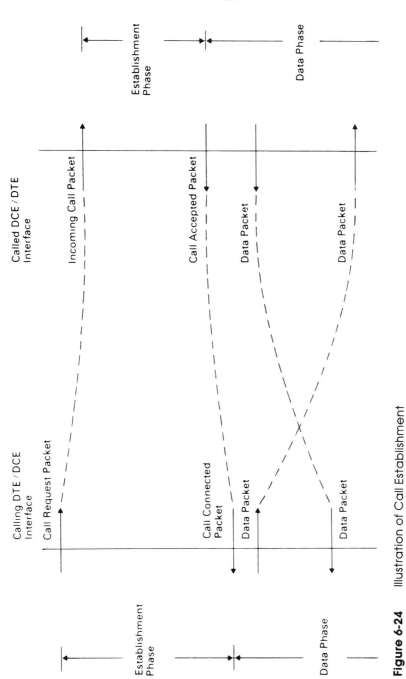

Figure 6-24 Illustration of Call Establishment

Source: Reproduced courtesy of Telecom Canada.

Data Transfer

Data transfer can take place only after the virtual circuit has been established. The format is shown in figure 6-25. P(S) is the packet send-sequence number. (Only data packets are numbered.) P(R) is the receive-sequence number used to locally confirm the receipt of packets. M is used in a full data packet to indicate continuation of the data on the next packet. Type=Data distinguishes this format from all the others. The maximum data field length is normally initialized to 256 bytes, but this may be revised by the user.

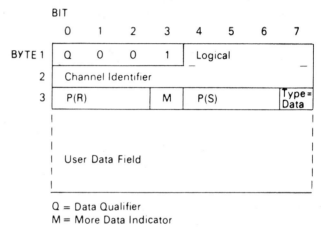

Q = Data Qualifier
M = More Data Indicator

Figure 6-25   Data Packet Format

Source: Reproduced courtesy of Telecom Canada.

Figure 6-26 offers another approach to understanding information transfer at the packet level. The following list of events at each logical channel will help in comprehending the diagram.

State 1:   A logical channel is in the ready state if there is no call in existence.

State 2:   A call request packet sent by a DTE puts the logical channel in the DTE waiting state.

State 3:   An incoming call packet sent by a DTE puts the logical channel in the DCE waiting state.

State 4:   A call accepted packet from a DTE, resulting from an incoming call packet, puts the logical channel in the data transfer state. Similarly, a call connected packet from a DCE, resulting from a call request, leads to data transfer.

State 5:   When a DTE and DCE transfer a call request packet and an incoming call packet, respectively and at the same time, a call collision occurs. The DCE will proceed with the request and cancel the incoming call.

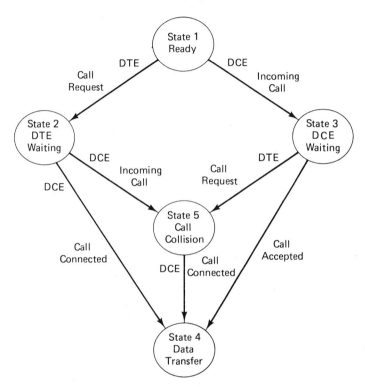

Figure 6-26   Call Setup State Diagram

Source: Reproduced courtesy of Telecom Canada.

THE TRANSPORT LEVEL (LEVEL 4)

This may be the busiest of all the architectural levels. Its protocol establishes network connections for a given transmission, for example, whether several parallel paths will be required for high throughput, whether several paths can be multiplexed onto a single connection to reduce the cost of transmission, or whether the transmission should be broadcast. This is the lowest level of strictly end-to-end communication, where the involvement or even the existence of intervening nodes is ignored.

The transport level provides the facilities that allow end users to transmit across several intervening nodes. Of the upper four levels, the transport level is the one which is relatively well defined; a good example is the European Computer Manufacturers' Association ECMA-72 transport protocol standard. The services provided by this level include the optimizing of:

— costs,
— quality of service,
— multiplexing,
— data unit size, and
— addressing.

The main purpose of the transport level is to free the higher levels from cost and reliability considerations.

THE SESSION CONTROL LEVEL (LEVEL 5)

It is at this level that the user establishes the system-to-system connection. It controls logging on and off, user identification and billing, and session management. For example, on a data-base management system, the failure of a transmitting node during a transaction would be calamitous, because it would leave the data base in an inconsistent state. Level 5 organizes message transmissions in such a way as to minimize the probability of such a mishap, perhaps by buffering the user's inputs and sending them all in a group, more quickly than they could be sent under control of a higher level.

This level provides the end users with the means of organizing and synchronizing their dialogue as well as managing their data exchange. It includes:

— initiation of the session,
— management and structuring of all session-requested data transport actions, and
— termination of the session.

THE PRESENTATION CONTROL LEVEL (LEVEL 6)

The presentation level provides for the representation of selected information. Any function that is requested often enough to justify a permanent place is held in the presentation level. Such functions include library routines, encryption, and code conversion. Three protocols are being developed for the presentation level:

— virtual terminal,
— virtual file, and
— job transfer and manipulation.

THE APPLICATION LEVEL (LEVEL 7)

This is the level seen by individual users. At this level network transparency is maintained, hiding the physical distribution of resources from the human user, partitioning a problem among several machines in distributed-processing applications, and providing access to distributed data bases that seem, to the user, to be concentrated in his CRT terminal.

The application level is the highest level of the ISO-OSI and is normally developed by the user. The user determines the messages used and the actions to be taken on receipt of a message. Other features include:

— identification of partners,
— establishment of authority,
— network management statistics,
— network transparency, and
— network monitoring.

SUMMARY

Although an absolute standard for protocol levels is not available, there is a definite trend towards the ISO-OSI seven-level architecture. This reference model attempts to provide a conceptual and functional framework that permits the independent development of standards for each of the functional levels.

The ISO has defined a seven-level protocol that is achieving widespread acceptance. The first three levels are the focus for network communications. The CCITT has developed a recommendation for the first three levels, which has gained acceptance as a basis for public packet-switched networks and for some private network architectures as well.

The first level defines the physical and logical interface betwen the DTE and the network. The standard is the RS-232-C interface, which specifies the signal characteristics for half- and full-duplex operation and synchronous and asynchronous communication.

The second level describes the way the data communication process between the DTE and the network is controlled. The data must be controlled in terms of its format, its accuracy, and its progress through the network. Additionally, the line must also be controlled in terms of the circuits connecting nodes, whether half- or full-duplex, and by either a centralized node or in a shared manner.

The third level is concerned with the movement of data within the network as packets, principally in terms of establishing efficient, accurate communication between network nodes.

The remaining levels are concerned with establishing end-to-end communication and with application considerations such as costs, session control, job handling, and network control.

Review Questions for Chapter 6

1. Identify the level of protocol associated with:

    a. flow control

    b. logging on

    c. asynchronous software

    d. message format

    e. full-duplex circuit

    f. code conversion

    g. error handling

    h. RS-232-C

    i. multiplexing

    j. encryption

    k. packets

    l. call establishment

    m. billing

    n. asynchronous data transfer

    o. network transparency

2. Complete the following hierarchy.

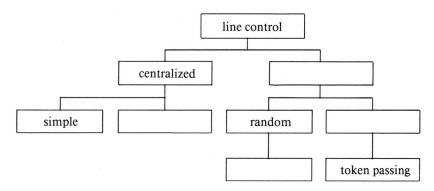

3. Complete the following table.

Message Format	Error Checking
BISYNC DDCMP X.25	

4. Calculate the checksum character and the blockcheck character for the message, "BCS470," in ASCII using odd parity.

5. Name the flow control method that contains the following:

    a) simultaneous packet transfer in both directions,

    b) transmission halt,

    c) resending multiple blocks, and

    d) "same block sent twice" detection.

6. List three BISYNC control characters and explain their function.

7. Identify three control mechanisms used in BISYNC transmission.

8. In point-to-point balanced 4-wire systems using X.25 what are the functions of each station?

9. How is the interpretation of an information code as a flag prevented?

10. Distinguish between a permanent virtual circuit and a switched virtual circuit.

11. What is the advantage of ATDM over TDM?

12. Which packet types are used to establish a call?

13. At each level of ISO-OSI, control information is added to the data transmitted, for example, an application header at the application level; a transport header at the transport level, etc. What control information is added at the datalink level?

14. What are the main differences between synchronous and asynchronous protocols?

15. Assuming they were being used for control purposes, how would you make the numeric characters of the EBCDIC code transparent to the user receiver?

16. Draw a detailed flowchart for the initialization routine of Fig. 6-20.

17. Using figure 6-27a-b answer the following questions:

    a) Which signal is used by the DTE to indicate clearing?

    b) Which signal is used by the DCE to indicate clearing?

    c) When the logical channel is the DTE clear request state, which signal does the DTE use to free the logical channel?

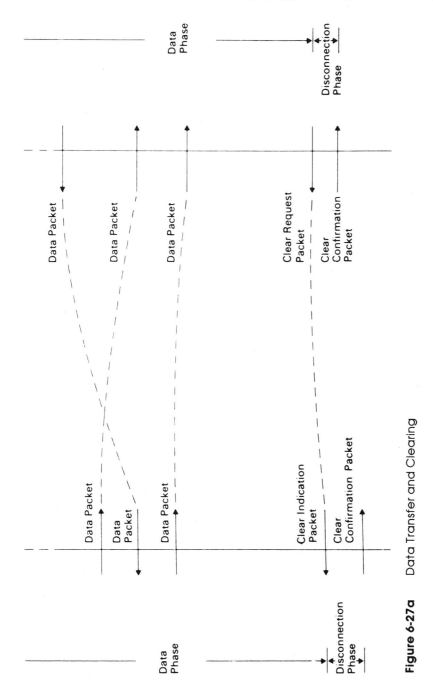

Figure 6-27a Data Transfer and Clearing

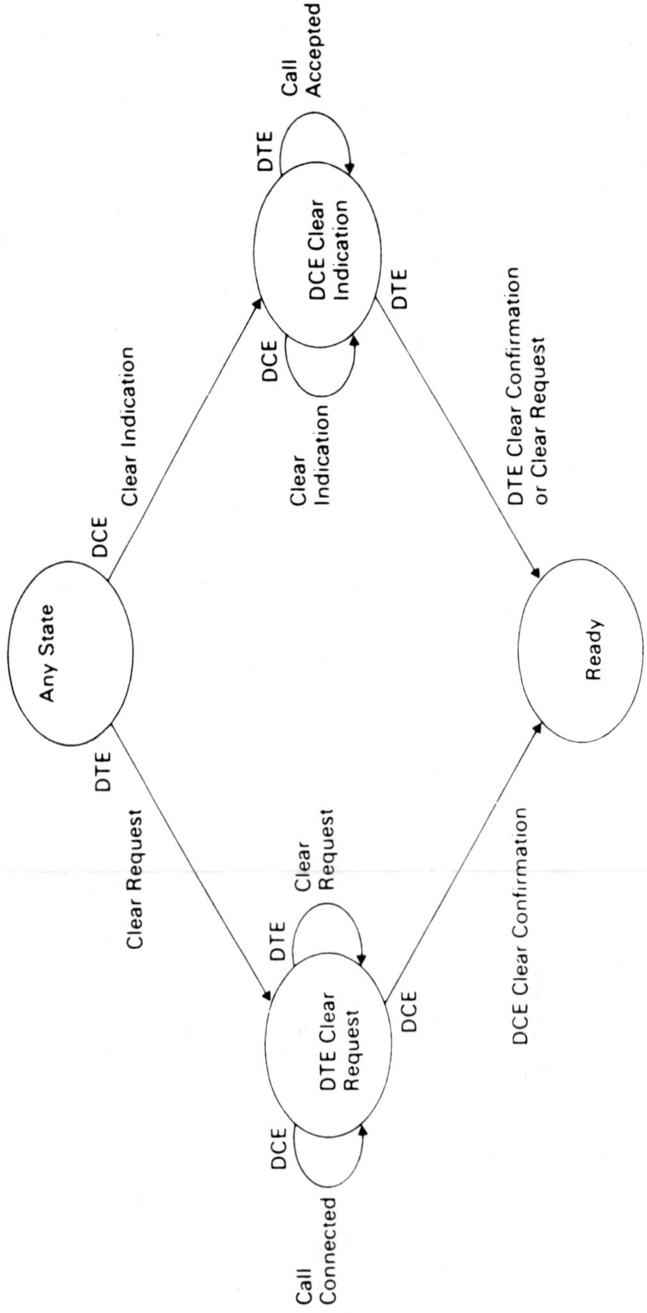

Figure 6-27b   Call Clearing

7

PUBLIC NETWORKS

INTRODUCTION

The public telephone system has been a major factor in the development of networks. Data network technology inherited a connection system that had been developed for voice communication. Voice signals are continuous, low frequency, and do not require a high degree of accuracy for the communication to be acceptable. Computer-generated data signals, on the other hand, are discrete, are most efficiently transmitted at high frequencies, and must be transmitted accurately. A variety of measures can be taken to make public telephone voice-grade lines more suitable for data transmission. An alternative is to consider replacement of the telephone connection system with a more suitable one. Telephone companies are at present implementing both approaches.

The scale of the problem is an important consideration for both approaches. For example, in Europe a telephone exchange may contain transistor and integrated circuit switches, as well as switches using large-scale integration and microprocessors. The interfacing, maintenance, and upgrading problems are considerable. This is somewhat ironic when one considers that the highly populated, highly developed countries may be hindered by their own initiative when they attempt to improve voice-grade lines for high-speed data communication. Canada is in the forefront of developing new international data networks. With less commitment to older technology, vast distances to span, and a national coordinating group, Telecom Canada, Canada is in an excellent position to contribute to international network development. In the United States, the free enterprise system encourages technological development through competition. At the same time, the creation of incompatible systems retards the development of national and international networks. The solution is to incorporate the standards of organizations like the International Standards Organization (ISO) and the Consultative Committee on International Telegraphy and Telephony (CCITT), into the competitive process.

NETWORK TYPES

An organization requiring a data communications network has a choice; it can select from a variety of leased communication facilities to build a private network, or it can use a public network. Whichever choice is made, the connection between two DTEs is complicated by the inclusion of the carrier facilities (fig. 7-1). This brings us to the heart of communication systems, which is *shared responsibility.* As networks become more complex, the problems that occur may be the responsibility of the user, the computer system supplier, or one of a number of public networks through which the data passes. Thus, network management, monitoring, and control become premium considerations for all concerned.

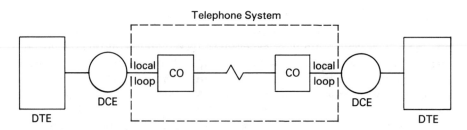

Figure 7-1   DTE to DTE Using the Telephone System

As well as the standard dial-up and private analog services that can be used for data transmission, there are three main categories of public digital data networks: circuit switching, packet switching, and dedicated digital transmission. All are available from common carriers.

Circuit switching is economical in low traffic volumes and batch-oriented applications.

Packet switching is more appropriate for efficient, flexible, higher-volume transmission as well as interactive applications (fig. 7-2).

No.	Circuit Switching	Packet Switching
1	physical connection	logical connection
2	messages not stored	messages stored
3	statically established path for complete message	the route is established dynamically for each packet
4	set-up time	negligible set-up time variable transit time
5	busy signal if receiver not available	busy signal if receiver not available
6	switching offices	switching computers
7	variable length messages	packet length messages
8	low-volume data	high-volume data
9	no speed or code conversion	speed and code conversion
10	fixed bandwidth	variable bandwidth

Figure 7-2 Circuit Switching versus Packet Switching

With the growth of satellite transmission and the conversion of higher-level telephone switching offices to digital switches, dedicated digital data transmission is one of the fastest growing areas in data communications.

Analog Transmission

Data transmission over voice-grade telephone lines requires modulation. Connections can be made temporarily or permanently.

Permanent connections over leased lines have no active switches. They can be arranged in either point-to-point or multipoint configuration. Multipoint connection reduces line costs. Leased lines are easily conditioned to improve their bandwidth (speed), but they require high usage to be cost effective. Conditioning of a line means that electronic circuitry has to be added to the line to compensate for attenuation and delay distortions in the signal.

Dial-up lines are connected when a call is placed. The time it takes to make the connection can be significant in applications where many short calls are required. Since the dial-up connection may be different each time a call is made, line conditioning is not possible. One solution is to use an automatic equalization modem to perform the same function.

Dial-up services are more flexible and less expensive than permanent services for low volumes of data to many locations but they suffer from lower data rates and electrically noisier environments. (fig. 7-3).

No.	Dial-up	Permanent
1	switched	leased
2	public	private
3	access to many other subscribers	access always available to other end
4	cost based on connect time	cost based on distance
5	noisy, unpredictable environment	can be conditioned
6	connect time	no connect time
7	up to 9600 bps	higher speeds due to conditioning

Figure 7-3   Dial-up versus Permanent Connection

Digital Transmission

Transmitting a digital signal causes degradation of the signal amplitude and shape. These problems can be solved by using repeater circuits appropriately spaced on the line to reshape the signal. The repeater circuit performs the same function as the conditioning circuits do on analog transmissions. As well as having high transmission speeds, digital transmission also facilitates direct multiplexing of a number of terminals. Problems include the cost of installing repeaters on transmission lines and the cost of replacing an already existing system.

Future Development

There are three ways in which data transmission services are improving:

1. The traditional approach is to adapt analog telephone networks for data transmission. In particular, the development of modulation techniques is significantly improving the performance characteristics of voice-grade lines.

2. The main thrust of development is towards special networks to handle data, such as packet-switching networks and dedicated digital data transmission networks.

3. The long-term solution appears to be an integrated network for voice, data, and video. The Integrated Services Digital Network (ISDN) is often referred to as "the network of the future." It is not a separate new network, but will emerge from the gradual transformation and enhancement of existing networks and services. The concept of ISDN has gained wide support. Its implementation will include:

   a) a single interface between the user and the telephone company for all services;

   b) a gateway to route information between the user and other networks (circuit-switched, packet-switched, digital) via the ISDN network;

   c) the ISDN core network, digital in nature; and

   d) network control for the interface, the gateway, and the core network.

THE CANADIAN SCENE

The Trans Canada Telephone System (TCTS) was formed in 1931 by an agreement among the companies providing communication services. Because of developments in office automation, electronic messaging, and data transmission, TCTS was changed in 1983 to Telecom Canada. Telecom Canada consists of the nine major carriers in the country and Telesat Canada, the satellite carrier. Each of the nine carriers provide a variety of telecommunications services for a geographically defined area such as a province. The main exceptions are Bell Canada, which operates in Ontario, Quebec, and part of the Northwest Territories; and Alberta Government Telephones, which serves all of Alberta except for Edmonton, which provides its own local services.

The companies that make up Telecom Canada have a variety of ownership structures, regulatory conditions and services unique to each company. Bell Canada, the largest company in the group, is privately owned, federally incorporated, and regulated by the Canadian Radio-Television and Telecommunications Commission (CRTC). BC Tel, the second largest company, is shareholder owned and federally regulated by the CRTC. AGT, Sask Tel, and Manitoba TelePhone System (MTS) are provincial Crown corporations. The New Brunswick TelePhone Company (NB Tel), Maritime Telegraph and Telephone Company Ltd. (MT&T), Island Telephone Company Ltd. (Island Tel), and Newfoundland Telephone Company Ltd. are all investor owned.

CN Telecommunications, a subsidiary of Canadian National, merged with CP Telecommunications in 1981 to form CNCP Telecommunications, which is Telecom Canada's only competition. Both organizations provide public digital data networks using circuit switching, packet switching, and dedicated digital transmission systems (fig. 7-4) as well as other communication services.

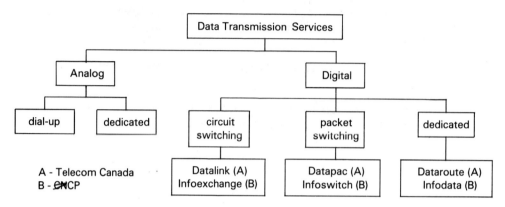

Figure 7-4   Canadian Data Services

Telecom Canada

Telecom Canada provides three basic digital data networks: Datalink, Datapac, and Dataroute. Datalink provides circuit-switched connections. Datapac is a public packet-switched network. Dataroute is a point-to-point leased service.

CIRCUIT SWITCHING: DATALINK

Datalink is a digital circuit-switched network particularly useful for meeting periodic data transmission requirements. The network operates in half- or full-duplex, using synchronous transmission and at speeds of 2400 bps to 9600 bps. Access to Datalink is via a dedicated loop from the user location to a Datalink switch on a four-wire channel. Applications are typically batch-oriented and include remote job entry, file transfer between host computers, digital facsimile transmission, and the exchanging of text between communicating word processors. Payment for Datalink is based on speed, time, and distance.

PACKET SWITCHING: DATAPAC

Datapac, the first commercially available packet-switched network in the world, was introduced in 1977. It is a national packet-switching network consisting of switching nodes and internodal high speed digital communication trunks (fig. 7-5).

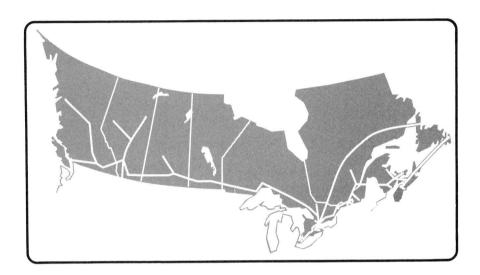

Figure 7-5 Datapac

Source: Reproduced courtesy of Altel Data.

Datapac uses a store and forward process that divides files into 256-byte packets and transmits them digitally on internodal trunks in full-duplex, synchronous mode at 56 kbps.

Applications best suited to Datapac are low- to medium-volume and interactive in nature, for example, data collection systems, inquiry/response systems, and time-sharing systems. Costs are based on the volume of data transmitted.

There are two kinds of access service to Datapac. Datapac 3000 connects equipment using the network's own X.25 protocol, and Datapac 3101, 3201, 3303, 3304, 3305 connect equipment using other protocols to the network. Datapac 3101 and 3201 services are used to connect asynchronous devices to the network. Datapac 3303, 3304, and 3305 services connect devices using IBM's BISYNC (sometimes referred to as BSC) protocol to the network. Nonstandard equipment must access Datapac through a PAD (fig. 7-6).

Datapac International Services provides for connection to other packet-switching networks such as Telenet in the United States and Transpac in France. The CCITT has established an international standard for connecting packet-switched networks called X.75. Datapac conforms to this standard.

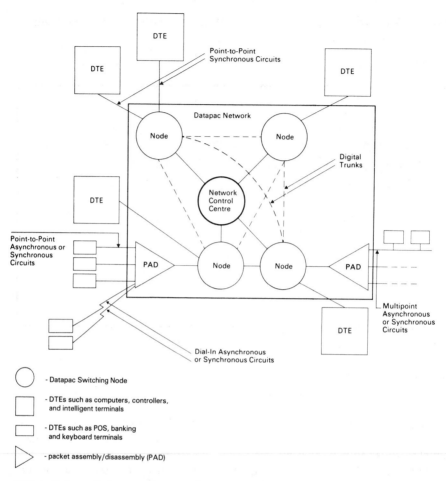

Figure 7-6   Datapac Connections

Source: Reproduced courtesy of Altel Data.

Datapac Access Software (DAS) provides an X.25 interface to IBM 370 systems. DAS runs in an IBM 3725 communications controller and interfaces with asynchronous terminals and IBM 3270 synchronous terminals operating in an IBM environment.

Recent developments in Datapac include Display Systems Protocol (DSP), access software for Datapac 3303 to enhance the Datapac/IBM 3270 interface. The Remote Access Protocol Interface Device (RAPID) is a concentrator that simultaneously supports multiple protocols. In the future, Datapac will be a major component in the development of ISDN systems.

DIGITAL TRANSMISSION: DATAROUTE

Dataroute is a dedicated digital data transmission service between certain Canadian cities that are called Dataroute serving areas (DSA). The service provides full-duplex transmission in a broad range of asynchronous and synchronous speeds up to 56 kbps on point-to-point and multipoint connections. It provides end-to-end digital connection for "on-net" users (users within the DSAs). "Off-net" users connect to the nearest DSA using dial-up or leased analog lines. Dataroute is particularly suitable for large-volume data transfers as well as high-speed access. Applications include host-to-host file transfer, load sharing, and remote job entry, as well as data collection, information retrieval, and database enquiry/response systems. Costs are based on a monthly charge for all communication facilities from DTE to DTE.

Dataroute Multistream is an enhancement to Dataroute that supplies users with multiple medium-speed synchronous lines between two DSAs. It allows the derivation of up to four 1200-bps, 2400-bps or 4800-bps sub-channels from one channel operating at 4800 bps or 9600 bps. This reduces communication costs and provides more data circuits through the same connection.

Dataroute International connects Canadian users with Dataphone Digital Services in the United States. Teleglobe Canada, the Canadian overseas carrier, connects Canadian users to international digital data networks.

VALUE-ADDED SERVICES

Value-added services can be defined as those services that are derived from other available services. By means of additional hardware or software, the facilities of the telephone system, a packet-switching network, or the postal service can be adapted to produce a valuable service.

Envoy 100

Envoy 100 is a national, bilingual, electronic message service. It provides time-flexible, delay-free communications and allows you to compose, edit, send, receive, and store written messages. Envoy 100 is accessible from anywhere in Canada, the United States, or the world through the telephone network, telex, and all the major international packet-switched networks. Asynchronous terminals, word processors, and personal computers can all access Envoy 100. Typical applications include messaging, scheduling, and ordering. Messages can be delivered in several ways:

1. Autodelivery means the messages are automatically delivered shortly after being sent or at scheduled times during the day.

2. Mailbox delivery means that the messages are stored for pickup at the receiver's convenience.

3. EnvoyPost allows Envoy 100 subscribers to send messages to non-subscribers by routing messages to the Canada Post electronic mail center nearest the receiver. Delivery can be either basic (next day) or special (next morning).

4. Envoy Courier provides national courier delivery of electronic mail transmitted on Envoy 100 to the Purolator Facsimile Center where it is printed and routed to a pickup and delivery depot and delivered within three hours.

iNet 2000

iNet 2000 provides access to international on-line databases supplying financial, economic, statistical, and technical data. iNet 2000 can be accessed from Datapac, by long distance dialing, or via a leased line. Access via Datapac means access can be extended to databases in the United States and overseas.

Teletex

Teletex, an economic option to mailing or courier service, provides 2400 bps of communication between any make of memory typewriter or word processor both nationally and internationally. Teletex conforms to the international Teletex standard defined by the CCITT and can handle a wide variety of terminal types. It can be accessed via the telephone system, circuit-switched networks, and packet-switched networks.

Satellite-based services

In 1983, Telecom Canada introduced two satellite-based services. Conference 600 is a two-way, fully interactive, point-to-point, color video conferencing service. It is designed to improve the productivity and efficiency of larger customers who have geographically dispersed locations.

Stratoroute 2000 is a business network designed to integrate voice, data, and image communication using time-division multiplexing. Users are able to monitor and control their traffic flow by dynamically reconfiguring their network resources. Applications include distributed data processing and facsimile transfer. Stratoroute 2000 services can be linked to Dataroute, Datapac, and the telephone system.

CNCP

CNCP has digital data networks that provide the same services as Telecom Canada. Their digital circuit-switching service is called Infoexchange. The dedicated digital data service is called Infodat, and the packet-switching network, Infoswitch.

There are several options within Infoswitch, including X.25 end-to-end synchronous transmission. SDLC services are available for access to the IBM world via an IBM PAD, integrated into the network's nodes. The X.28 service, based on the CCITT asynchronous terminal interface standard, provides asynchronous device interface to the network, as well as dial access, and international interconnection.

CNCP's Network Management Control Center (NMCC) provides monitoring and control of the company's "backbone" facilities, Infodata and the Microwave Network. NMCC also monitors Infoswitch.

CNCP value-added services include Teletex, Dialcom Services for electronic messaging, and MACH III, a high-speed, point-to-point network that offers an integration of voice, data, and image at 1.54 Mbps in a system evolving towards ISDN.

THE U.S. SCENE

In the United States the picture is much more complicated than in Canada. The American Telephone and Telegraph Company (AT&T) has been divested of 22 operating companies that have subsequently formed themselves into seven organizations referred to as the Bell Operating Companies (BOC). The BOCs are regionally based and provide services within their own areas of the country. AT&T itself now includes AT&T Communications, AT&T Information Systems and Bell Laboratories, which offer both data communication and data processing services. Other companies that vie for the same market include United States Transmission Systems Inc., RCA American Communications Inc., and Western Telecommunications Inc. The Bell Operating Companies provide most of the switched and leased public networks in the country. In addition, the FCC has approved value-added networks (VANs), which provide services that go beyond simple end-to-end transmission. Typical examples include the major public packet-switching networks, Telenet and Tymnet.

There are four basic types of transmission facilities suppliers. These are the common carriers, specialized carriers, value-added carriers, and international carriers.

The traditional common carriers are regional and local telephone companies including the Bell Operating Companies and the telegraph companies. They provide facilities for the transmission of voice, data, video and facsimile information.

The specialized carriers provide interstate communication to most large metropolitan areas. The range of services include voice and data access transmission through dial-up, leased line, satellite channel, and packet switching. The specialized carriers use common carriers to connect the user to their facilities.

Value-added Carriers are specialized carriers that enhance common carriers facilities to provide additional services. Most Value-added Carriers use packet switching.

There are two kinds of international carrier. International Carriers are limited to voice and data transmission, but International Record Carriers (IRC) transmit voice, data, video, and facsimile information. Services include leased digital transmission, message switching, and packet switching.

Data can be transmitted over analog lines via direct distance dialing (DDD) and on the wide area telecommunications service (WATS) of the public telephone network.

Digital transmission facilities include AT&T Communications' Dataphone Digital Service, which provides full-duplex, point-to-point, and multipoint synchronous private line transmission up to 56 kbps. Terrestrial digital circuits (T1) provide point-to-point digital transmission at 1.544 Mbps.

Packet-Switching

Packet-switching services form the basis for high-speed international data transmission. Major packet-switching networks in the U.S. include Telenet, Tymenet, and Net 1000.

TELENET

Telenet introduced the first public packet-switching network in 1975 and became part of General Telephone and Electronics Corporation in 1979. It uses hybrid terrestrial links connecting X.25 protocol nodes that provide more than 300 access points in the United States, as well as connection to many foreign packet-switching networks (fig. 7-7). Telenet operates up to

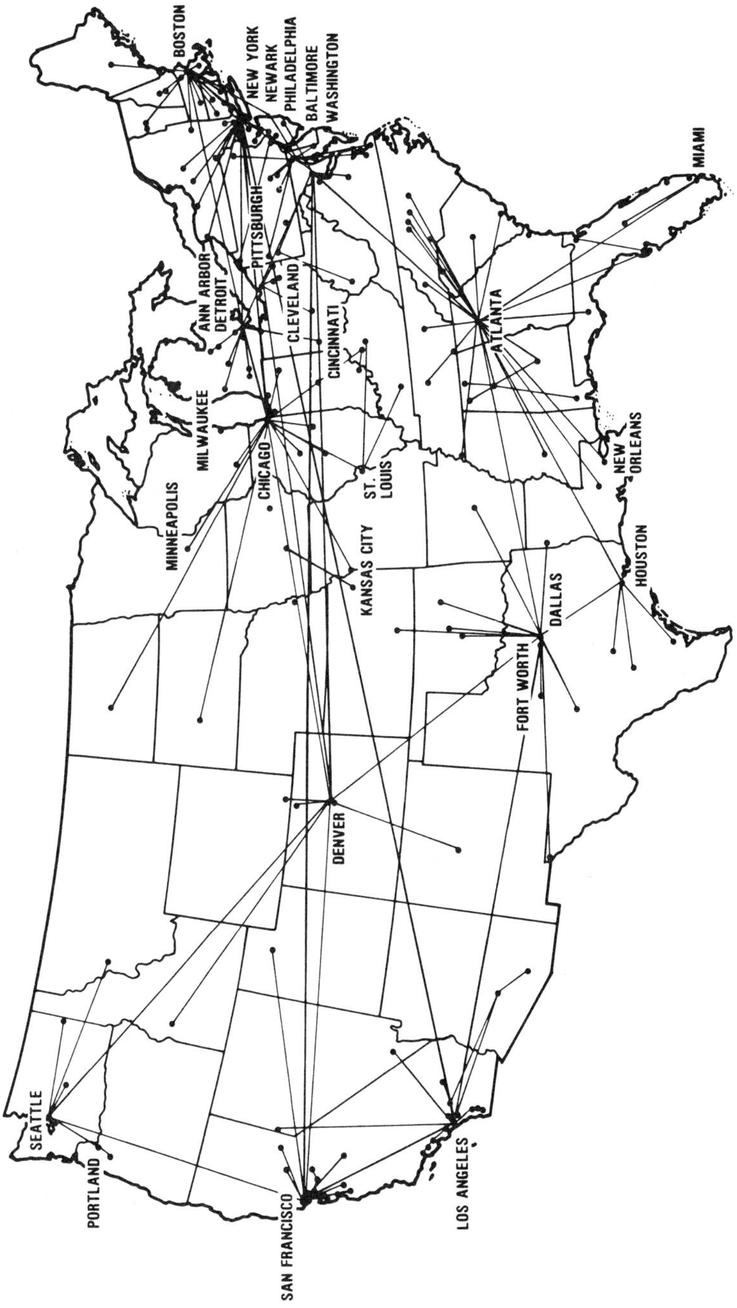

Figure 7-7   The Telenet Packet-switching Network

Source: Reproduced courtesy of GTE Telenet Communications Corp.

2400 bps for dial-up connection and up to 14.4 kbps for dedicated access. Telemail is a store and forward electronic mail/message service offered to Telenet subscribers. Message entry and delivery is made via the DDD network or user-dedicated lines.

The Telenet node is called a Telenet Central Office (TCO). A message from a source termination is converted into packets and sent into the network. The packets are transmitted from TCO to TCO according to routing information stored in the TCOs. At the destination TCO the packets are reassembled and the message is transmitted to the destination termination. The TCOs are also responsible for monitoring lines and equipment as well as generating performance and accounting information.

TYMNET

Tymnet was established in 1969 by the McDonnell Douglas Network Systems Company and operates a packet-switched network based on intelligent processors connected by leased lines, microwave links, and satellite channels. Tymnet supports X.25, BISYNC, and SDLC protocols. It also installs private networks based on its own communications processor, referred to as the Tymnet Engine. The Tymnet public network currently consists of over 2400 nodes (fig. 7-8).

There are two kinds of nodes: base and remote. The base node provides the network interface for mainframe terminations. Any one of four base nodes can be used as the network control center. The remote nodes provide an interface for the whole range of terminals from simple to user-programmable.

Tymstar is a digital satellite network capable of handling voice, data, and image for both point-to-point and broadcast nodes. The Tymstar network consists of:

a Master Hub Facility: a large earth station that is the switching and control center for thousands of Micro Earth Stations.

a Micro Earth Station: with a four-foot diameter dish installed on the user's site.

a Satellite: with a 12/14 Ghz transponder capacity.

Besides packet-oriented data protocols, Tymstar provides full-duplex circuit-switched digital services. As well as using the broadcast mode for video, Tymstar can transmit broadcasted messages to any selected set of Micro Earth Stations.

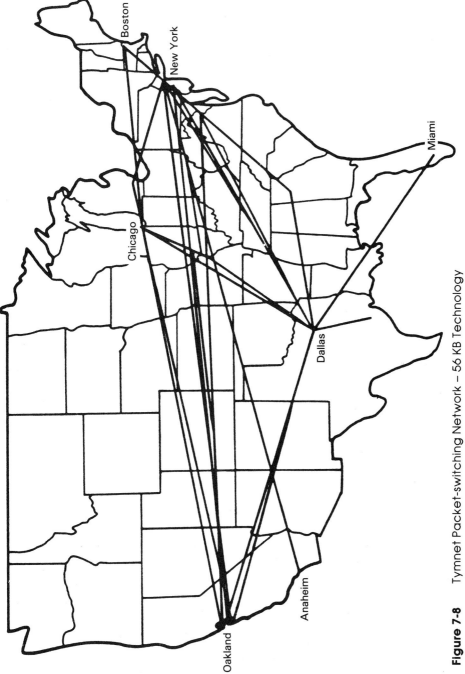

Figure 7-8   Tymnet Packet-switching Network – 56 KB Technology

Source: Reproduced courtesy of Tymnet, McDonnell Douglas.

NET 1000

AT&T's Net 1000 is a relative newcomer to the value-added network scene. It supports bidirectional full-duplex interactive communication between incompatible end-point devices. It also provides communication between devices and programs and between different programs within the network. It is different from Telenet and Tymnet in that users can store applications programs and data throughout the network and process entered data using these programs. Net 1000 has a limited number of processing nodes and access points. Its success is dependent on its expansion potential.

INTERNATIONAL PACKET-SWITCHING NETWORKS

As organizations grow and diversify and as international trade flourishes, so does the demand for data communication services at the international level. An important consideration for international data communication is the provision of standards and interfaces. The X.25 protocol provides both a world-wide standard for packet switching as well as interface standards for non-X.25 terminals and hosts.

The United Kingdom

British Telecom's national packet-switching network, Packet SwitchStream (PSS), supports a wide range of terminals and host computers. Access facilities are categorized by terminal type (packet or character), and connection type (dataline or dial-up).

Packet terminals operate via datalines that are dedicated, synchronous full-duplex links to the packet-switching exchange at 2400, 9600, and 48 000 bps.

Character terminals connect to PSS via a PAD using either the public telephone network or by a directly connected dataline. Character terminals operate in asynchronous full-duplex mode at access speeds of 300 and 1200 bps.

Access to PSS is also provided by a multistream service that consists of:

EPAD which provides error protection over local access links to PSS for asynchronous devices;

VPAD which provides videotex transmission over PSS;

BPAD which provides a directly connected IBM 3270 BISYNC service over PSS; and

SPAD which provides a directly connected IBM SDLC service over PSS.

PSS can be connected to other networks nationally via InterStream gateways, and internationally via International Packet SwitchStream services (IPSS).

The IPSS is accessed via PSS using passwords and international network addresses. It is a 24-hour service to approximately 50 countries and includes satellite access by ships at sea.

France

Transpac is the French public packet-switching network. It conforms to the international protocol standard, X.25. It also accommodates X.28 for asynchronous communication, and X.75, the CCITT protocol, for gateways between packet-switching networks. Operating speeds range from 300 bps to 48 kbps. Numerous international links are already available through the Transpac International Transit Node.

Atlas 400 is the French integrated services network that supports videotex, teletex, facsimile, and message transmission. Access to this service is via the telephone network, telex network, and Transpac.

Interpac is the French interface of an international private network called Infonet. This network was created by Transpac, France Cables and Radio (FCR), and Computer Science Corporation (CSC), which is based in the United States.

Japan

Data communications in Japan are geared to international service. The Kokusai Denshin Denwa Company Limited (KDD) provides an international telex service (Datel), an international message handling service, an international telegraph network (Automex), international leased circuits, and an international packet-switched network called VENUS-P.

VENUS-P is directly interfaced to the domestic packet-switched data network, Digital Data Exchange Packet (DDX-P), owned by the Nippon Telegraph and Telephone Company. It handles X.25, X.28, and BISYNC at speeds of up to 48 kbps.

Figure 7-9 shows the relationship between VENUS-P and other international networks. The connection of both CNCP's Infoswitch and Telecom Canada's Datapac is through Teleglobe Canada. The public packet-switching networks of the United States are multiply connected to the international grid through several carriers. The United Kingdom carrier provides connections to Spain and Norway, the French carrier provides connections for Luxembourg, Belgium, French Guiana and Gabon.

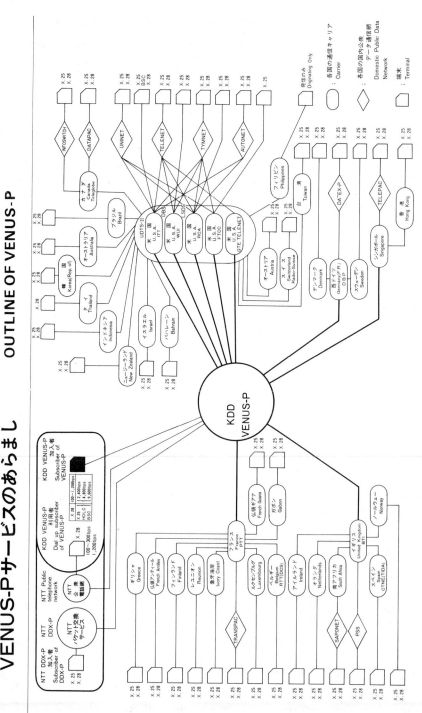

Figure 7-9 Venus-P Packet-switching Network

Source: Reproduced courtesy of KDD Co. Ltd., Japan.

The VENUS-P service has been created to cover a broad range of international business, scientific, and technological applications.

SUMMARY

Data communications networks are already dominated by digital transmission, which is used in circuit switching, packet switching, and dedicated line configurations. Circuit switching is used for batch processing applications, packet switching for interactive applications, and dedicated digital lines for high-volume host-to-host applications. The international standard for data communication is packet switching using the X.25 protocol.

A wide variety of data communication services are available to meet the data processing needs of the business community in Canada, the United States, the United Kingdom, France, Japan, and other developed countries. These services provide the means of tailoring an organization's communications needs to its budget and of responding dynamically to changes in those requirements. At the same time the increasing complexity of the data communications world demands more knowledge and expertise within a user organization to reap the benefits of effective data communications.

Review Questions for Chapter 7

1. Which connection types are used in public networks for analog transmission?

2. How can transmission on leased lines be improved?

3. Under what conditions is circuit switching superior to packet switching?

4. List three advantages of leasing lines over using dial-up lines.

5. How can digital signals be transmitted directly over long distances?

6. Match the following:

    packet switching   Datalink
    digital transmission   Datapac
    circuit switching   Dataroute

LOCAL AREA NETWORKS

INTRODUCTION

A local area network (LAN) is a system for interconnecting data communicating components within a relatively confined space. A system is a group of interrelated parts with a focus on the interrelationship. LANs are principally concerned with methods of communication among their components, which are mutually compatible devices and include microcomputers, disk storage, and printers. The emphasis on compatibility in a LAN is purely practical. Incompatible microcomputers may be able to share a printer but not programs or data. The phrase "a relatively confined space" is used in conjunction with the distinction between LANs and wide area networks. LANs are most commonly contained within one building but may spread to contiguous buildings. Wide area networks, on the other hand, usually operate between cities, countries, or continents. LANs are restricted to intra- and inter-building communication, the maximum distance depending on the medium used to connect components.

Other significant characteristics of LANs, which did not appear in the above definition, include ownership, speed, and availability. LANs are privately owned and therefore not subject to regulation by public bodies or networks. This fact, coupled with the simple, symmetrical topologies used in LANS, facilitates most acceptable speeds of between 1 and 10 megabits per second. The speed of a LAN is limited by the way the software interacts with the network and by the access speed of shared storage rather than by the speed of the medium that connects the nodes. Although a large number of LANs are now commercially available, the variety of technical options is limited. There are three major media, three topologies, and two protocols.

LANs are, by definition, distance limited. The access potential of a LAN node is greatly increased by gateways and by connection to other LANs through a metropolitan area network.

An alternative approach to using a LAN is to incorporate data transmission facilities into a private branch exchange, the switchboard that provides telephone facilities for most organizations.

Before considering the technology, we should look first at the purpose of LANs.

PURPOSE OF LANs

This discussion centers around two considerations: first, the technological role of the LAN and second, the application spectrum. The initial impetus for LAN development came from the need to interconnect a growing number and variety of intelligent machines in the office. These intelligent machines were purchased to automate office functions and to augment data-processing development, where, in many cases, it was thought that the data-processing center was experiencing enormous backlogs and was unresponsive to the needs of the small user. Initially, the purchase of office machines was on an individual-need basis and independent of broad organizational planning. Inevitably, some form of coordinated effort was made to consider such functions as compatibility, standardization, and interdepartmental communication. This led quickly to the possibility of connecting these systems to improve efficiency, to facilitate the integration of the applications, and to share the resources.

Resource Sharing

The major advantage of LANs is their ability to share equipment, data, and software. The physical resources to be shared are the expensive parts of small systems, namely, file space (disk handlers) and reporting capability (printers). By allowing several workstations (terminals, wordprocessors, personal computers) to share equipment, information costs can be drastically reduced and spread over a number of departments.

The ability of a group of workstations to share each other's data facilitates the integration of work in different departments and decreases duplication of effort. A single master copy of a file promotes consistency, accuracy, and reliability of data. Under such conditions, changes to a master file by one user are immediately available to all other users.

Shared software means an immediate cost savings. In the educational environment, for example, a typical personal computer laboratory could have 30 microcomputers. Instead of buying 30 copies of a spreadsheet program, the coordinator can simply divide the laboratory into a system of three LANs, serving 10 workstations apiece and needing only one copy of the software for each network. Further benefits include the saving of disk storage space and the consistent use of the same version of the software by all users.

The benefits of resource sharing, however, are accompanied by corresponding restrictions. Incompatible microcomputers may share disks and printers but not files and programs. The integration of incompatible devices can be more costly than the installation of a new system. The user can choose, however, between a single-vendor system that minimizes compatibility and maintenance problems and a multiple-vendor system with its cost benefits and corresponding human communication problems.

APPLICATION SPECTRUM

Local area networks are used primarily in the business data-processing environment. They are usually employed at the operational level of the organization for the automation of clerical procedures, and at the planning and control levels (management levels) for decision making. More recently, their application potential in manufacturing and process control has been investigated.

Personal Computer Networks

With the introduction of personal computers to the office and their interconnection by LANs, comes a new potential for increased productivity. Sharing data files on customers, parts, and vendor information gives all users fast access to consistent word processing packages that facilitate memo, letter, and report writing. These packages can be standardized on the LAN. Spreadsheet and graphics software provide figures and diagrams to enhance reports. By sharing these programs, software costs are reduced considerably.

Office Automation

The interconnection of intelligent machines in the office integrates the job of managing information. Again the emphasis is on increased productivity, in this case of secretarial functions such as electronic filing (data collection), scheduling (calendar and reminder files), data base inquiry (customer, parts, vendor), word processing (memo, letter, report), and information dissemination (memo, letter, report).

The overlap of functions in these two applications is intentional and highlights the changing role of the computer as a direct aid to managers and the changing role of secretaries to office and information managers.

Process Control

The use of LANs in chemical plants and manufacturing factories is less well developed. Microcomputers are commonly used to monitor physical data (temperature, pressure, and flow), and they control these physical variables with switches and motors. The use of LANs to improve the economics of manufacturing, and to provide flexibility and backup, constitutes a new development.

In a production-line environment, individual microcomputers can be used to monitor and control a particular stage of production, while receiving data from the microcomputer at the previous stage and passing information forward to the next stage.

LAN TECHNOLOGY

The terminal nodes of a LAN are usually either special- or general-purpose microcomputers. The compatibility of these terminal nodes is crucial to the maximization of resource sharing. The junctions on a LAN are interface boards that are capable of generating and receiving control and data signals for the network. These interface boards are housed in the workstation (microcomputer) and file server (hard disk control unit). In addition, a junction box is used at specific points in the network to connect workstations physically to the network. The most significant component is the line, that is, the medium of communication. There are three popular media: twisted pair, coaxial cable, and fiber optics. The technology of LANs, as distinct from distance networks, is simple and contains a high degree of symmetry. As discussed in chapter 5, there are three principle topologies: bus, ring, and star.

LAN protocol, the network's way of controlling traffic, is also distinguishable from wide area networks, which normally use some form of polling, because the workstations have an equal say in controlling the traffic. There are two main protocols or access methods for LANs: carrier sense multiple access/collision detection (CSMA/CD) and token passing.

PROTOCOL

The International Standards Organization's reference model of Open Systems Interconnection (ISO-OSI) discussed in chapter 6 may also be applied to LANs. Since LANs are primarily concerned with the transmission of information over a physical medium, only the first two levels, physical and data link control, need be addressed.

The physical level has already been defined as consisting of an interface card coupled to an appropriate medium. The data-link control level can be discussed in terms of message format (the frame), error handling (CRC), flow control (buffering), and line control.

Line control can be subdivided into two categories: polling (for networks with a control node) and distributed-access methods (for LANs in which each node has equal control). Two distributed-access methods have emerged to dominate the LAN market: contention, in which any node has the ability to initiate transfer at any time, and token passing, in which each node must wait its turn.

Contention

The most common form of the contention protocol is CSMA/CD, which is usually associated with bus/tree topology. Carrier sense is the ability of each node to detect traffic on the channel by "listening." Nodes will not transmit while they "hear" traffic on the channel. Multiple access lets any node send a message immediately upon sensing the channel is free of traffic. This eliminates the waiting that is characteristic of non-contention protocols. One problem that can arise is that because of propagation delays across the network, two nodes can detect that the channel is free at the same time, since each will not have detected the other's signal. This causes a collision. Collision detect is the ability of a transmitting node to "listen" while transmitting, identify a collision, abandon transmitting, wait, and try again. Figure 8-1 shows the sequence of events for this protocol. CSMA/CD is a highly efficient form of distributed access.

Token Passing

Token passing is most often used with ring topologies, although it can be applied to bus/tree topologies by assigning the nodes logical positions in an ordered sequence with the last member followed by the first, in other words, as a logical ring.

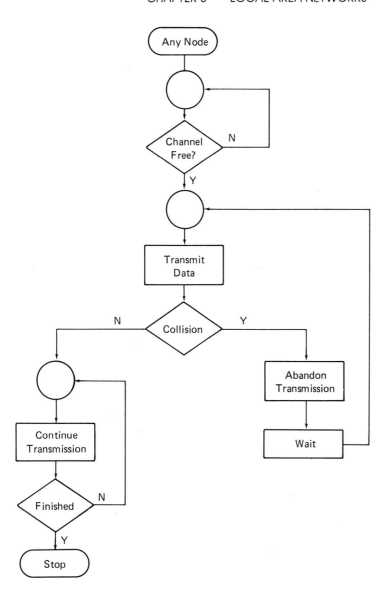

Figure 8-1   Contention Protocol

Tokens are special bit patterns that circulate from node to node around the ring, when there is no traffic. A node can take possession of the token. This gives the node exclusive access to the network for transmitting its message. This technique eliminates the possibility of conflict among nodes.

For example, suppose that node A holds the token and sends a message specifying node D. All the nodes on the ring check the message as it passes. Each node is responsible for identifying and accepting messages addressed to it, as well as for repeating and passing on messages addressed to other nodes. Node D accepts the message and sends the message to Node A to confirm its receipt. When node A receives confirmation that the message arrived and was accepted, it must send the empty token around so that another node will have a chance to take over the channel. Figure 8-2 shows the sequence of events for both the transmitting and receiving nodes.

A variation of token passing, known as slotted access, is found exclusively in ring topology. Instead of a token, the nodes circulate empty data frames, which a node may fill in its turn. Usually, a fixed number of slots or frames of fixed size circulate. Each frame consists of source and destination addresses, parity and control, and data. Note that the slotted access technique limits not only when a node transmits but how much it sends at a time.

LAN Software

The major purpose of LANs is the sharing of resources. To do this we need a way of connecting the workstations, that is, a medium, a topology, and a protocol. Then we need to control the sharing of equipment, data, and software, in other words, a local-area-network operating system is required. This is not as formidable a task as it may sound, since microcomputers already have well-developed operating systems such as MS-DOS, CP/M, and UNIX to name but a few. The problem then becomes one of interfacing network function software with the workstation operating system already available. The LAN software will add its own restrictions to those of the workstation operating system. It will also increase the file storage space available to the workstation, as well as provide for private and shared files and for printer capability at convenient locations.

Most LAN software packages come with modules for logging on and off the network, disk/file sharing, and print spooling. The logging-on and logging-off network module may include such considerations as password security, validation of user access to specific files and software, and an automatic log-on feature for specific workstations. It will also provide for releasing reserved files on log-off. Other features may include password changing, help menus, and error messages for log-on problems.

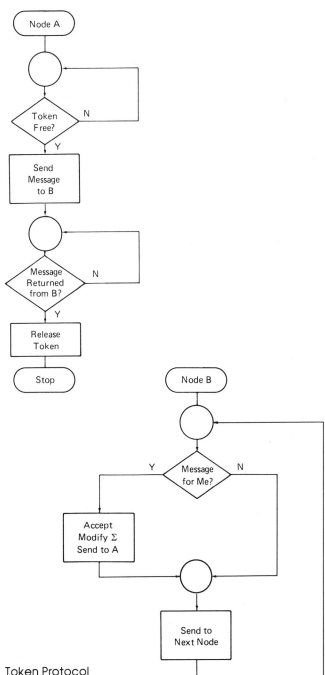

Figure 8-2   Token Protocol

It is important to realize that sharing files is different from sharing disk space. With simple LAN software it may be possible that each station is allocated a portion of the hard disk for its own use, but sharing data or programs in such cases may not be possible. Each work station takes its own copy of the data or the program. Changes to a file by one workstation will not automatically be passed on to other users. This type of LAN software is called disk-sharing software.

Data-sharing software involves either write-protecting a file or allowing multiple changes simultaneously. The write-protection method is simple and involves a software switch that allows access to a file by one workstation at a time. Other users are informed that the particular file is not available for access.

The multiple simultaneous update of a file requires software that permits simultaneous access to a file but that prevents simultaneous attempts to change the same piece of information. The distinction is between write-protecting the whole file or write-protecting specific records in the file.

Print spooling is an integral part of printer sharing. It is the process of copying a file to a temporary storage area on the file server until it can be printed. While the file is in the spooler it is queued, that is, each file, as it arrives, is given a number and the files are printed in the order of the assigned numbers.

EXAMPLES

Local area networks use two methods of communication between nodes: baseband transmission and broadband transmission.

In baseband transmission, the entire bandwidth is used for one data channel. The digital signals are transmitted directly without modulation. Baseband LANs use CSMA/CD and token-passing protocols on a variety of topologies.

In broadband transmission, a single physical channel, usually coaxial cable, is frequency-divided into a number of independent channels. These independent channels are allocated different bandwiths and can be used for voice and video, as well as for data transmission. Since this is an analog signal technique, the digital signals must be modulated. High frequency modems are required to provide channel-carrier frequencies that do not interfere with each other.

One distinction between broadband and baseband systems is that signals in baseband systems must travel in one direction, whereas on broadband the signal travels in both directions. Both use the modified bus or tree topology.

In broadband LANs, separate send and receive channels allow two-way exchange of information.

Baseband LANs: VictorLAN

The VictorLAN is an adaptation of the Corvus Systems' Omninet. It is a baseband LAN of two to 64 Victor computers, each with its own interface card called a transporter. The transporter is an intelligent interface, containing a microprocessor and its own firmware (permanently stored programs), to reduce the communications load on the workstation's microprocessor. Network junction boxes are used to connect the transporter to the network trunk and to insure matched impedance and minimum interference. The trunk line cable is a shielded twisted pair.

The VictorLAN fileserver is a 10-megabyte hard disk with 256 kilobytes of RAM and a 1.2 megabyte floppy disk, as well as having one parallel and two serial ports. The hard disk stores user files and may be divided into two, four, or eight equal-sized sections at installation time. The sections are then accessible as if they were separate physical disk drives. The floppy disk can be used to transfer files between LANs or for archiving. The VictorLAN hardware characteristics are summarized in figure 8-3.

Medium	twisted pair
Topology	bus
Protocol	CSMA/CD
Speed	1Mbps
Maximum number of nodes	64
Maximum trunk length	450m

Figure 8-3   VictorLAN Characteristics

VictorLAN resources are assigned to users, not to workstations. Users have access to the same hardware and software regardless of which station they use. Each user can be assigned up to 15 disk volumes that can be distributed among hard and floppy disks on different servers as well as on the workstation being used. Server volumes may be shared among several users or restricted to one user. Printers can also be assigned selectively. The resources associated with each server are managed by the software installed on that server. Files sent to a server for printing are spooled and sequenced automatically.

The VictorLAN Server Operating System is transparent to the workstation user. In addition to the MS-DOS commands, which all operate both locally and on the network (except for FORMAT, DCOPY, and CHKDSK which only operate locally), there are 11 network commands, tabulated in figure 8-4.

Command	Function
LOGIN	Logs the user on to network
LOGOUT	Ends session, protects files, allows new log-in
NETPRINT	Sends file to spooler for printing
NETSTAT	Displays network status information
NETUSERS	Displays active users
PASSWORD	Allows password to be changed
PROTECT	Changes status of server file
RESERVE	Temporarily restricts file access
RELEASE	Cancels RESERVE
SHOWLIST	Identifies active printers
STATION	Displays workstation status

Figure 8-4   Victor LAN Commands

NETWORK CONFIGURATIONS

The simplest possible network consists of a single workstation and a server (fig. 8-5). The trunk can be extended anywhere along its length, not only from its ends. The cable, of course, will physically go around corners and up and

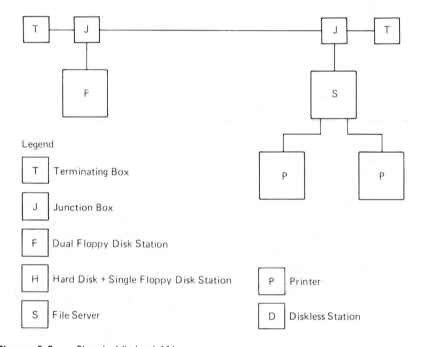

Legend

T   Terminating Box

J   Junction Box

F   Dual Floppy Disk Station

H   Hard Disk + Single Floppy Disk Station   P   Printer

S   File Server   D   Diskless Station

Figure 8-5   Simple Victor LAN

down walls, but it must remain as a bus. Figure 8-6 shows the expansion of the previous network by two nodes.

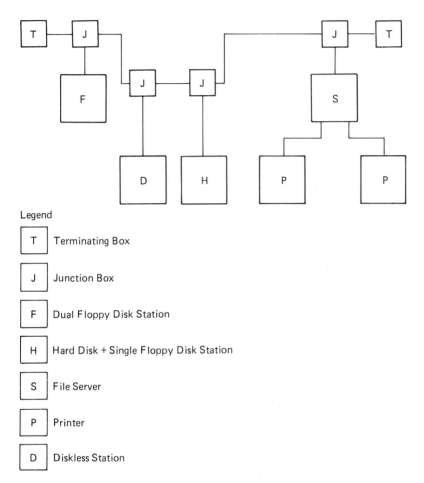

Legend

T	Terminating Box
J	Junction Box
F	Dual Floppy Disk Station
H	Hard Disk + Single Floppy Disk Station
S	File Server
P	Printer
D	Diskless Station

Figure 8-6   Expanded Victor LAN

More typical networks consist of one to 54 workstations and one to 10 servers, each supporting a maximum of three printers. Figure 8-7 shows a typical configuration. Note that the printer attached to the hard disk station cannot be used by other stations in the network. Servers may be equipped with keyboards and displays, both of which are inoperarable during network operation but may be used in the stand-alone mode.

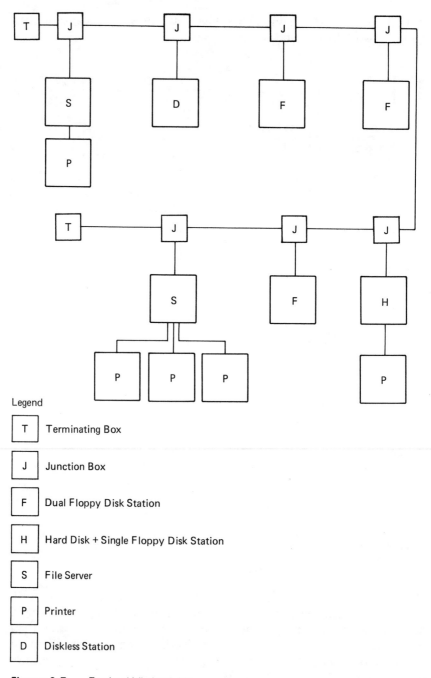

Legend

T	Terminating Box
J	Junction Box
F	Dual Floppy Disk Station
H	Hard Disk + Single Floppy Disk Station
S	File Server
P	Printer
D	Diskless Station

Figure 8-7   Typical Victor LAN

Baseband LANs: Ethernet

In 1980, Digital Equipment Corp., Xerox Corp., and Intel Corp. joined forces to advance the Ethernet approach to LANs. This resulted in a precise, detailed specification for a baseband LAN. In this network, the workstation interface card, called the transceiver, is connected to the coaxial trunk cable by means of four twisted-pair wires, each of which carries one of the four signals: transmit, receive, collision presence, and power. Ethernet is described as a branching bus topology with a maximum distance of 2.8 kilometers between the two furthest nodes of the network. Up to 1024 nodes can be tapped onto the Ethernet coaxial cable. Hardware characteristics are summarized in figure 8-8.

Medium	coax
Topology	bus
Protocol	CSMA/CD
Speed	10 Mbps
Maximum number of nodes	1024
Maximum trunk length	2.8km

Figure 8-8   Ethernet Characteristics

Ethernet provides the local environment for print and file servers to share storage and I/O resources, and for terminal servers to convert dumb terminals to intelligent ones.

One version of the Ethernet implementation for personal computers is that of 3Com Corp., and it is called the 3Com Etherseries. Software for this LAN includes Ethershare, which provides sharing of hard disk and printers. Subdivision of hard disk volumes can be public, private, or shared. Etherprint allows all network users to share up to two printers attached to each server.

CONFIGURATIONS

A small Ethernet LAN would consist of a simple bus topology with perhaps three workstations sharing one file server, all within the maximum coaxial cable limit of 500 meters (fig. 8-9).

A more sophisticated Ethernet LAN would be configured as a tree with a repeater being used to link the segments together. A repeater enables two cable segments to function as if they were one. It amplifies transmission signals and passes data between the coaxial cable segments. A local repeater connects two segments within a limited distance of up to 100 meters (fig. 8-10).

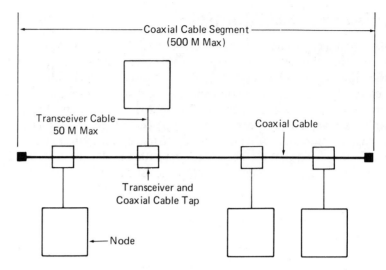

Figure 8-9   Small Ethernet

Source: Reproduced courtesy of Digital Equipment Corporation.

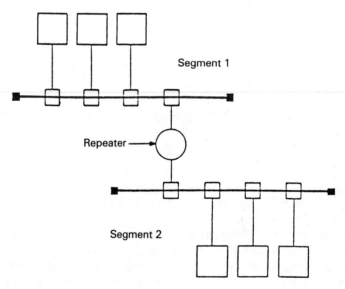

Figure 8-10   Medium Ethernet

Source: Reproduced courtesy of Digital Equipment Corporation.

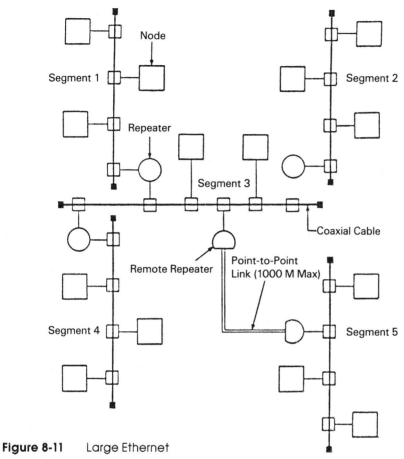

Figure 8-11   Large Ethernet

Source: Reproduced courtesy of Digital Equipment Corporation.

A large-scale Ethernet configuration would include remote as well as local repeaters. A remote repeater connects two coaxial cable segments over a distance of up to 1000 meters. The remote repeater consists of two local repeaters connected by a fiber optic link (fig. 8-11).

Baseband LANs: The IBM Token-Ring Network

The IBM token-ring LAN conforms to the Institute of Electrical and Electronic Engineers' (IEEE) 802.5 standard, which defines the characteristics and operation of a token-passing LAN with a ring topology. The acceptance of the standard, the marketing power of the IBM name, and the support of other LAN manufacturers, guarantee this LAN a large share of the market.

Although this LAN logically operates as a token-passing ring, it is constructed physically like a star. The central node is called a multistation access unit, and in it the multiconductor cables (either twisted-pair or coax) are connected to form a ring (fig. 8-12). The advantages of this arrangement are that the network is operational during workstation location changes and, since all the connections are available in one unit, troubleshooting is easier. Each multistation access unit has the capacity for eight workstations and the facility for connection to other multistation access units. Hardware characteristics are summarized in figure 8-13.

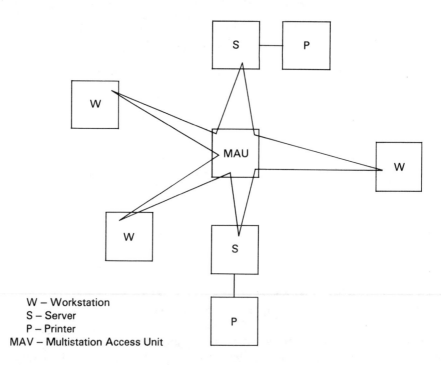

W – Workstation
S – Server
P – Printer
MAV – Multistation Access Unit

Figure 8-12   IBM Token Ring LAN

Medium	twisted pair/coax
Topology	bus
Protocol	token passing
Speed	4 Mbps
Maximum number of nodes	8 per MAU
Maximum trunk length	2km between MAUs

Figure 8-13   IBM Token-Ring Characteristics

The IBM token-ring software is called the PC Local Network Program. One difference between this and other LANs is the ability of each node on the network to operate simultaneously as a workstation and a server. This allows other users on the network to share one's disk space or printer. This advantage is offset by a reduction in performance during simultaneous activity.

Commands in the PC Local Network Program include:

NET SHARE   permits the sharing of complete drive directories on a drive, individual files, or printers.

NET USE   links a shared device to a particular user.

NET PATH   provides a path for an applications program to find its data files (just like the PATH command in DOS).

Broadband LANs

Broadband LANs use frequency division multiplexing (FDM) to subdivide the coaxial cable into several channels, each of which can have the capacity of a baseband LAN. Since this is an analog signal technique, the digital data signals must be converted. The main drawback of broadband LANs is the cost of the modems and FDMs. The major benefit lies in the fact that the network can transmit data, voice, and video signals simultaneously. The coaxial cable used in broadband LANs is the same as that used in cable television (75ohm). Its capabilities include a bandwidth of 300 megahertz and a transmission rate of up to five megabits per second per channel.

To accommodate transmissions of data, voice, and video, the cable is divided into bands that are multiplexed into many subchannels. Figure 8-14 shows a possible allocation of bands for low-speed data, switched voice and data, and video channels, with capacity reserved for future expansion.

On single cable systems, compatible with cable television, this is accomplished by halving the capacity of the cable. A central retransmission facility (CRF) remodulates lowband (send) to highband (receive) signals. Figure 8-15 shows the IEEE 802 working group recommendation for a broadbend standard and establishes a 108-162 megahertz guard band between high and low band nodes.

In a dual cable system the entire bandwidth is available in both directions. The coaxial cable loops around to pass each node twice. Nodes use one-half of the cable for sending and one-half for receiving. Figure 8-16 shows a simple dual cable link-up.

The trade-off between the systems is between cost and bandwidth. The single-cable broadband LAN is less expensive but supplies only half the bandwidth of the dual-cable broadband LAN.

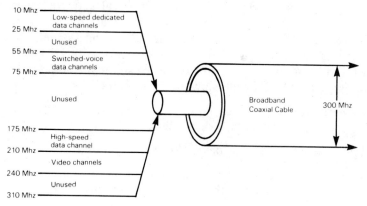

Figure 8-14   Broadband Subchannels

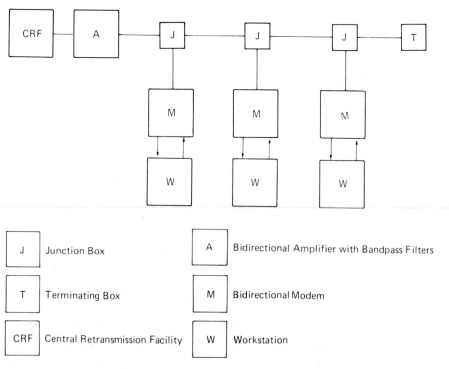

Figure 8-15   Single Cable Broadband LAN

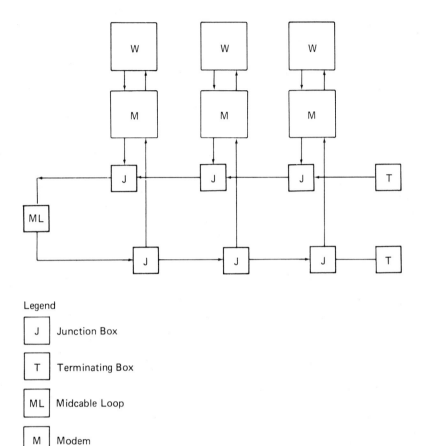

Figure 8-16 Dual Cable Broadband LAN

Gateway

A *gateway* is a device for connecting two systems that use different protocols. A gateway has intelligence and acts as a communications controller and protocol converter. Gateways can be used to connect LANs to a mainframe computer or a public packet-switching network, or to connect limited intelligence terminals to the LAN.

Metropolitan Area Networks

Distance networks are used for intercity communication, LANs for inter-office/interbuilding. Many organizations, banks, insurance and finance companies, and retail outlets have enough data traffic within a city to make intracity networking a viable means of reducing high communication costs. The need exists within a metropolitan area for a network that supports data, voice, video, and facsimile transmission. These demands are not well catered to by public telephone companies. LANs are also criticized for having failed to fulfill their potential in terms of resource sharing and savings. Nevertheless LANs remain a major contender in office automation and have obvious potential in the industrial area. A more reasonable criticism is that LANs are not connected to other computers. Their future may lie in the development of sophisticated gateways that will combine LANs spread across a city into a metropolitan area network and connect them as well to distance networks.

Private Branch Exchange (PBX)

The Private Branch Exchange provides a viable alternative to the LAN as a way of exchanging both data and voice communication and as a means of resource sharing. Using time-division multiplexing and an all-digital, computer-controlled switch, PBX replaces the traditional office switchboard. The transmission medium, twisted-pair, provides analog voice signals that must be converted at the switch to digital and converted back to analog after being rerouted. Data signals are converted by modulation prior to transmission. The PBX is capable of interconnecting a variety of office equipment including workstations, intelligent copiers, facsimile transceivers and printers. Figure 8-17 shows a brief comparison of PBX and LAN systems and identifies some of the factors that may influence user selection.

Factor	LAN	CBX
Speed	1-10Mband	64Kband
Data	All LANs	Yes
Voice	Broadband	Yes
Video	Broadband	No
Cost	Higher	Lower
Installation	Required	Already there

Figure 8-17   LAN versus PBX

SUMMARY

LANs provide a viable means of information exchange and resource sharing within a building complex. New LANs are being introduced on the marketplace with regularity, yet only a few technologies compete for prominence. Twisted pair and baseband coaxial cable compete for the lower end of the market, most often using bus or ring topology and CSMA/CD or token-passing protocol. The future may lie with the baseband coaxial cable system initially, but in the long term, with the broadband system that combines the transmission of data, voice, and video in an extremely flexible but expensive system.

Other factors that will have an important impact on LAN development include the need for communication between LANs and wide area networks via a gateway, the introduction of metropolitan area networks and the competition from private branch exchanges.

Review Questions for Chapter 8

1. What is the main technical difference between LANs and distance networks?

2. Which resource shared by LAN workstations contributes most to increased productivity in office automation?

3. What would be the main advantage of a bidirectional ring over a unidirectional ring topology?

4. Complete the following table:

Characteristic	ISO-OSI level
bus token passing fiber optics transporter network operating system	

5. What is the main purpose of the RESERVE command in VictorLAN?

6. Identify two characteristics that distinguish "local" from "remote" repeaters on Ethernet.

7. The CRF and the ML in broadband networks are sometimes referred to as the "headend." What is the main hardware difference between the headend on a single-cable system and the headend on a dual-cable system?

SECTION A: CONCLUSION

The aim of this section was to describe the key concepts of data communications and to provide the anatomy of a network. The network was defined as a system of interconnected nodes. The function of each node-type, the physical and logical relationships among nodes, the medium of interconnection, and the control of networks were all evaluated in the context of wide area networks, public data networks, and local area networks.

What emerges from all the detail is that however complicated it may seem, the fundamental concerns are repeated throughout all aspects of the network. Each network node is concerned with establishing connection with another node and ensuring that the data it transmits or receives is error free. Each level of protocol is concerned with controlling this process and with supplying appropriate control information to the next level above it. The confusion that arises when studying networks is usually caused by complexity. There are few difficult concepts involved but there is a lot of detail. Just as in building a jigsaw puzzle, learning about networks requires patience and a conviction that it is not beyond your powers.

Section C reviews these first eight chapters and provides questions, exercises, and hands-on laboratories, most of them using a minimum of equipment. Included in this section are demonstrations that will provide an understanding of the material covered and also give you an opportunity to build your own framework for the material.

Section B describes the way networks can be used to solve those problems of data processing that are concerned with aspects of information management.

SECTION B
APPLICATIONS

Networks have become an integral part of data processing. Few installations operate without remote access to their own systems or to external systems. As in other fields, there is usually a gap between the possible and the actual. In production environments where data processing participates in the day-to-day running of an organization (as with on-line systems), there is a natural tendency towards caution in implementing new technologies. This tendency is often offset, however, by rapid changes in technology and the need to stay competitive.

The present trend in the application of networks is towards distributed data processing (DDP). This is a simple concept involving the decentralization of data processing resources, but it is also a complex and difficult system to implement. Because of the complexities involved and because a philosophical change has to be engineered in an organization's perspective, from centralized to decentralized, progress has been slow in the development of wide area networks for DDP. A more practical example of DDP occurs in the field of local area networks where shared software, hardware, and data are basic to the design of such networks.

Although there are a few distributed database management systems (DDBMS) available for commercial use, these applications remain rooted in the research/university arena of activity.

A more practical example of network development lies in the micro/mainframe link. Because of the microcomputer's increasing power and decreasing price, it is possible to solve sophisticated data processing problems on the microcomputer using productivity tools such as spreadsheets, local databases, and graphics. When the microcomputer can also be used to access corporate databases, locally and remotely, and to upload and download files, a powerful combination is created.

The possibility of user implementation of DDP has decreased in recent years as computer manufacturers concentrate on developing network architectures based on their own hardware. It has become critical for them to provide interfaces to public packet-switched networks, local area networks and other manufacturers' networks. This is the most realistic way of developing DDP systems in wide area networks.

The Northern Alberta Institute of Technology network (chapter 13) is an example of an educational network. The applications include student laboratories (a large number of small jobs), computer-managed learning, and college administration applications.

The Alberta Government network (chapter 14) is an example of a large, province-wide, IBM Systems Network Architecture network. It also shows the relationship between data and voice networks and the potential for the integration of these.

The Interprovincial Pipe Line network (chapter 15) is an example of an international (Canada/U.S.) network based on DEC's Digital Network Architecture. This network uses multiple autonomous hosts and interfaces with Ethernet local area networks and a public packet-switched network.

Chapter

DISTRIBUTED DATA
PROCESSING

EVOLUTION

Three major forces contributed to the development of distributed data processing (DDP). The organizational structure of large corporations that becomes fragmented through geographical dispersal, the focus on information as a valuable resource, and the technological potential and cost effectiveness of handling information in a new way, all contributed to an increased awareness of DDP as a solution to data processing problems.

As organizations grew, they created functional groups that specialized in a particular aspect of the business, for example, sales or accounting. The creation of these groups led to a need for formalized communication and then to a group responsible for the communication of accurate, timely information. This functional group became the data processing department. The centralization of information services developed further when branches of the organization in other geographical areas were connected to the computer as remote access terminals.

The next stage in evolution had a dual emphasis and came from the end users of data processing services. First, the remote users demanded local access, control, and processing capability for their own data. Second, the large centralized system was under fire from its own local users. This led to the development of end-user languages, the concept of the information center, and local area networks (fig. 9-1).

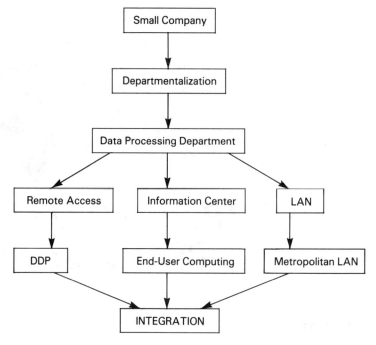

Figure 9-1 Evolution of DDP

The future development of DDP points to the integration of LANs, metropolitan, and distance networks in a complex but productive end-user environment.

STRUCTURE

There are two facets to the issue of centralization versus decentralization. One relates to organizational philosophy, the other to information handling.

The hierarchical nature of organizations and the need for company-wide goals leads to the idea of centralized control. The head-office mentality has been criticized lately and yet it has its strengths: relatively simple decision-making paths, consistent company-wide policy implementation, and a high degree of organizational control. At the other end of the spectrum, in organizations with geographically dispersed sites, there are good arguments for local control and autonomy: familiarity with local conditions, faster reaction to changing conditions, and the motivational need for control over one's own destiny. The conflict is often viewed as a power struggle. Certainly, there is evidence at all levels of society of a growing awareness that individuals and groups should be given the chance to direct their own lives.

In terms of decentralizing information services, the first solution was to access a centralized system by remote terminal. It was thought that this would provide for decentralized decision-making (optimum solutions to local problems are achieved by those who are there), as well as for overall monitoring and control by the central site. This did not satisfy, however, either the remote end user's information needs nor, for that matter, the needs of the local end users. In addition, the perception that the head office can operate on the basis of summaries or summaries of summaries is also open to question.

The *end user* can be defined as the person who needs specific information to make decisions that will fulfill the organizational goals of profit and service. Whether located at the head office or in a branch office, the end user is a manager who directly affects organizational performance. All other groups in the organization provide support for the end user, whether they are in personnel, data processing, or senior management. This perception of the end user as the driving force in an organization has led to an emphasis on providing the information and productivity tools necessary for the end user to do the job wherever he or she is located.

DDP is not a process or a technology, but a concept that enables hardware, software, and communication strategies to meet the needs of the end user. A centralized information system reflects a shared approach to information resources. A decentralized system, on the other hand, tends towards the dedicated, autonomous use of information. A distributed system lies somewhere in between: the system's control is usually only partly decentralized, but the information used is decentralized almost completely.

DEFINITION

DDP has evolved from an attempt to satisfy organizational information systems goals to an emphasis on end-user productivity. Because of its conceptual simplicity but complex and varied implementation, DDP has been defined in many ways. Consideration of several definitions (fig. 9-2) may provide insight into the breadth of meaning, the variety of emphases, and the changing perception of DDP.

The first three definitions are broad and emphasize the relationship between goals and resources. Definitions four and five emphasize the processing needs of distributed systems; six and seven focus on the software and data aspects of DDP, while eight and nine are very specific. Eight defines DDP in terms of the three words: distributed, data, and processing. Definition nine attempts to identify functional responsibility. Number 10 encompasses both local and remote processing and reflects the more recent preoccupation with productivity tools for the end user.

---

1. The concept of arranging hardware, software, and networks to meet organizational needs.

2. The philosophy of placing computers geographically and organizationally close to the application.

3. Putting resources where the people are.

4. The use of multiple computers in a cooperative arrangement to support common systems objectives.

5. The transfer of data processing functions from a central system to the small dedicated processors where the information is used.

6. Programs and data reside in processing nodes that are integrated by networks.

7. The interconnection of components of a system permitting shared resources and databases.

8. Placement of intelligent devices at multiple sites to execute user-written applications to update and store local files and access remote databases.

9. A local site connected to a remote host via a network in order to access the corporate database and provide local processing, data entry, and printing.

10. The provision of an integrated computer network for end-user productivity.

Figure 9-2 DDP Definitions

ADVANTAGES AND DISADVANTAGES

The decision to implement a distributed data processing system usually involves a series of trade-offs or compromises. The factors on which the decision is based must be clearly identified and carefully weighed. The prior commitment to one strategy (a centralized information system, for example) means that the case for change should significantly outweigh the decision to stick with the present system. The nature of the organization (conservative or risk-taking), the application, the potential rewards, and the present performance of the organization are all factors that can swing the decision one way or the other. The choice is such a fundamental and important one, and it is so heavily influenced by the world economy and market strategy, that a relatively cautious implementation may be appropriate. The advantages and disadvantages of the problem, often different sides of the same coin, are summarized in figure 9-3.

Advantages	Disadvantages
response time	maintenance
end-user applications control	loss of data control
flexibility	complexity
costs	costs

Figure 9-3   Advantages and Disadvantages of Distributed Systems

Response Time and Maintenance

The traditional argument for centralized systems is based on Grosch's Law, which states that there are economies of scale available when building computer systems. The bigger the system, the more you save. In other words:

cost/number of machine instructions = 1/(size of computer)**2

This may have been true in the mainframe world but it is not true for minicomputers or microcomputers. In addition the vast overhead incurred in operating large mainframes has led to the unloading of database and communication functions to separate processors.

A major criticism of the centralized information system has centered on its poor response time. This in turn has led to pressure for distributed systems based on the relatively low equipment costs of mini- and microcomputer systems, and on the impracticality of asking a single mainframe to service thousands of terminals.

The main reasons for the improvement in response time are the elimination of communications time, the reduction of the number of users sharing a specific system, and the power of the local minicomputers and intelligent terminals.

By distributing the hardware and providing better system response time we run the risk of maintenance and service problems because of the remoteness of some locations and the problems of multi-vendor suppport.

Control

The trade-off here is between providing better end-user control of applications and the risk of losing corporate control of the data. Problems involving both the backlog and the hidden backlog (the backlog caused by users not submitting requests because of the backlog) of applications in the data processing department have led to the development of productivity tools for the end user. These tools, together with the ability to download portions of the corporate database, have provided:

— end-user control of applications;
— user-friendly systems; and
— easy development, implementation, and installation of applications.

The main problems with distributing in this way are in preserving data integrity, maintaining data standards, and providing the facility for data auditing.

Flexibility and Complexity

Again these are different views of the same entity. Their characteristics are summarized in figure 9-4. The inherent modularity of a distributed system provides a good illustration of its ability to adapt to changing conditions, for example, peak demands, additional nodes, and technological change. Implementation and upgrading of such a system can be carried out piecemeal, one geographical area at a time, in this way minimizing the system's downtime.

On the other hand, the replication of resources (data, software, hardware, people, and space) are major contributing factors in any cost comparison.

Flexibility	Complexity
adaptability	incompatibility
backup	duplication
resource sharing	training
failsafeness	newness

Figure 9-4   Flexibility versus Complexity of Distributed Systems

RESOURCE SHARING AND TRAINING

It may be useful, in multiple sites with similar configurations, to share expertise, storage space, and application software. Conversely, the fact that the systems are similar but not the same may cause the users significant levels of frustration. For instance, the user may have to learn more than one system. This consideration leads to the widely held belief that distributed systems, being more complex than centralized systems, require a higher level of user education. Apart from the consideration of cost, the significant thing here is that the user is motivated to solve his problems, not merely to learn the idiosyncracies of computer systems.

FAILSAFENESS AND NEWNESS

A major advantage of distributed systems over centralized systems is their failsafe nature. Disruptions in a centralized system affect all users. The bigger the system and the greater the number of users affected, the more effort and expense is devoted to security and recovery procedures. In distributed systems, disruptions affect a relatively small percentage of the total user population. In other words, most of the processing capability will be available to most of the users most of the time.

A counterbalancing effect is that the relative newness of the distributed system means a higher degree of unfamiliarity on the part of the user, and a higher level of hidden technical problems that can affect the design, implementation, and management of a DDP system.

Costs

A comparison of the relative costs of distributed and centralized systems is complex and must take note of the following:

— computer hardware costs are falling more rapidly than communication costs;
— by using local processing, DDP decreases communication costs;
— replication of hardware, software, data, people, and space resources increases DDP costs;
— economies of scale do not apply in this comparison; and
— centralized systems have a much larger operating-system overhead.

The calculation of relative costs is best handled in a cost/benefit context. The major benefits of distributed systems lie in their responsiveness to end users, and this in turn increases user productivity, the key to the survival and growth of any organization.

CLASSIFICATION

Network topology describes the relationships of communication nodes. In distance networks the topology is dictated by geography, in LANs by the network manufacturer. The termination nodes of a network may also be classified by different topologies, the most common of which are vertical, horizontal, and functional topologies.

Vertical Topology (Hierarchical)

This topology (fig. 9-5) parallels the classical organizational structure, and for that reason it is the most popular topology. Because the vertical model pervades everyone's thinking, however, it may be over-utilized. Typically, we have three levels of processing: at the host, at the remote site, and in intelligent terminals. Transactions enter and leave at the lowest levels. Processing not possible at the intelligent terminal is passed to the remote-site processor. Processing not possible at the remote site is passed to the host or primary site. The lower levels can perform partial processing before passing the data up the hierarchy. Each level may support its own database, which may or may not be shared with other levels. IBM's Systems Network Architecture (SNA) provides this environment.

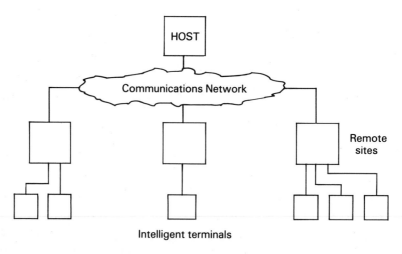

Figure 9-5   Vertical Topology

Horizontal Topology

Horizontal topology (fig. 9-6) is characterized by peer (equal) relationships among nodes. Every node in the network can communicate with every other node without having to consult a central node. The advantage of such a configuration is that each node can be equally responsive to user requests. A network user at one node can easily gain access to applications and facilities at other nodes. Since every data exchange and remote access operation does not have to pass through a central node, communication overhead is reduced and network performance increases in efficiency. The Digital Equipment Corporation's DECnet network is a good example of horizontal topology for distance networks. Both ring and bus LAN topologies are also examples of this form of distributed processing.

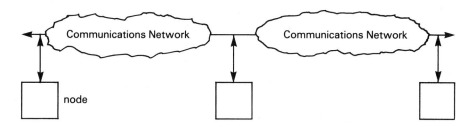

Figure 9-6 Horizontal Topology

Functional Topology

This topology (fig. 9-7) involves the separation of processing functions into separate nodes. Typical functional separations are:

— database processing,
— application processing,
— communication processing, and
— transaction processing.

The major advantage of this type of topology at the host end is the offloading of database searching and retrieval and the communication handling of large numbers of terminals. This improves the applications throughput on the host significantly.

Another important aspect of computer network configuration is the compatibility or incompatibility of the machines. A homogeneous network avoids the problems of protocol conversion, the need for gateways from one manufacturer's system to another, emulation software, and multi-vendor servicing problems. The heterogeneous network takes advantage of manufacturer strengths and price breaks.

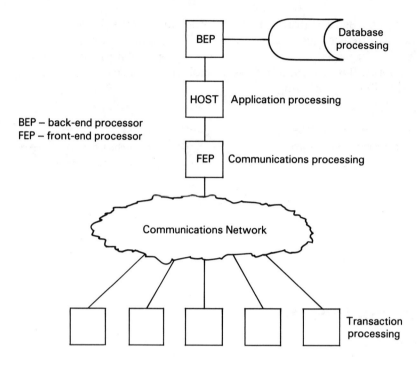

Figure 9-7 Functional Topology

Review Questions for Chapter 9

1. DDP as a solution to an organization's communication problems is designated by two characteristics. Name them.

2. Define DDP.

3. Why can DDP be defined in a variety of ways?

4. In what ways can DDP be classified?

5. Identify the major advantages of DDP.

6. Identify the major problem areas in implementing DDP.

DISTRIBUTED
DATABASE

A distributed database (DDB) is a collection of data that belongs logically to the same system but that is spread over the computer nodes of a network. Distributed applications are applications that access data from more than one database, for example, when an account is transferred from one bank branch to another. A DDB can also be implemented on a LAN where the nodes not only share server data, but each other's files. Rather than emphasize the geographical dispersion of data that applies to distance networks, we may broaden our definition as follows to include LANs:

> A distributed database application is one in which a node accesses databases connected to other nodes in the network.

The characteristics of a centralized database are well known. They are compared with the requirements of a distributed database in figure 10-1.

WHY DISTRIBUTE DATABASES?

It turns out that the reasons for distributing databases are similar to those used to justify DDP. This is not surprising since DDB is a major application of DDP. The main difference lies in the emphasis on data access in DDB rather

173

Characteristic	Centralized Database	Distributed Database
Centralized control	database administrator (DBA)	global DBA, local DBAs
Data independence	schema	distributed transparency
Reduction of redundancy	avoid inconsistencies, share data	redundancy desirable: - replication - failsafeness
Complex physical structures for efficient access	indexes, chains, 2-way-circular linked lists	different solution: - distributed access plan
Integrity, recovery, concurrency control	transactions must be completed or cancelled	more difficult in distributed databases
Privacy and security	authorized access through DBA	local protection schemes; network is the weak link

Figure 10-1 Centralized versus Distributed Database

than on distributed processing. The factors are listed here for completeness:

1. DDB fits naturally into the decentralized structure of many organizations.

2. It is a natural solution when several databases already exist in the organization.

3. It supports a smooth incremental growth with a minimal impact on already existing nodes.

4. It reduces communication costs.

5. It improves system performance through parallelism (true for any multiprocessor system).

6. It has a higher degree of availability and reliability (failsafe).

The development of commercially available DDBs is dependent on the continuing low cost of microcomputers and minicomputers, on network technological developments that facilitate DDB communication and on DDBMS (distributed database management system) software developments to solve the problems of concurrency and recovery.

COMPONENTS OF A DDBMS

The main parts of a DDBMS are:

— the DBMS component,
— the data communication component,
— the data dictionary component; and
— the DDB component.

A DDBMS provides the following facilities:

• access by an applications program to data in databases connected to other nodes of the network;
• a degree of distributed transparency;
• support for database administration and control; and
• support for concurrency control and recovery of distributed transactions.

DDBMS ACCESS

There are two approaches to accessing a DDBMS:

a) The direct approach involves an application issuing a database access request to its local DDBMS. The request is routed to the DDBMS at the remote site, executed there, and the result returned to the original site. This is a simple approach that enables the application program to access the remote database directly.

b) The database access is executed at the remote site by an intermediary program that has the capability of performing multiple database accesses, if required, before transmitting the results to the original site.

The direct approach provides more distribution transparency while the indirect approach is more efficient if many database accesses are required.

A homogeneous DDBMS is one that uses the same DBMS at every site. These DDBMSs are easier to implement and are more commonly available for the commercial market. Heterogeneous DDBMSs use at least two different DBMSs and are therefore more difficult to design and implement. They are used at present as research prototypes. The need for heterogeneous DDBMSs grows as the requirement for integrating pre-existing databases grows.

TYPES OF DATA DISTRIBUTION

There are three choices available for the distribution of data:

1. *Centralization,* in which one copy of the data resides at a central node, for example, in the principal host of a wide area network or the server of a LAN.

2. *Partitioning,* in which the single copy of the data is split into parts and allocated geographically or functionally to specific nodes.

3. *Replication,* in which copies of key data files are stored at each site.

Centralization

This is the classical approach to locating DBMSs and is included for comparison purposes (fig. 10-2). The advantages include centralized data control, clear standards implementation, and simple security. The problems include

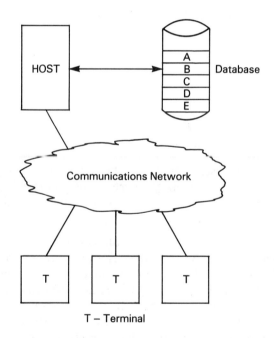

Figure 10-2   Centralized Database

high operating-systems overhead, a poor response time, and the increased reliability emphasis associated with dependence on a single system.

Partitioning

In this case, queries must be decomposed and sub-requests sent to different nodes (fig. 10-3). This approach is used with relational databases in which the data is stored in two-dimensional tables called relations. These relations are composed of entities, which are either concrete or abstract objects, and attributes, which describe the objects. For example, a bank account is an example of an entity that has an account number and a balance as attributes. A relation can be partitioned by entity or attribute. Entity, or horizontal, partitioning would subdivide a relation by geographical location. For example, all the accounts at a particular branch of a bank could be listed together. Attribute or vertical partitioning can distinguish between different kinds of information, for example, financial and personal.

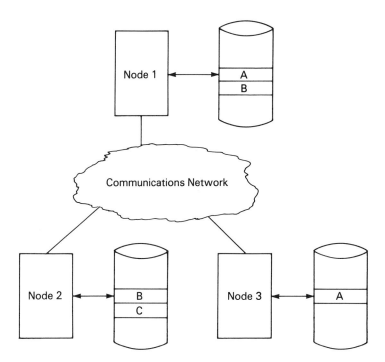

Figure 10-3 Partitioned Database

Replication

When a database is replicated (fig. 10-4), the DDBMS must choose which copy or copies should be used in the request. For a query, any copy will satisfy the request, assuming all copies are updated through update synchronization. However all copies must be the object of an update request.

The particular choice of partitioning or replication depends on the size of the file and the frequency of use of each node. A design starting point is summarized in figure 10-5. Normally, some combination of partitioning and replication is appropriate (fig. 10-6).

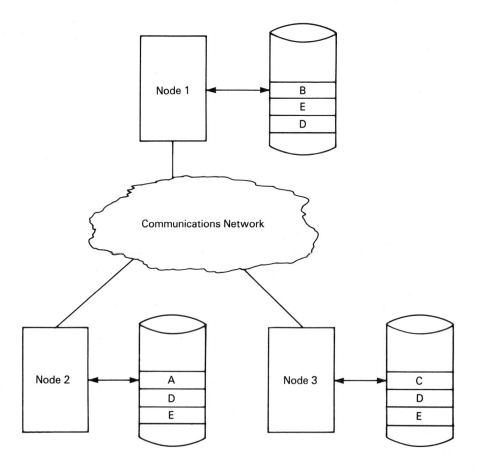

Figure 10-4   Replicated Database

File Size	Remote Access	Method of Distribution
small	none	replicate
large	low	partition
large	high	centralize

Note: Remote Access = number of non-local requests/total number of requests

Figure 10-5   A Design Starting Point

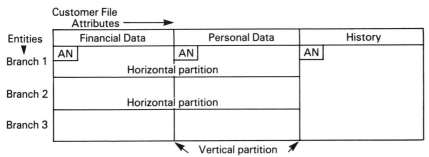

AN - Account Number
Partitioning - vertical: financial/personal history   horizontal: branch
Replication - financial data at head office

Figure 10-6   Partitioning and Replicating a File

PROBLEMS IN DISTRIBUTED DATABASE MANAGEMENT

The distributed database faces the same kinds of control problems that are associated with the management of a centralized database. These problems are complicated by the fact that the data is physically located in different sites.

Recovery

A transaction is a program unit whose execution preserves the consistency of the database. It must be executed to completion or not at all. In a distributed database it is more difficult to ensure that this happens. The failure of one site may result in erroneous computations. It is the function of the transaction manager to ensure transactions are executed to completion or cancelled. The transaction manager maintains a log for recovery purposes and participates in concurrency control.

Concurrency Control

Most computer installations operate in a multiprogramming mode in which several transactions are executed at the same time, that is, concurrently. There are several schemes for controlling the interaction of concurrent transactions to prevent them from destroying the consistency of the database in a centralized database. These schemes involve a transaction locking portions of the database so that other transactions cannot access specific data till it is unlocked. These schemes can be modified for use in a distributed environment.

Deadlock Handling

A serious problem that can occur in concurrent processing is called "deadlock." A system is in a deadlock state if there exists a set of transactions such that every transaction in the set is waiting for another transaction in the set. There are two ways of dealing with the deadlock problem. A deadlock prevention protocol ensures that a deadlock state is never entered. Alternatively, a deadlock detection and recovery scheme allows the system to enter a deadlock state and recover from it. Deadlock prevention and recovery schemes can be implemented in a distributed system.

Review Questions for Chapter 10

1. List the two main characteristics of a DDB.

2. What are the four main parts of a DDBMS?

3. Explain distributed transparency.

4. List two ways of accessing a DDBMS.

5. Identify two ways of partitioning data.

6. Why is replication avoided in DBMSs yet used in DDBMSs?

11

MICRO/MAINFRAME LINKS

INTRODUCTION

DDP and distributed database are major network applications that require considerable additional resources and the reorganization of a centralized data processing environment. These areas are still relatively undeveloped technologically (except for LANs) and still face considerable design and implementation problems. The proliferation of low-cost, powerful microcomputers has encouraged many organizations to seek ways to interface these devices both locally and remotely to their mainframes.

PURPOSE

The main encouragement for the development of micro/mainframe facilities came from the end user who already had a personal computer on his desk for use with productivity tools such as spreadsheets, data management programs, and graphics. The simplest idea was to use the personal computer as a terminal for separate access to mainframe data. It was recognized that it would be helpful for the end user to be able to switch from using a productivity tool on his personal computer to using, for example, a mainframe program to access the corporate inventory control system without changing machines.

Terminal emulation has become a major concern of software suppliers. An important feature of it is the ability to emulate a variety of terminals and gain access to different in-house mainframes as well as national financial and statistical databases. These applications led quickly to the demand for access to mainframe data for incorporation into end-user solutions and for transmission of results to the mainframe. There are two ways of exchanging data: downloading and uploading. Downloading a segment of data from the mainframe to the micro for reprocessing, integrating, and incorporating into a report is straightforward. It has the advantage of dealing with current information. Uploading data to the mainframe from the micro is useful for linking together reports. For example, department reports can be combined to produce a company-wide report with appropriate summaries and graphs.

In addition, the data processing department saw the advantage of using the micro as a development tool to save mainframe resources. The possibilities range from editing on the micro and uploading from it to the mainframe for compilation and debugging to applications development. The micro can also be used to build a prototype of a system with a fourth-generation language that can be converted to another language on the mainframe or used with the mainframe version of the productivity tool. A number of organizations are finding the combination of PC FOCUS and mainframe FOCUS useful as a way of off-loading the mainframe during project development while using the multiple-user capability of the mainframe version for running the finished product. Since the two versions of FOCUS are compatible, the exchange is simple:

> Downloading   ON TABLE PCHOLD AS d:filename.ext
> Uploading   XFER ddname FROM d:filename.ext

The micro/mainframe link improves end-user productivity by making data more easily available, and by providing local processing capability. The incorporation of the micro/mainframe link into a distributed database application is a good possibility for the future, when local and remote data access may be combined in a way that is transparent to the user.

CLASSIFICATION

There is some confusion about the options available for micro/mainframe connections. Contributing factors include:

— microcomputers support asynchronous transfer as their standard user-terminal interface;
— IBM supports synchronous communication with its standard 3270 series terminals;

— asynchronous terminal communication uses ASCII, as do micros and minis;
— IBM uses EBCDIC (as do some other mainframe manufacturers);
— mainframe computers often unload display processing onto the terminal (or the terminal-emulating micro); and
— the ANSI terminal standards are interpreted in different ways.

The characteristics of micro/mainframe tools can be classified in the following way. Simple programs that are used to allow the microcomputer to behave like a terminal are called terminal emulation software. Asynchronous communications packages include terminal emulation facilities, file transfer capabilities, and other features (fig. 11-1). They usually have to be present at both ends of the link for full operation. A combination of hardware and software tools are used to supply the very important synchronous terminal world. The products available on the market add to the confusion by supplying overlapping features for a variety of applications.

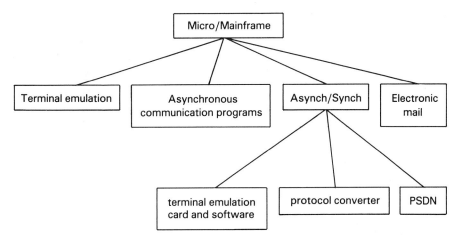

Figure 11-1   Micro/Mainframe Classification

Terminal Emulation

This is a relatively simple aspect of micro/mainframe communication. PCs can emulate simple (dumb) terminals using software to act like a specific asynchronous terminal, for example, TTY, VT52, or the very popular VT100 terminal specifications. A simple terminal emulation program is normally used to communicate with a host mainframe or mini computer. Many packages have the ability to emulate more than one terminal.

Asynchronous Packages

These communications programs have the following features:

a) *terminal emulation,* as described above.

b) *file transfer.* This is the ability of the program to transfer (upload and download) files between the user's micro and another micro, mini, or mainframe.

c) *configuration setting.* This is the ability to create communications sets, macros, or script files. These names describe the files that provide initializing information for the communications programs, such as a table of telephone numbers for dial-up routines, setting parity, the number of bits per character, the number of stop bits, and the transmission rate.

d) *softkey programming.* This is the ability to program function keys so that a single key can be used to sign on to a specific mainframe, set up the micro for unattended access and file transfer, or provide help facilities. These procedures are sometimes called command or script files.

e) *error detection.* The methods range from simple checksum in hobbyist environments to the standard CRC-16 of commercial environments.

f) *editing.* Some programs provide for insertion, deletion, and creation of data, as well as for copying, renaming, and deleting files without having to exit the program to an editor or the operating system.

A number of modem manufacturers, for example Hayes, are now supplying communications software as an option with the modem. This guarantees compatibility between the software and the modem and can be less expensive than making separate purchases.

Async/Sync

Synchronous techniques are used in direct, coaxial cable connection to an IBM mainframe or remote controller (fig. 11-2). Since the micro market is dominated by PC-DOS and MS-DOS, there are many vendors who produce hardware and software products for linking PCs as emulators of IBM 3270 terminals.

The IBM 3270 terminals are the most widely used synchronous devices on the market. The emulation of these devices provides a major market for many vendors who produce hardware and software to perform this task. Problems with this process begin with the different keyboards. PC keys must do double duty to represent all the 3270 keyboard keys. The video control is different, and PCs are limited in what they can simulate. The IBM mainframe expects to

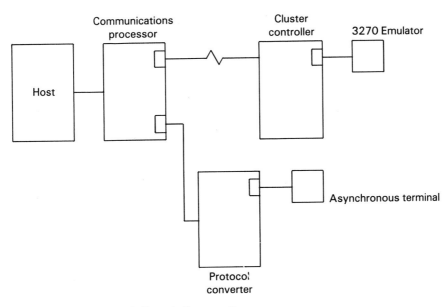

Figure 11-2   Asynch/Synch Connections

treat a printer attached to a PC as a separate device. These difficulties must be addressed by the emulator's hardware and software.

The main problems in using a PC for 3270 emulation are:

1. The async to/from sync protocol conversion
   TTY <------> SDLC
   TTY <------> BISYNC

2. The code conversion
   ASCII <------> EBCDIC

These problems are usually solved in one of three ways: by use of the terminal emulation card, the protocol converter, or the PSDN.

THE TERMINAL EMULATION CARD

A terminal emulation card with accompanying software allows the PC to communicate with an IBM mainframe directly, via a communications controller, or via a remote cluster controller. A number of variations in terminal emulators are available:

1. *Emulation of the 3278/9 terminals.* The 3278 is a monochrome display, the 3279 is the color graphics version. The card is designed to communicate with

the 3274 (32-device cluster controller) or the 3276 (a single, integrated control unit and display unit).

2. *Emulation of the 3274 controller.*

3. *Emulation of the 3276 controller.* These cards, with the accompanying software, provide:

- 3270 emulation,
- file transfer, and
- windows for multiple 3278 sessions.

Typical packages include:

- Data Communication Associates' IRMA board plus the IRMA link software,
- Blue-Lynx 3270 Advanced Coax, and
- IDEACOMM 3278.

PROTOCOL CONVERTER

This is an intelligent device that converts ASCII to/from EBCDIC, twisted pair to/from coax, and the PC screen to/from the 3270 screen. Most protocol converters have a single port attachment to the mainframe (replacing the 3274) and multiple ports that can be attached to PCs, modems, terminals, printers, LANs, and statistical multiplexers.

Despite having a variety of features, a protocol converter's principal function is to convert asynchronous to synchronous communication.

VIA PUBLIC DATA NETWORKS

When there are many remote users, the mainframe can be equipped with a direct link to a public packet-switched network. Asynchronous micros can dial into the network with a local number and be connected to a remote host. The network can treat the microcomputer as a simple terminal or provide protocol conversion for 3270 operation.

Electronic Mail

Designed specifically for message transmission, electronic mail systems are used for accessing on-line services like the Source, the Dow Jones News/Retrieval and Compushare. Another facet of this application is the interface with Telecom Canada's ENVOY 100, which offers customers access, via their PCs, to each other through

— DATAphone,
— Datapac,
— TWX,
— Telenet, Tymnet,
— Telex, and
— international networks.

Review Questions for Chapter 11

1. List the four categories of micro/mainframe tools.

2. How is the micro/mainframe link used as a development tool? Identify two ways.

3. What are the three problems associated with connecting a micro to an IBM mainframe?

4. What is a communications set or macro used for?

5. What is a command file used for?

6. List three ways of solving the async/sync communication problem.

Chapter

NETWORK ARCHITECTURE

Network architectures facilitate operation, maintenance and growth of the communication and processing environments by isolating the user and the application programs from the details of the network. Many network architectures are based on the ISO-OSI seven-level protocol discussed in chapter 6. The main producers of network architectures are public packet-switching networks and computer manufacturers. We have discussed the X.25 architecture developed by the CCITT for the first three levels of the ISO-OSI model and used by most public packet-switching networks. Two widely used network architectures are:

— IBM's Systems Network Architecture, based on a hierarchical computer topology; and
— Digital Equipment Corporation's (DEC) DECnet, based on a horizontal topology.

SYSTEMS NETWORK ARCHITECTURE (SNA)

Because IBM has a large share of the mainframe market, SNA is a de facto standard for network architectures. SNA formally defines the responsibility of communication system components in terms of nodes or devices and paths. Both nodes and paths are arranged hierarchically in several levels. The nodes provide functional distribution under a central control. A typical IBM network configuration (fig. 12-1) consists of hosts (370 series), front-end processors or communication controllers (3705/3725), cluster controllers (3274/3276/3174), and terminals (3270) or personal computers. Each device controls a specific part of the network at its level in the hierarchy and operates under the control of a device at the next level. The paths provide flexibility and multiple routing.

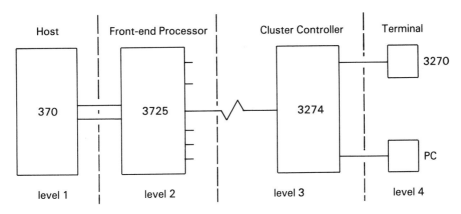

Figure 12-1   A Typical Network Configuration

IMPLEMENTATION

SNA was specifically designed for the System/370 architecture, which includes the 4300 series of small mainframes, the 303X series of medium-sized mainframes, and the 308X/309X series of large systems. The 3705/3725 communications controllers can be used as remote communications controllers and as front-end processors for a host. The 3270 Information Display System is a family of display devices that can be configured as a system: display stations, printers, PCs, and control units. The 3274 cluster controller connects display devices to a host via a local or remote hook-up. All current IBM operating systems (OS, MVS, and DOS) support SNA to some extent. The advanced communication function (ACF) is the standard access method for SNA. An access method is a system program that provides a single interface to communication facilities for all applications running under a single computer's operating system. There are two versions of ACF: ACF/TCAM (derived from the TeleCommunications Access Method) and ACF/VTAM (Virtual Telecommunications Access Method). They are similar but have different strengths and weaknesses (fig. 12-2).

VTAM	TCAM
More efficient for host	More efficient for terminals
Requires Network Terminal Option for asynchronous transfer	Requires less buffering
Looks like the long-term standard	Handles asynchronous transfer better
	Handles BISYNC with the Emulation Program (EP) and the Partitioned Emulation Program (PEP)

Figure 12-2   A Comparison of VTAM and TCAM

Network Architecture

The direct users of an SNA network are devices and applications programs such as TSO or CICS. Network addressable units (NAU) are communications programs that represent a specific device or applications program in the network. There are three kinds of NAU: the system services control point (SSCP), the physical unit (PU), and the logical unit (LU).

The SSCP resides in the host and is responsible for the overall control of the network. It uses the network's address and routing tables to establish connections between nodes and select routes and to control network flow.

Each device in the network has a PU. The PU is a program for hosts and front-ends, but is usually implemented in hardware (ROM chips) for cluster controllers and terminals. There are five types of PU in SNA, four of which have been defined:

— PU1 is for a terminal;
— PU2 is for a cluster controller;
— PU4 is for a communications controller; and
— PU5 is for a host computer.

Each application in the network has an LU. An application is any process that requires communication facilities, for example, data entry, database enquiries, file transfer, or remote printer spooling. The LU is the interface between the application program and the network. A PU may be associated with several LUs. There are eight types of LU in SNA; LU0 and LU5 are undefined. The others are:

— LU1, which describes a session between a host and a remote batch terminal;
— LU2, which describes a session between a host application and a 3270 terminal;
— LU3, which describes a session between a host application and a printer;

— LU4, which describes a session between a host application and a word processor;
— LU6, which describes a session between two applications on two different hosts;
— LU6.2, which describes a session between an application in a host and an application in an intelligent terminal; and
— LU7, which describes a session between a host application and an IBM 5250 display terminal.

All communications between NAUs occur within a session. A session is a logical two-way connection between two NAUs over a specific route for a specific time. The main ones are:

— SSCP-PU sessions are used for status and diagnostic requests;
— SSCP-LU sessions are used for the same purpose;
— SSCP-SSCP sessions are used to exchange information between hosts, and establish sessions between two LUs under the control of different SSCPs; and
— LU-LU sessions are used for end-user communication.

The data link control level of SNA uses SDLC, a protocol which is very similar to, but not compatible with, HDLC, the X.25 data link control protocol. It contains the same control parameters: flag, address, control, and frame-check sequence. Imbedded in the SDLC frame is the IBM equivalent of the packet called the path information unit (PIU). The PIU contains the transmission header (TH) to identify the source and destination addresses, the request/response header (RH) which contains the conversation rules, such as who speaks first, and the request/response unit (RU) which contains the data (fig. 12-3).

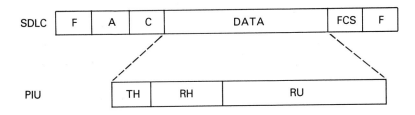

F - Flag
A - Address
C - Control
FCS - Frame Check Sequence

TH - Transmission Header
RH - Request/Response Header
RU - Request/Response Unit

Figure 12-3 The SDLC/PIU Relationship

The inter-relationship between SSCP, PU and LU can be explained by looking at a simple network containing one host, one communications controller, two cluster controllers and a number of terminals. Figure 12-4 shows how a host application is connected to a particular terminal, via a network control program table contained in the communications controller, using the SDLC frame.

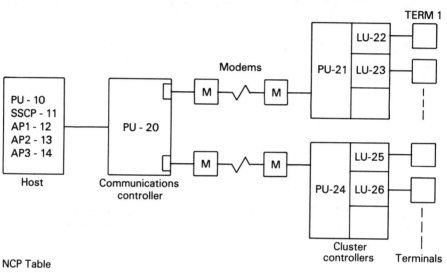

NCP Table

Entry	Contents	Symbolic Name
1	line-0	
2	PU-21	
3	LU-22	
4	LU-23	TERM 1
5	PU-24	
6	LU-25	
7	LU-26	

Frame for TERM 1

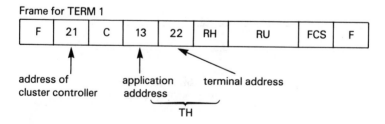

Figure 12-4 SNA Example

Advanced Program-to-Program Communication

SNA is more than a protocol. It is a collection of hardware and software products for the development of communication programs which are, to a large extent, independent of network changes. SNA began as a host/terminal environment but has gradually changed to support distributed processing. It now supports IBM's minicomputer lines: System/3X, Series/1, 5520, and 8100 computers, and the IBM Personal Computer.

The IBM minicomputer and microcomputer support by SNA is through advanced program-to-program communication (APPC), also known as LU 6.2. For example, SNA supports IBM PCs in the form of 3270/SNA terminal emulation as well as through LU 6.2, thus providing more complex user interactions at a lower cost. The main benefit of the LU 6.2 development is the maintenance of communications compatibility among IBM mainframes, minicomputers and microcomputers.

SNA Layers

SNA protocol is similar to the ISO-OSI model in that it has several levels or layers. The general approaches are comparable, but the specifics are quite different. The levels of SNA are identified and defined in figure 12-5. Each level communicates only with the level above and below it. All messages between end users must pass through all layers.

Layer	Function
Application	user's application processing
NAU services manager	data formatting, data compression, data compaction
Function management data services	connection/disconnection of sessions, network operator interface, network management
Data flow control services	flow control using chaining and brackets, high-level error control
Transmission control services	encryption, pacing
Path control	routing, segmenting, blocking
Data link control	addressing, sequencing, error checking using SDLC
Physical	high-speed I/O channels, parallel links, peripheral links, coax

Figure 12-5   SNA Layers

DIGITAL NETWORK ARCHITECTURE (DNA)

Digital Network Architecture is the structural and functional model, "the framework of specifications," on which DECnet is based. DECnet is a family of hardware and software communication products that form a network environment for Digital Equipment Corporation's (DEC) computers. The DNA model is closely based on the ISO-OSI model. The protocol layers have the same function. This means the DECnet/X.25 interface is relatively straightforward.

Implementation

The DECnet network can contain any combination of the PDP-11, VAX, and DECsystem 10 computer families. DEC provides communications hardware and software for communication between their own products (DECnet), to connect systems to IBM and other vendors' systems (Internets), and to interface with packet-switched networks (Packetnets). The incorporation of Ethernet LAN technology into DNA provides for the integration of local computing facilities at each node of the network. Hardware communication products include asynchronous devices for multiplexing terminals and synchronous devices such as communications controllers, modems, statistical multiplexers, and matrix switches.

DNA has been developed in phases starting in 1976. Each phase has included new features that extended its network capabilities. Consideration of the sequence in which these features have been incorporated provides insight into the evolution of network architectures.

Phase 1: – program-to-program communication
      – file transfer

Phase 2: – remote file access
      – network management
      – point-to-point configurations

Phase 3: – adaptive routing
      – network terminals
      – multipoint lines
      – X.25 protocol

Phase 4: – Ethernet
      – communications servers
      – virtual terminal
      – SNA gateway

The DNA allows for the construction of a DECnet that will interconnect WANs, LANs, and PDNs. The WAN routing program ensures node-to-node communication via intermediate nodes where necessary. Adaptive routing is used to find alternate paths during peak loading. Area routing provides for routing within an area of a large network (level 1 routing) and routing between areas (level 2 routing). Ethernet baseband LANs operating at 10 Mbps can be incorporated into the network via communications servers (nodes dedicated to performing communications for other nodes). These nodes increase network performance and reduce the cost of implementing baseband LANs. The incorporation of X.25 into DNA Phase IV gives DECnet easy access to public packet-switched networks. This feature allows remote users inexpensive access to DECnets as well as a simple interface between DECnet and other network architectures. Figure 12-6 illustrates the combination of WANs, LANs, and PSDNs within a DNA model.

Network Architecture

The seven layers of DNA are identified and described in figure 12-7. There are two kinds of relationships within these layers: interfaces and protocols.

Interfaces are the definitions of specific function boundaries between DECnet software components residing within a single node. The boundaries are structured as a hierarchical set of layers and arranged according to function, as modules within these layers (fig. 12-8). A module can provide services to modules in the next higher layer and can use the services of modules in the next lower layer. Modules in the network management layer can interface directly with modules in each of the lower layers for access and control purposes.

Modules with equivalent functions in the same layer, but residing in different nodes, communicate using protocols. A protocol (by DEC's definition) is both a set of messages and the rules for exchanging messages. DNA defines the message formats and the rules. DNA does not define the protocol for the user layer. Some layers support multiple protocols. For example, there are three data link control protocols: DDCMP, X.25, and Ethernet.

A node is a network entity, capable of processing, sending, and receiving information. It consists of hardware and software that implement the DNA specifications. Every node has a unique numeric address. In area-based networks the address includes an area number. Data travelling between nodes is enveloped in control information. The node addresses are assigned names at the session level of the DNA for user-friendly communications. The data passes from a source process in the user level down through each level of the

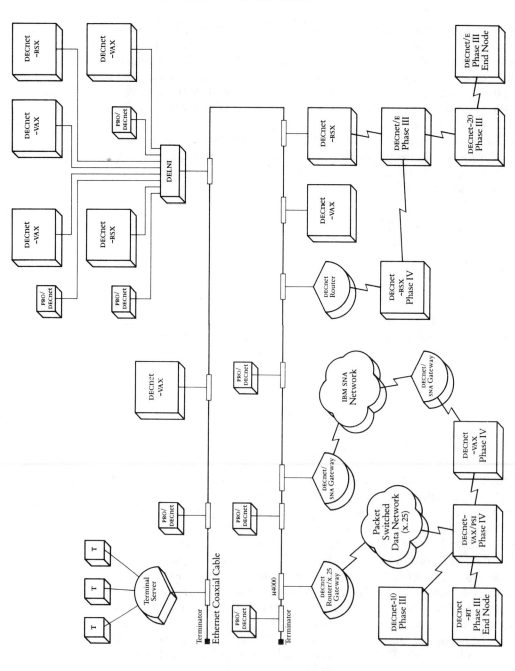

Figure 12-6   WAN + LAN + PDN

Source: Reproduced courtesy of Digital Equipment Corp.

Layer	Function
User	user programs, user services including file transfer, remote access, database management
Network management	planning, controlling, maintaining functions used by operators and managers, performance monitoring
Network application	remote file access, file transfer, terminal control, access to X.25, SNA gateways
Session control	name-to-address translation, process addressing, access control
End-to-end communication	connection management, dataflow control, end-to-end error control, assembly/disassembly of messages
Routing	congestion control, packet lifetime control
Data link control	point-to-point and multipoint communication DDCMP, X.25, and Ethernet
Physical link	monitoring channel signals, clocking interrupts, informing DLC when transmission complete.

Figure 12-7   DNA Levels

DNA hierarchy of the source node before being transmitted. If the destination node is not adjacent to the source node, the data travels up to the routing layer of the adjacent node, where it is routed, sent back down through the two layers, and transmitted to the next node in the path. At the destination node, the data passes up the hierarchy of layers to the destination process in the user level (fig. 12-9).

Network architectures are at the heart of most data networks at the present time. Most computer manufacturer architectures and public packet-switched networks were developed from the ISO-OSI standard. IBM's SNA architecture is unique. The various architectures continue to develop, to provide more services, and to become more flexible and integrative. The main user problems continue to be with the incompatibilities of different networks.

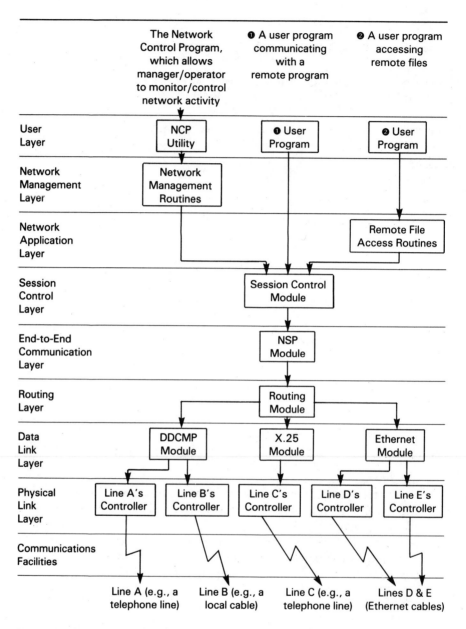

Figure 12-8 DNA Modules in a Typical Node

Source: Reproduced courtesy of Digital Equipment Corp.

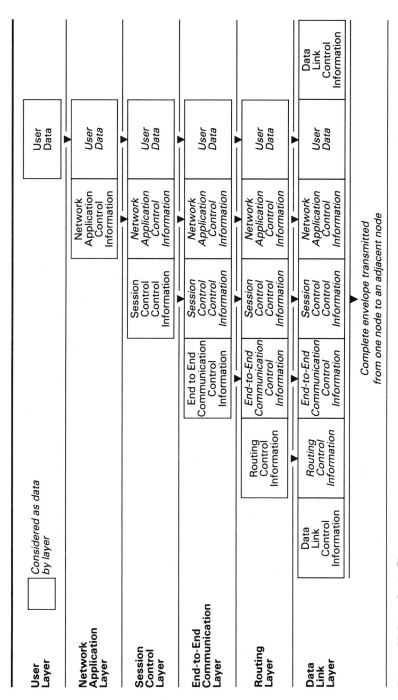

Figure 12-9   Data Flow

Source: Reproduced courtesy of Digital Equipment Corp.

Review Questions for Chapter 12

Systems Network Architecture

1. What is the purpose of an SNA node?

2. Match node to PU:

host	PU1
front-end processor	PU2
cluster controller	PU3
terminal	PU4
	PU5

3. How does the SSCP control the network?

4. Why is the LU6.2 such an important development?

Digital Network Architecture

5. Which facilities connect DECnets to:

   (a) other vendor networks?
   (b) packet switched networks?

6. What is the purpose of adaptive routing?

7. To which other architectures can DNA interface?

8. Draw a routing diagram showing the communication between node A and node C through an intermediary node B for DNA architecture.

Chapter

AN ACADEMIC NETWORK

THE NAIT NETWORK

The Northern Alberta Institute of Technology (NAIT) network is a small communications network contained within the city of Edmonton; nevertheless, it contains many of the hardware elements discussed in the first section of the course. It is a good example of the way in which many networks operate. Its most notable characteristic is the sharing of local and remote computing facilities among a large number of users (students, faculty, and administration). As a result, software requirements are not complex and consist of:

— terminal emulation (VT100 and 3270);
— resource sharing (printer spooling);
— file transfer (Kermit); and
— micro/mainframe links (PC plus IRMA boards).

The NAIT network consists of two campuses and three satellites (fig. 13-1). The main campus contains the major components of the network:

- IBM4381 for academic use;
- VAX8200 for student records;
- MAI8030 for financial systems; and
- PACX1V for switching.

The Plaza users connect directly to one of three VAX750 systems via a Develcon switch primarily for CML applications and indirectly through 56 lines to the main campus.

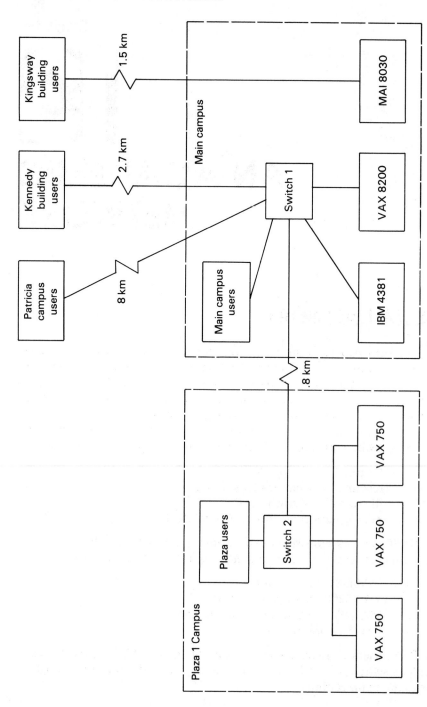

Figure 13-1   NAIT Network Geography

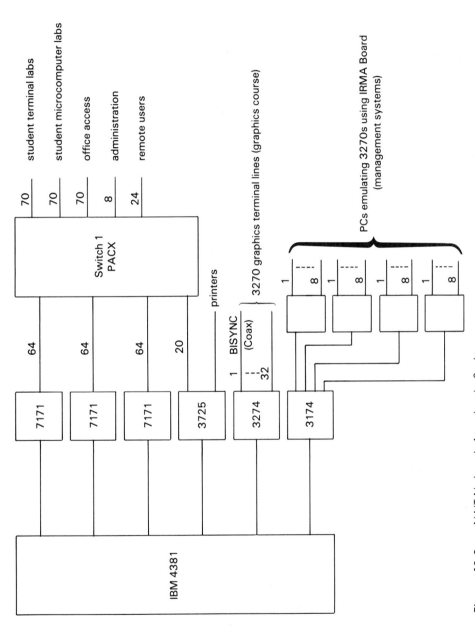

Figure 13-2   NAIT Network Academic System

The satellite communities are the Patricia Campus (automotives), the Kennedy Building (purchasing), and the Kingsway Building (accounting).

ACADEMIC APPLICATIONS

The heaviest users are computer systems technology students who program applications in COBOL, Pascal, SQL, and FOCUS. Business administration, mathematics, earth resources, and chemistry students use application packages and program in BASIC.

One of the main problems associated with the academic applications is the increasing demand for hardware resources by both users and applications (ISPF, PROFS, SQL, and FOCUS) in the context of budgetary constraints. Solutions include running non-interactive applications in batch mode and deferring them to off-peak periods, and restricting access to applications for parts of the day.

The network nodes for academic applications include a communications controller (3725), cluster controllers (a 3274 and the 3174/3299 used to extend the coax range), and three protocol converters (7171s used for asynchronous to BISYNC conversion) (fig. 13-2).

FINANCIAL SYSTEMS

These applications are typical of most educational organizations and include general ledger and inventory control systems. Remote access from the Kingsway Building is handled using statistical time division multiplexers (STDMs) on two 4800 bps leased lines (fig. 13-3). The STDMs are:

a) A Gandalf PIN9103 that has 32 asynchronous lines converted to one synchronous line using HDLC protocol with dynamic line allocation up to 9600 bps.

b) The Gandalf SWITCHMUX 2000 converts 16 asynchronous lines to a synchronous line operating at speeds up to 19.2 kbps using HDLC protocol. (A similar configuration is used for the Kennedy Building-to-Main-Campus interface.) The terminals are asynchronous devices emulating VT100 operation.

STUDENT RECORDS

Principally used by the Registrar's Office and the Continuing Education Department, student records are available to other departments on a limited access basis. The main applications are:

— admission processing,
— registration, and
— mark processing.

Communication is via the PACX switch. The system is based on the POISE Data Management System tailored to NAIT's requirements. The applications operate in an online enquiry and update mode.

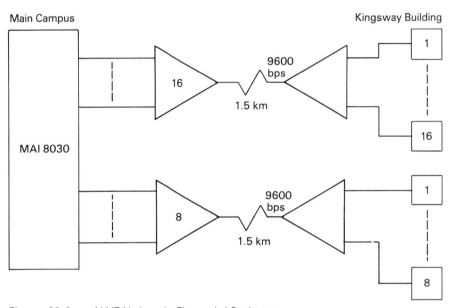

Figure 13-3   NAIT Network: Financial Systems

CML

Computer Managed Learning is growing into a major application at NAIT. Many departments make use of the software by providing their own test banks. These include:

— power engineering,
— electrical engineering, and
— health sciences.

The communications facilities consist of 56 lines to the main campus, 14 dial-up lines, and a VAX/Ethernet cluster to optimize resource usage (fig. 13-4) The single entity concept, of sharing storage among several processors,

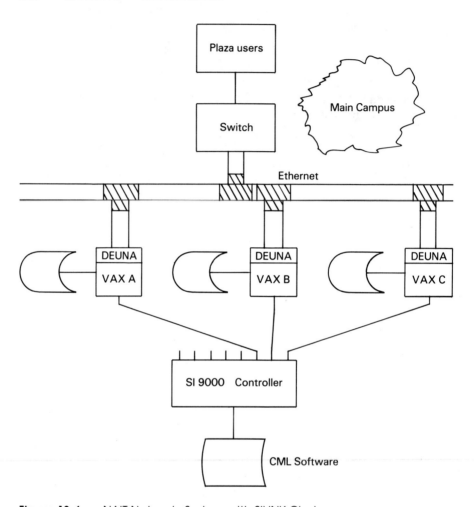

Figure 13-4   NAIT Network: System with SILINK Cluster

is used to smooth user demand for access. The Develcon switch allocates users to each VAX on a rotational basis and in increments of four. The terminals are asynchronous devices emulating VT100 operation.

The application is an online update system, since students are evaluated as they enter results. Hard copy terminals are provided to optimize terminal availability, to enable students to consult reference materials (for example, steam tables) and for back-up in the event of machine downtime. An optical scanner input device is provided for high-speed multiple choice examinations.

The VAX cluster should not be confused with a network. A cluster has an integrated file and record system, can use common batch and print queues, and is confined to a small area. A cluster offers resource sharing and a common security database. It is often part of a network.

In a SILINK cluster all nodes are connected to a shared disk using a Systems Industries 9900 disk controller, and they are interconnected through a DEC Ethernet System. Each node has a DEC Unibus Network Adapter (DEUNA). Up to eight SI disks may be shared in a single cluster. The Plaza to Main Campus interface running between the Develcon and the PACX switches is an STDM configuration using Gandalf SWITCHMUX 2000s (fig. 13-5).

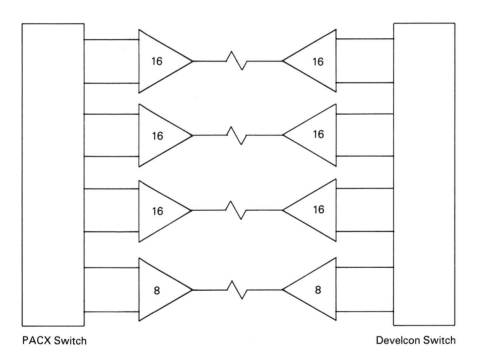

PACX Switch   Develcon Switch

Figure 13-5   NAIT Network: Main Campus/Plaza Interface

THE FUTURE

The NAIT network is expanding and evolving. There are already problems developing in line connections. Twisted pair connection conduit is reaching maximum capacity. Consideration is being given to the use of thin coaxial cable.

The main issue being addressed at present in the network is that of connectivity between network nodes. Microwave links are ruled out because of the closeness of the Edmonton Municipal Airport. Sometime in the future, fiber optic trunks may be installed. The software interfaces for non-compatible hosts are available from computer manufacturers, independent software companies, and telephone companies. As with most telecommunication systems, the only constant in the evolution of the NAIT network is change.

Chapter

A GOVERNMENT NETWORK

INTRODUCTION

In most large organizations that are geographically dispersed, the volume of information flowing between centers is increasing. Although voice traffic predominates, there is a growing demand for improved data transmission facilities and greater connectivity. At the same time, developments in the communications industry are directed towards an information transport system that will encompass a variety of services including voice, data, image and video. The advantages of an integrated approach to information transmission are reduced costs, improved response, greater flexibility and better control. The Alberta government is planning the evolution of a province-wide integrated services network.

GEOGRAPHY

The Alberta government network (AGN) (fig. 14-1) consists of three completely separate networks carrying various types of traffic:

— a voice network handling all the telephone traffic for government departments throughout the province;

— a data network to carry all the traffic for the IBM SNA network;
— a mobile radio network providing voice communications in those areas that are not easily serviced by other methods.

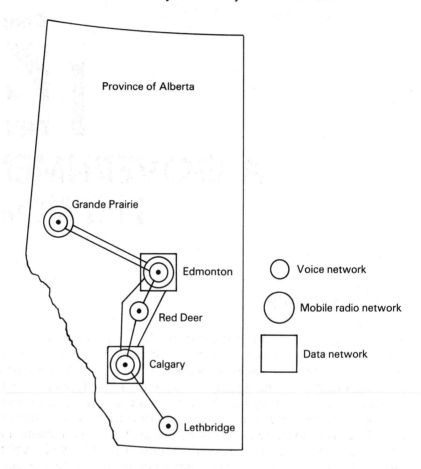

Figure 14-1   Alberta Government Network

Voice/Telephone Network

Some 30 000 telephone sets serve the needs of the government departments throughout Alberta. These use a mixture of technologies, including key systems, PBXs and large central office (CO) switches. This equipment is purchased or leased from the telephone companies but operated separately from the public telephone service (except CO switches, which are shared).

The voice network is based on five large central office switches in Grande Prairie (Northern Telecom DMS-100), Edmonton (Northern Telecom SP-1), Red Deer (DMS-100), Calgary (DMS-100) and Lethbridge (DMS-100). These switches are shared with the public voice network. About 100 smaller private branch exchanges (mainly Northern Telecom SL-1 PBXs) serve smaller centers in Alberta and the telephone needs of the various government departments.

This equipment is connected via leased trunk facilities (tie-lines) into a private telephone system (the RITE network). Users throughout Alberta can make toll-free calls to other users using this telephone network. The network connects to the public telephone network allowing access to and from the public telephone service.

SNA DATA NETWORK

Three main computer centers (two in Edmonton, one in Calgary) provide most of the computer power for the government departments. These computer centers are predominantly large mainframes (IBM 3084/3090) running MVS/XA or VM/CMS. These support most of the applications used by the government departments. However, a growing number of minicomputers are supporting more distributed applications. The major data communication requirements are handled by an IBM SNA network. The mainframe computers are connected to a number of front-end processors (IBM 3725 type) at each data center (fig. 14-2). These front-end processors (FEPs) support a number of access protocols using different software packages:

— SDLC and 3270 BSC protocols are supported by NCP;
— 2780 BSC (RJE) is supported by PEP or EP;
— asynchronous terminals are supported by NTO; and
— X.25 protocol is supported by NPSI.

These software packages run in various combinations on the FEPs to support the required protocols. In addition, the FEPs are interconnected using high-speed links and the MSNF software (Multi-System Networking Facility). This facility allows terminals connected to one FEP to access a host computer connected to another FEP. Thus terminal users anywhere can access any of the host computers.

The data network supports the needs of the IBM host computer users throughout the government departments. Over 4000 terminals (IBM 3270 type or equivalent) are distributed throughout the province and are connected to cluster controllers (IBM 3274 type or equivalent), which are sited usually in

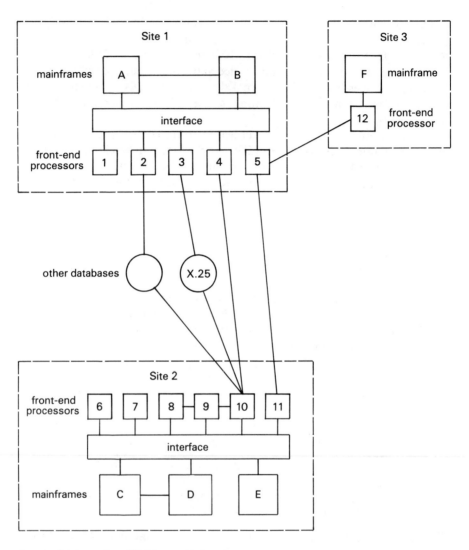

Figure 14-2 The SNA Data Network

the same building as the terminals (up to 32 terminals per cluster controller). Some 500 leased lines at speeds between 2400 bps and 9600 bps connect from the FEPs in Edmonton and Calgary to these cluster controllers. This results in a star topology IBM SNA network. The leased lines connect back to front-end processors at the data centers (fig. 14-3).

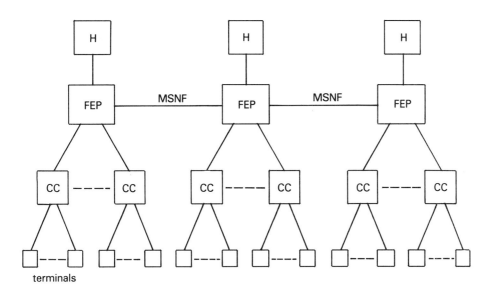

H - Host
FEP - Front-end processor
CC - Cluster controller
MSNF - Multi-system network facility

Figure 14-3 Data Network Topology

MOBILE RADIO NETWORK

The mobile radio network (fig. 14-4) uses base and repeater stations throughout the province to support voice communication for government departments needing it for mobile units or remote areas such as forest lookouts. This network is shared between departments and is known as MDMRS (multi-departmental mobile radio system). Several hundred mobile radio users throughout the province are able to communicate with one another and with any public or private telephone user. About 116 repeater sites using UHF frequencies are distributed throughout most areas of the province. These are connected to about 13 regional switches enabling mobile communications to be switched between repeaters or connected to the public telephone network. A control center located in Edmonton allows mobile calls to be switched to other regional switches and so communicate with any other mobile users. The network is of particular use to forest workers, wildlife workers, and those responsible for the highways throughout the province.

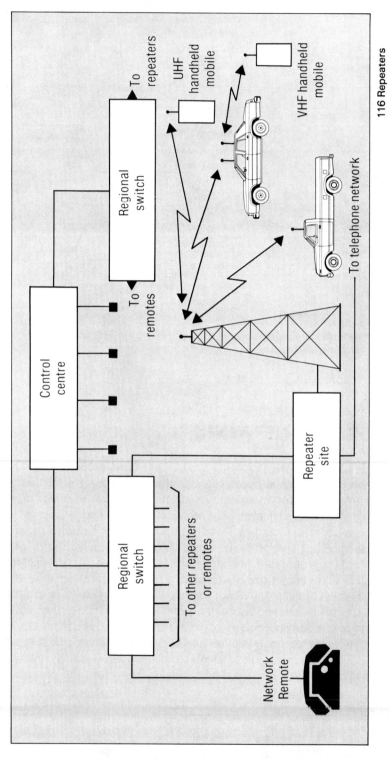

Figure 14-4   Mobile Radio Network

Source: Reproduced courtesy of Mobile Communications, AGT.

PACKET SWITCHING

A packet-switched network (based on X.25) is being developed to support not only the SNA network users but also the word processor and microcomputer users throughout the government departments. The present SNA network supports the requirements of users requiring access to the main data centers. Throughout the government, there are a growing number of word processors, microcomputers, and minicomputers that have requirements for inexpensive communication facilities. The packet-switching network will establish concentration and switching points throughout the province to serve the needs of these users plus the needs of the SNA network users. This will allow the large numbers of leased lines to be replaced by a small number of high-speed digital links, and this will reduce costs substantially.

THE FUTURE

The long-term communication network directions of the Alberta government are towards the implementation of ISDN (integrated services digital network) services throughout the province. This will provide a uniform means of supporting voice and data communication requirements for all users. The ISDN specifications provide for simultaneous voice and data transmission over a standard telephone-jack-type connection at speeds up to 144 kbps. All computer and terminal facilities within the government will be connected using this type of connection; switching will be possible between any terminal and any computer. The benefits of this ISDN network are:

- common network management,
- shared transmission facilities for voice and data,
- unified building wiring scheme (twisted pair) for voice and data,
- common international standard protocols for access, and
- simple reconfiguration of the network.

The migration of the present data network and voice network to ISDN will be a long, multi-step process, since many user departments and tens of thousands of users are involved, not to mention millions of dollars of investment. The steps to be followed are:

1. Establishment of a packet-switching network throughout the province with concentration and switch points at major towns.

2. Migration of star SNA data network onto this packet network.

3. Migration of other data networks (such as small minicomputer-based networks) onto packet-switching network.

4. Use of packet network by word processors and microcomputers.

5. Establishment of digital cross-connect and trunking facility throughout the province to allow for provision of high-bandwidth services and easy sharing of digital trunks.

6. Connection of packet switches and voice PBXs to this digital trunking facility. This enables voice PBX and data switch to share the same trunk facility.

7. Integration of voice and data switches into ISDN switches, including migration to standard building wiring scheme.

Many of these steps can be undertaken simultaneously, but the ultimate goal is the same – a shared voice and data network with a unified connection for voice or data terminals and complete connectivity allowing any terminal to connect to any other terminal or computer.

Chapter

15

AN INTERNATIONAL
NETWORK

INTRODUCTION

Interprovincial Pipe Line Company and its United States affiliate, Lakehead Pipe Line Company Inc., own and operate the largest crude oil pipeline system in the western hemisphere, stretching some 3700 kilometers (2300 miles) from Edmonton, Alberta to Montreal, Quebec. The system consists of three parallel lines from Edmonton to Superior, Wisconsin; two lines from Superior to Sarnia, Ontario, one via the Straights of Mackinac and one via Chicago; two lines from Sarnia to Toronto, Ontario, with a lateral extension to Buffalo, New York, and a second lateral to Nanticoke, Ontario; and one line from Sarnia to Montreal, with a lateral extension to Clarkson, Ontario (fig. 15-1).

The company operates as a common carrier for the transportation of approximately 50 different types of crude oil and other liquid hydrocarbons. The oil is moved across two thirds of a continent – through five Canadian provinces and seven American states. The company also owns and operates an 868 kilometer (539 mile) pipeline between Norman Wells, Northwest Territories and Zama, Alberta.

The company's Oil Movements department, located in Edmonton, is responsible for the movement of all oil in the system and for ensuring that the right amount of a specific oil reaches the proper destination. The department

217

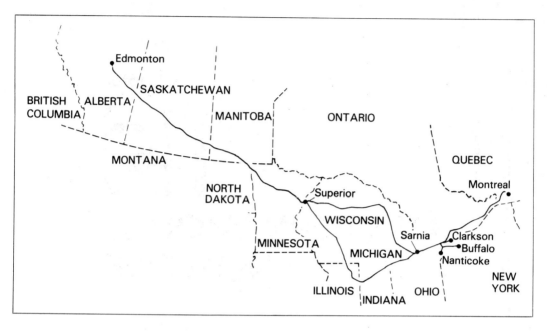

Figure 15-1   The IPL Network Geography

coordinates all receipts and deliveries in the system, establishes the sequence and amounts of the various oils to be pumped, and controls the operation of the pumping stations.

PIPELINE CONTROL

The pumping operation is remotely controlled from four locations, Edmonton, Superior, Sarnia, and Norman Wells. Additionally, the Edmonton control center monitors operations at Superior, Sarnia, and Norman Wells. At each of the remotely controlled pumping stations, minicomputers are installed that communicate with the central computers. Ninety-seven computers assist in controlling the operation of more than 400 units at 91 locations on the Edmonton/Superior/Sarnia network. There are 25 computer-controlled sites on the Norman Wells/Zama network. This is one of the largest and most advanced remote control systems in use today (fig. 15-2).

HARDWARE

The Edmonton control center provides control of all pumping locations between Edmonton and Superior, and of the south line from Superior to

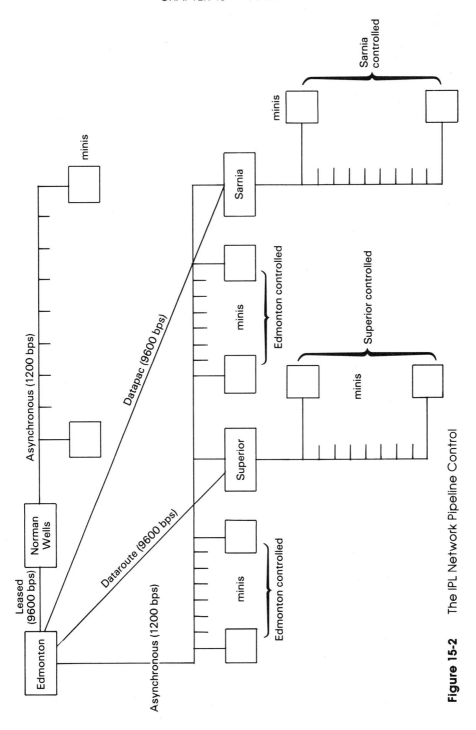

Figure 15-2   The IPL Network Pipeline Control

Sarnia via Chicago. Superior controls locations on the north line between Superior and Sarnia. Sarnia controls all the pumping locations east of Sarnia. Norman Wells controls all pumping locations in the Northwest Territories.

The major components of the computerized system at Edmonton are two Digital VAX 8530s. The computers are located at separate sites for contingency reasons. They exchange data via a communications link at 56 kbps. Each site is also equipped with a VAX-11/785 for backup. At Superior and Sarnia the control system consists of two VAX-11/780s. At Norman Wells, the control system consists of two VAX-11/750s. One minicomputer exists at each location regardless of the number of pumps present at that location.

At all of the control centers only one of the computer systems at a time is actively monitoring and controlling the pipeline, while the other serves as a hot standby.

The major responsibilities and functions of each of the control systems include:

— control of the multidrop, privately leased, asynchronous data circuit that links the remote locations to a particular control center;
— display of pipeline information;
— interpretation, validation, and transmission of operator commands to the remote computer; and
— automatic surveillance and pipeline protection in certain instances.

The functions of the remote computers at the pumping station are:

- continuous scanning of all station readings and alarm points;
- receiving, checking, and executing commands from the control centers;
- transmission of all readings, alarms, and status information to the control centers; and
- performing automatic control functions independently.

SOFTWARE

The computer software at each control center for the Pipeline Control System consists of a series of modular programs that interact under the control of an operating system and include:

— traffic scheduling and data validation of all data traffic (the satellite computer systems report all system activity [except for that at the Norman Wells control center] to Edmonton);

— data logging;
— data displays for pumping units, valves, alarms, gravitometers/ densitometers, maximum/minimum pressures and current line status, using colour graphics and audible alarms; and
— power limiting, to schedule monthly requirements and take advantage of off-peak power discounts.

The Pipeline Control System is a continuously evolving system designed to adapt to changes in operating conditions and computer hardware, as well as to expansion of the system.

THE FUTURE

Development of the IPL computer system network is directed towards upgrading the computer system configuration and implementing a standard communications protocol for pipeline control.

Computer System

Upgrading of the computer system network includes the creation of VAX-clusters and the integration of the Pipeline Control System with other data processing applications and end-user computing on Ethernet LANs. A possible scenario for the Edmonton Computing Center is shown in figure 15.3.

The Local Network Interconnect (DELNI) is a concentrator that allows up to eight Ethernet-compatible devices to be grouped together. The DELNI reduces the cost of multiple connections to the Ethernet coaxial cable and increases the number of devices that may be connected to a single 500-meter coaxial cable segment.

The DECnet Router is used to interface high-speed synchronous interfaces to the DECnet (a maximum of eight channels at 56 kbps) via the DELNI concentrator. Here, the Router is used for 9600 bps lines between Edmonton and Superior and Norman Wells as well as a 56 kbps line to the other Edmonton site. The Datapac packet-switching network is used for communications between Edmonton and Sarnia.

The DEMPR is a multiport device that provides eight ports for connection to eight thin wire Ethernet segments, each of which can be up to 185 meters (600 feet) long and can accommodate up to 29 stations for a total of 232 stations per DEMPR.

The *star coupler* is a "passive" hub device, containing only transformers and cable connectors, and providing a dual path and electrical isolation between processor nodes (fig. 15-4).

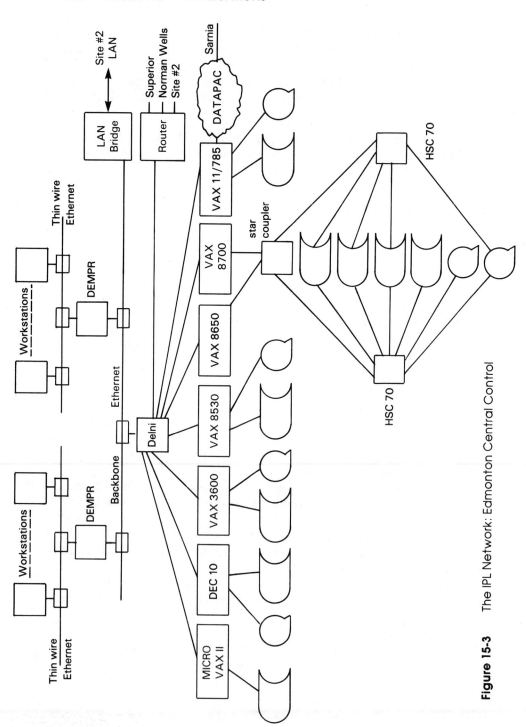

Figure 15-3   The IPL Network: Edmonton Central Control

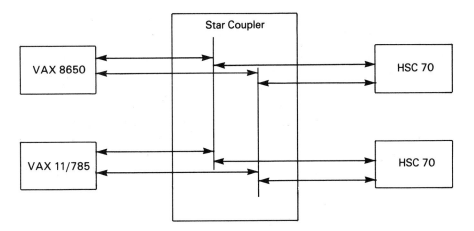

Figure 15-4   The IPL Network: The Star Coupler

The HSC70 is a storage server that autonomously manages input/output (I/O) requests from a maximum of 15 hosts for up to 32 disk or tape drives and provides optimal throughput, data integrity, and accessibility to data. Volume shadowing is an important feature that can be added for those systems that put a premium on reliability. An operator command will direct the HSC70 to treat any group of identical disk drives as a "shadow set," which appears as a single drive to an application. Each write request from an application is performed on all drives in the shadow set, each read is performed by the single volume that will provide optimal performance. Because reads generally outnumber writes, performance of a "shadow set" can be expected to be better than the single drive performance. So, as well as providing immediate backup, the shadow set also enhances performance.

The most significant aspect of the application as a whole is the importance of backup. The dual VAXs, with separate multiple disks and associated hardware attest to the need for a failsafe system.

The IPL Standard Protocol

A standard protocol is in the process of being implemented on all data circuits used for pipeline control. The specification parameters of this protocol include:

— a byte-oriented protocol;
— efficient movement of single- and multiple-byte messages;
— comprehensive control and status information;

— error checking facilities; and
— capability of incorporating subprotocols.

The IPL Standard Communications Protocol has two basic message types: the data message and the control message. The message formats are illustrated in figure 15-5.

One interesting feature of the protocol is the inclusion of a bit-extensible field that can convert the fixed length protocol into a variable length protocol. The bit-extensible field is defined as one or more bytes whose low-order, seven-bit portions can be strung together to form one field of bits. The bit-extensible fields apply only to the message header as shown in figure 15-5.

All private line circuits from pipeline control centers will implement the IPL Standard Protocol.

Data message format

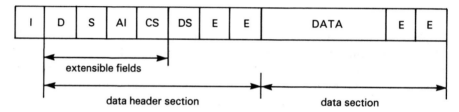

Control message format

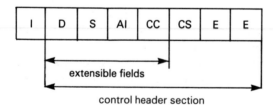

I - identifier byte
D - destination address
S - source address
AI - application invariant information field
CS - communication status field
DS - data size field (2 bytes)
CC - control code
E - error checking (checksum or CRC)

Figure 15-5   IPL Standard Protocol

SUMMARY

A DECnet network consists of two or more Digital Equipment Corporation computer systems, enhanced with DECnet software and linked by physical channels or communication lines. Implementations of DECnet are based on a model of structure and function known as Digital Network Architecture (DNA). The IPL network is a DECnet network that includes Wide Area Networks, Local Area Networks and a packet-switching network interface.

Interprovincial Pipe Line Ltd. is continuously engaged in the development and construction of loop lines, extension of the mainline station tankage, and other facilities. These improvements, together with technological changes in the computer and communications industries, signify continued change and growth for the IPL network.

SECTION B: CONCLUSION

Since data communication networks are so widely used in data processing, it is important to distinguish between what is theoretically and technologically possible on the one hand, and what it is actually practical to implement now and in the near future.

Distributed data processing is a concept that has been discussed for many years in broad terms. These discussions have centered on the connecting of mainframe computers by communication networks for the sharing of an organization's data processing resources.

The practical problems involved in such an arrangement include the availability of software to:

— manage partial processing at different installations on different configurations,
— monitor and control the distribution of data,
— resolve conflicts,
— provide backup and recovery procedures in the event of hardware/software problems, and
— provide protection from accidental or deliberate breaches of security.

All this must be done in the context of a geographically dispersed system.

In practical terms, there are three kinds of systems that partially fulfill the requirements of distributed data processing.

1. The LAN, a local distributed network, that allows for the sharing of hardware, software, and data.
2. The micro/mainframe link that provides shared processing and file transfer.
3. The network architecture that provides a means of building wide area networks, principally for a particular computer manufacturer's product.

Although all three of these systems continue to expand their facilities and improve their capabilities, the trend in network applications at present seems more directed towards integrating an organization's data, voice, and video communications needs in an ISDN network.

SECTION C
PRACTICAL

It is one thing to read a book or listen to a lecture and understand the ideas and explanations. It is another to make that information your own. In this book, while Section A provides a description of data communications networks, Section C allows you actually to develop data communications skills based on the knowledge acquired from Section A.

Section A provides a logical, sequential outline of the conceptual material. It covers fundamentals, components, and network applications.

Section C considers those aspects of networks that can be tackled practically. Although these practical units are small in scale, they illustrate several key characteristics of networks:

- the meaning of terminology,
- the nature of the connections,
- terminal-to-computer communication,
- the optimization of network configurations,
- the importance of response time,
- the implementation of protocols,
- network performance, and
- communications programming.

As far as possible, this material has been sequenced to correlate with the sequence of chapters in Section A, but it has not always been possible to do so. For example, the exercise on optimizing configurations (unit 4) is based on both the variety of junctions available (chapter 4) and the ways in which they can be connected (chapter 5). Unit 7 on communications programming has an integrating function. It relates the need for terminal emulation (chapter 3) and the micro/ mainframe link (chapter 11) to the programmer's perspective on communications software.

Each unit in section C adheres to a general pattern:

1. *Objectives,* which describe the intent and content of each chapter and its relation to the material of Section A.

2. *Background,* which provides supplementary theory on the concepts, equipment, and software for the assignments of each chapter.

3. *Assignments,* which may be one or more of the following:

   a) paper exercises in which the student solves the problems provided,
   b) laboratories in which the student must demonstrate facility in performing the required tasks and must provide supporting documentation,
   c) demonstrations in which the student must observe and answer questions on the effect of parameter variations within the demonstration.

The correlation between sections A and C is given in figure C-1.

SECTION A		SECTION C	
chapter	title	unit	content
1	Fundamentals	1	oscilloscope monitoring asynchronous protocol
2	Media	2	line continuity
3	Terminations	3	softkey programming
4	Junctions	4	optimizing configurations response time comparison
5	Connections		
6	Protocol	5	packet flow uploading/downloading packet transfer
7	Public Networks		
8	Local Area Networks	6	LAN interaction
		7	terminal emulation USART programming file transmission

Figure C-1   Correlation between Section A and Section C

Unit

FUNDAMENTALS

OBJECTIVE

The purpose of this unit is to use basic communications equipment and software to clarify your understanding of the terms and concepts of chapter 1. We will use a microcomputer, a modem, a break-out-box, (a device for providing access to communications signals), and an oscilloscope to perform the demonstrations. We will use this equipment to monitor electrical noise (a common problem in data transmission), to monitor the transmission of a single asynchronous character, and to monitor the modulated signals created by the modem. Our focus will be on the information that this equipment provides, not on the equipment itself, some of which will be explained later.

For the laboratory we will use a standard communications package to distinguish between half-duplex, full-duplex, and echoplex as well as to relate baud rate, file size, and transfer time.

BACKGROUND

Electrical Noise

Electrical noise interferes with the achievement of accurate information transfer and limits the speed at which information can be transmitted. The three most common sources of noise in a data communications environment are:

1. *Electrical equipment* used for other purposes, for example, an electric drill generates electromagnetic waves that can interfere with the signals in a cable running close to the operating drill.

2. *Crosstalk,* which is the interference caused by one signal on another. This is a particular problem for multiwire cable in which two signals may travel in close proximity and in parallel for long distances.

3. *Switching noise,* which is caused by making and breaking the physical connection between two points in a network. This problem is particularly severe on older electromechanical equipment and for high-speed (more sensitive) signal transmission.

Using a Communication Package

There are many asynchronous communication packages on the market as well as a number of good reliable ones that are in the public domain. Their main characteristics are:

1. Terminal emulation facilities that vary in terms of the number of terminals emulated as well as in the choice of terminal emulated.

2. A configuration setting that involves the preselection of the transfer speed, the parity, the number of bits per character as well as many other options. This process is often menu driven.

3. A file transfer capability that is used for uploading and downloading files between a microcomputer and a mainframe or for transferring files between microcomputers. This feature usually requires copies of the communication software at both ends of the link.

4. Softkey programming that provides a means of simplifying the communication between computers by automating such processes as remote sign on, unattended operation, and printer control.

In this unit the terminal emulation and file transfer facilities are used to illustrate the difference between half-duplex and full-duplex connection and the relationship between file size and transfer rate.

Most packages have the means of providing both half-duplex and full-duplex operation. The question of which mode to use becomes crucial when using a microcomputer as a terminal to access a remote host whose operating mode is unknown. By connecting two microcomputers together with an RS-232-C cable and running the communication package on both machines, it is possible to check the operating modes by:

1. running both machines in half-duplex,

2. running both machines in full-duplex, or

3. running both machines in the same duplex mode but at different baud rates.

From the first two experiments, it becomes apparent that there is a need for terminals that have the facility for displaying the information sent to another machine on their own screens. This is called echoplexing (fig. U1-1). In full-duplex operation the remote device automatically retransmits the received information to the sender's screen (fig. U1-2).

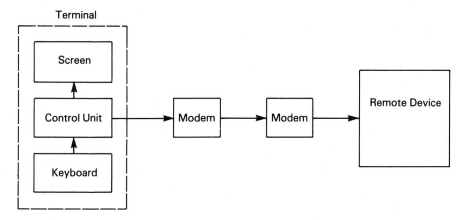

Figure U1-1   Echoplexing

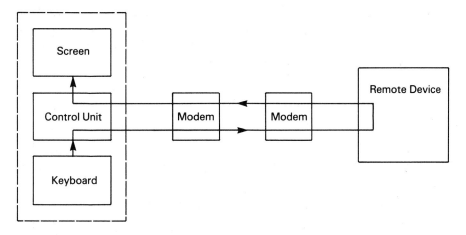

Figure U1-2   Full-Duplex

The third experiment can be used to relate the resultant garbage received to the difference in baud rate between the two terminals. For example, if you receive at twice the speed you send, each bit of the character sent is sampled twice and the character received can be predicted from the pulse train that was transmitted (fig. U1-3).

A typical asynchronous communication package that can be used for the experiments described is ASYNC, designed by IE Systems, Inc.

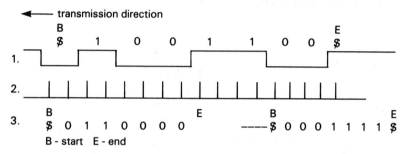

1. Transmits $4C_{16}$.
2. Shows the clock for receiver operating at twice the baud rate.
3. Two characters are received 30_{16} and $0F_{16}$.

Figure U1-3   Sending and Receiving at Different Baud Rates

ASYNC

ASYNC allows you to sign on to a remote host as well as to upload and download files. File transfer is block oriented with continuous error checking and automatic retries. The format for an ASYNC block is shown in figure U1-4. ASYNC can operate in three modes:

1. *Terminal mode* uses the microcomputer as a terminal in full-duplex operation.

2. *Terminal echo mode* treats the microcomputer as a terminal in half-duplex mode.

3. *Datalink mode* is used to transfer files between the microcomputer and another computer (normally a mainframe).

There are three ways of communicating with ASYNC:

1. Selecting requirements via a series of menus may be a relatively slow process but it is very useful to the first-time user.

Transmission Direction ⟶

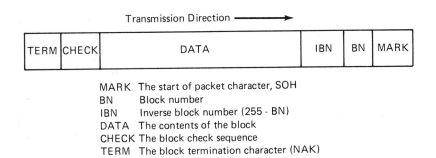

TERM	CHECK	DATA	IBN	BN	MARK

MARK The start of packet character, SOH
BN   Block number
IBN   Inverse block number (255 - BN)
DATA The contents of the block
CHECK The block check sequence
TERM The block termination character (NAK)

Figure U1-4   The ASYNC Block

2. Once you are familiar with ASYNC, you can use a command line, which is really an extension of the command used to invoke ASYNC and has the format:

    A>ASYNC   PS.BB   FILENAME.EXT$TELEPHONE

    where P identifies primary options:

R   receive a file with error-correcting protocol,
S   send a file with error-correcting protocol,
T   act as a terminal with full-duplex,
E   act as a terminal with half-duplex,
D   disconnect the phone, and
Esc return to main memory.

    where S identifies secondary options:

A   answer phone,
C   use CRC-16 error checking instead of checksum,
D   disconnect phone on exit,
E   revert to terminal echo mode after file transfer,
G   get a file from mainframe,
H   enable handshaking to prevent overfilling of receiving buffer during a SEND,
I   inform receiver of file size,
P   put a file to the mainframe,
Q   enable quiet mode of transfer,
T   revert to terminal mode after file transfer, and
X   disable direct cursor addressing during file transfer.

Note that: a) You can use only one primary option but up to seven secondary options.

b) Put(P) and Get(G) are used to send raw ASCII files in terminal and terminal echo modes (without error correcting).

c) Send(S) and Receive(R) are used in datalink mode to transmit and receive blocked records with automatic error retransmission.

3.   A third way of operating ASYNC is by means of a single-screen cursor-controlled menu select which is faster than the first method yet supplies more reference information than the second.

Figure U1-5 shows the file transmission protocol for sending a file. The process is started by a negative acknowledge (NAK) signal from the main-

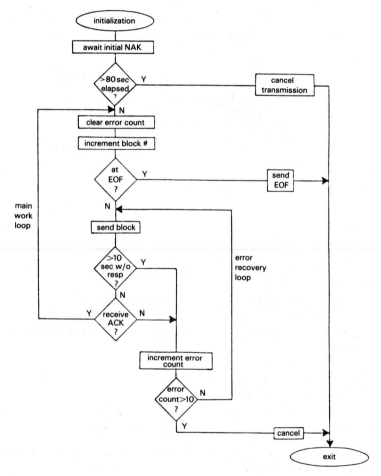

Figure U1-5   Sending a File in ASYNC

frame. Notice the time-out limit of 80 seconds and the error count which allows for 10 retries before aborting.

Figure U1-6 is the flowchart for the corresponding protocol used when receiving a file. Here the time-out limit is 10 seconds although the retry counter is still set for 10. Note too, the ability of the protocol to accept the most likely possibility of a block being sent twice without incrementing the blockcount.

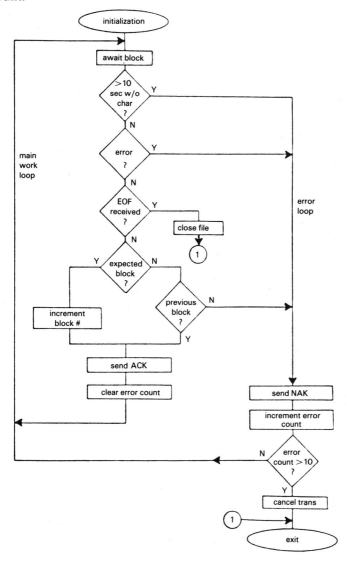

Figure U1-6   Receiving a File in ASYNC

Sample Session

Use of the command line in datalink mode to transfer a microcomputer file to the DECsystem 10 is illustrated in figure U1-7.

The following sample laboratory (page 240) provides insight into the way full-duplex, half-duplex, baud rate and file size affect data transfer.

```
A > ASYNC T.30                    ; invoke ASYNC
• LOGIN 123,456                   ; Log-in to mainframe
Password:_____
• RUN MICRO
/RECEIVE MYFILE. DAT              ; Tell MICRO to receive
^ V ^ E                           ; Exit to micro
A > ASYNC S.30 MYFILE.DAT         ; Send file

file  transferred
A > ASYNC T.30                    ; Sign off
/EXIT
KJOB
^ V ^ E
A>
```

Figure U1-7   A Typical ASYNC Session (user input underlined)

DEMONSTRATION

Oscilloscope Monitoring

An oscilloscope provides the means of visually monitoring the signals being transmitted by a microcomputer. It verifies that old cliche that "a picture is worth a thousand words" and provides dramatic evidence that keyboard input is converted into serial electrical pulse trains and transmitted in that form. This demonstration requires the use of an oscilloscope, a break-out-box for access to the signals being monitored, and a short BASIC program of the type that you will become very familiar with before the end of this section (fig. U1-8). The demonstration set-up may be used to illustrate electrical noise, the asynchronous protocol, and modulated signals.

Electrical Noise

Electrical noise is invisible but can be displayed by holding the end of the oscilloscope probe (when it is not connected to anything else) and using your body as an antenna. The messy picture that results can usually be resolved into a spiky sine wave of 60 hz, showing the predominance of the a.c. mains signal.

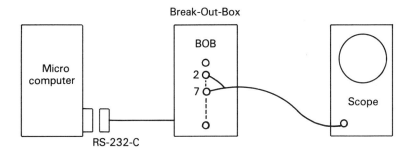

Figure U1-8 Asynchronous Transmission (Hardware)

Asynchronous Protocol

The asynchronous protocol defines the number, type, and order of bits in an asynchronous character. The transmission of characters can be monitored on the oscilloscope using the setup in figure U1-8. The break-out-box is connected to the microcomputer and provides access to all the signals travelling between the microcomputer and a modem. In this case we want to connect the oscilloscope to pin 2 on the break-out-box which is the data transmit signal, and we also want to provide a common ground by connecting the oscilloscope ground clip to pin 7 (ground) on the break-out-box. A short BASIC program is run on the microcomputer, and it continuously transmits any keyboard key struck until another key is struck. The continuous transmission of a character allows the oscilloscope to display a stable picture. The oscilloscope should be externally triggered on the data transmit signal. The flowchart for the program (fig. U1-9) is similar to that for a standard transmit-a-character routine.

Modulation

Connecting a modem to the microcomputer permits the monitoring of the modulated signal on the oscilloscope (fig. U1-10). The information can be transmitted using any asynchronous communication package. To provide time to monitor the signals effectively, use a large file. At 300 bps, standard modems use frequency modulation and at 1200 bps they use phase shift modulation. Depending on the modem used it may be possible to monitor both types of modulation. The usual sequence of commands issued to the communication software is itemized in figure U1-11. Triggering the oscilloscope for a stable picture is more difficult for a modulated signal but the process of transmitting blocks of information is clear and so is the difference between frequency modulation and phase shift modulation.

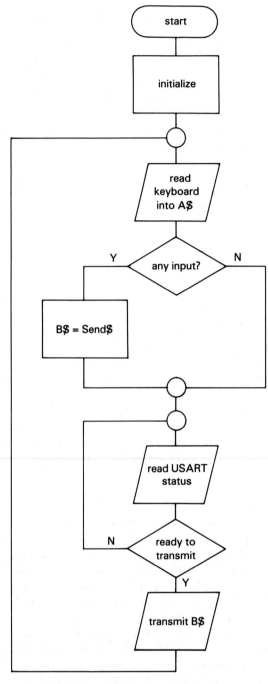

Figure U1-9a   Asynchronous Transmission (Software)

```
5     B$="x"
10    CONTROL = 2
20    DATAPORT = 0
30    DEF SEG = &HE002
40    POKE 3, &H36
50    POKE 0,8
60    POKE 0,0
70    DEF SEG = &HE004
80    POKE CONTROL, &H3
90    POKE CONTROL, &HC1
100   SEND$ = INKEY$
110   IF SEND$<>"" THEN B$=SEND$
190   STATUS = PEEK (CONTROL): STATUS = STATUS AND 4
200   IF STATUS THEN POKE DATAPORT, ASC(B$)
210   GOTO 100
220   END
```

Figure U1-9b   Asynchronous Transmission (Code)

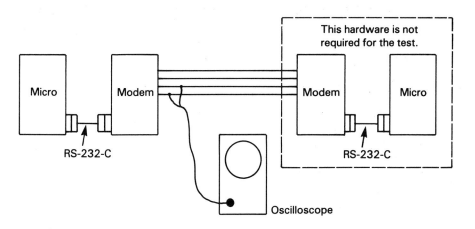

Figure U1-10   Modulation (Hardware)

1. Invoke the communication software for a specific baud rate and parity.

2. Initiate receive mode in one micro.

3. Initiate send mode in the other micro and specify file name.

4. Begin transfer.

Figure U1-11   Modulation (Software Sequence)

LABORATORY

Basic Terms and Relationships

Objectives

Upon completion of this lab you should be able to:

a) Distinguish between half-duplex, full-duplex, and echoplex.
b) Explain the effect of baud rate and file size on transfer time.
c) Pass error-checked files between microcomputers.

Purpose

To reinforce the terminology and concepts explained in Section A, chapter 1.

Background

a) ASYNC is a communications package that can be operated in:

i. Terminal Mode
ii. Terminal Echo Mode
iii. Datalink Mode

and can be invoked via:

i. menu
ii. default screen
iii. command line
iv. command file

We will use the command line method.

b) Because of the different levels of MSDOS, ASYNC can be invoked as follows:

```
A>ASYNC    PS.BB    FILENAME.EXT
       or
A>CD    ASYNC (subdirectory)
A>CPM    ASYNC    PS.BB    FILENAME.EXT
```

Exercises

Requirements: a) Two units connected by RS-232-C cable with pins 2 and 3 reversed.
   b) Units connected from serial port A to serial port A.
   c) Students work in pairs.

Exercise 1. Half-duplex, Full-duplex, Echoplex

1) Run both machines in terminal mode at the same baud rate. What happens?

2) Run both machines in terminal mode at different baud rates. What happens?

3) Run both machines in terminal echo mode at the same baud rate. What is the difference between exercises 1 and 3?
   If a terminal communicates with a mainframe computer in half-duplex, does it require echoplexing?

Exercise 2. Baud Rate and File Size

1) Use the command line to transmit three files of different sizes at 300 baud. Use a stopwatch to time the transfers.

2) Repeat (1) at 1200 and 4800 baud.

3) Complete the following table.

File Name	Size	BAUD RATE		
		300	1200	4800

What is the relation between transfer time and baud rate?
What is the relation between transfer time and file size?

Lab requirements

The purpose of this demonstration is to ensure that you can a) locate the communications package on your workstation, b) work in cooperation with another student to establish mutually-agreed-upon communications parameters such as baud rate, and c) transfer a short file between workstations. It is important before starting to check that the cable is DTE-to-DTE configured and that it is connected between two appropriate ports.

1.   Student 1 creates a short file containing:

TERMINAL 1
<Student name>
INITIAL FILE

2.   Using ASYNC transmit the file to the diskette on terminal 2.

3.   Student 2 lists the file and adds

TERMINAL 2
<Student name>
MODIFIED FILE

4.   Using ASYNC transmit the file to the diskette on terminal 1.

5.   Student 1 lists the modified file using TYPE.

Unit

2

MEDIA

OBJECTIVES

This unit briefly considers the physical construction of the standard types of communications cable described in chapter 2: twisted pair, coax, and fiber optics. The matter of testing cables is also treated.

Cable testing involves the detection and repair of broken cables. This is particularly significant for the terminal-to-modem connection. The break-out-box is a very useful device for detecting and correcting problems and for designing the initial interface. It is used here to demonstrate how an RS-232-C cable can be checked for continuity and to identify the common problems encountered by the telecommunications specialist.

BACKGROUND

Media Types

From samples of coaxial cable and twisted pair wire it is clear that the more elaborate coax construction with its low impedance connectors is more expensive. The shielding of the coax signal with the copper mesh adds to the cost. Another important factor in comparing the two is the volume of twisted pair required for the telephone industry. This contributes to its lower cost. The most impressive characteristics of fiber optics cable are its size and weight. When placed alongside a piece of coax and twisted pair it becomes clear that although such fine wire is more difficult to handle, its physical compactness is a major advantage. In addition, copper as a raw material is in much shorter supply than the sand used in glassmaking. The main problems associated with fiber optics are its incompatibility, its relative newness, and the cost of interface equipment. The relative costs of the media are summarized in figure U2-1.

Medium	Cost/metre (Canadian)
twisted pair	$0.50 – $3.00
coax	$2.00 – $21.00
fiber optics	less than $1.00 (monomode)

Figure U2-1   Media Costs

The Break-Out-Box

DTE (data termination equipment) to DTE communication over the telephone system is implemented using DCEs (data communication equipment). When DTEs are located in close proximity (up to 15 meters), the DCEs are not required. This means that for proper communication the DTEs must be made to emulate the data conversion and control functions of the DCEs. This necessary emulation is produced in the external cable connecting the two DTEs.

The break-out-box (BOB) is a device that provides the means of examining the logic state of each line in the cable and of reconfiguring the cable to match the DTE to DTE requirements (fig. U2-2). The BOB was used in unit 1 to facilitate monitoring signals for the oscilloscope. Here we shall examine its general capabilities and use it to perform the simple but important task of testing the RS-232-C cable for line continuity, open circuits, and bridging (a condition in which several lines can be electrically coupled together).

The BOB, or interface tester, can be used to establish a working data link. There are a wide variety of these devices on the market that can be categorized in terms of:

1. the interface which they support, for example RS-232-C, X.21, RS-449;

2. the functions available:
    — monitoring interface signals either by permanent connection or by patching of LEDs to the signal lines;

— enabling, disabling, jumpering, crossing over, or busing interface signals using jumper cables;
— cable testing, which can include an optional loopback module; and
— gender matching.

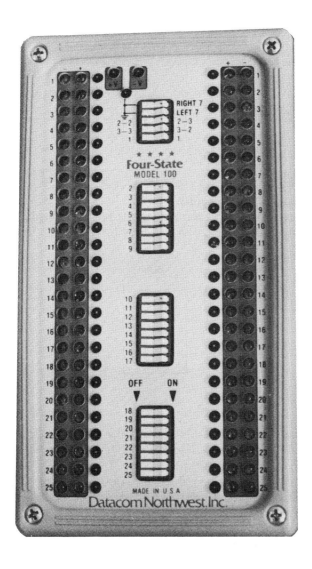

Figure U2-2   Break-Out-Box

The BOB is a tool for reconfiguring non-standard devices and enabling DTEs to communicate directly or via DCEs. A common way of using the BOB is to cross-connect pins 2 (transmitted data) and 3 (received data) of the RS-232-C cable to allow two DTEs to communicate directly by permitting the transmitted data of device A to be received on the received data line of device B and vice versa (fig. U2-3).

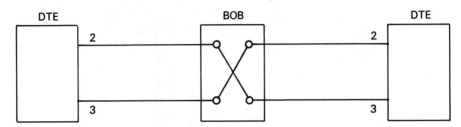

Figure U2-3   Cross Connection

By providing jumpering facility for all 25 lines of the RS-232-C, the BOB enables devices that have to receive signals for their operation to literally supply these signals for themselves, merely by requesting them (fig. U2-4).

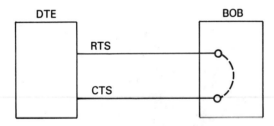

Figure U2-4   Jumpering

The RTS signal is normally used to initiate the CTS signal from the modem. Since there is no modem present in this DTE to DTE connection, the BOB is used to let the RTS signal generate its own CTS.

Signals are monitored using red LEDs to indicate positive signals (logic 0) and green LEDS to indicate negative signals (logic 1). When the signal is alternating between 1 and 0, both LEDs will light (fig. U2-5).

Signals may be enabled (set to logic 1) or disabled (set to logic 0) or grounded by pins supplying logic 1, logic 0, and ground respectively (fig. U2-6).

Busing describes the ability of the BOB to connect several lines together to form a bus (fig. U2-7).

The loopback module acts as a data verifier by echoing data back to the transmitting device for diagnostic testing (fig. U2-8).

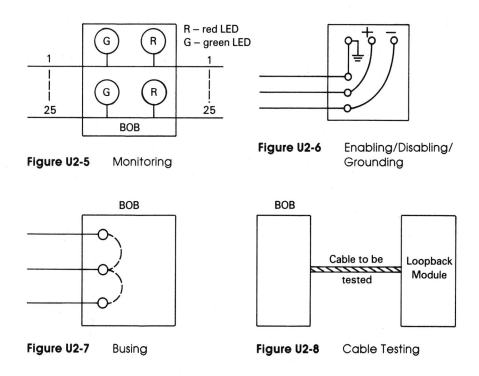

Figure U2-5   Monitoring

Figure U2-6   Enabling/Disabling/ Grounding

Figure U2-7   Busing

Figure U2-8   Cable Testing

Some BOBs provide both male and female RS-232-C connectors to enable hook-up to any combination of terminated devices. This is referred to as gender matching (fig. U2-9).

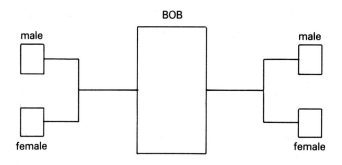

Figure U2-9   Gender Matching

A representative example of the BOB is the Four State Model 100 (fig. U2-2), which has the following characteristics:

GENERAL

Two nine volt batteries to enable (−9v) and disable (+9v) control signals and provide power for the LEDs during cable testing.

THE TOP FOUR SWITCHES

(a) Two switches are used to connect the battery and LED ground lines to pin 7, which is defined as the RS-232-C ground. These switches are normally closed when testing RS-232-C interface circuits. To isolate the BOB both switches should be open.

(b) The third and fourth switches are used to reverse pins 2 and 3 quickly and easily for DTE to DTE connection (fig. U2-10).

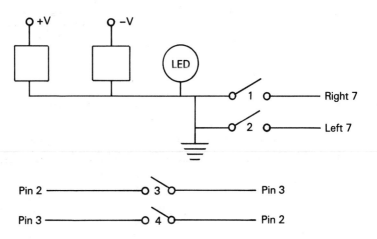

Figure U2-10   The Top Four Switches

THE REMAINING 25 SWITCHES

All 25 lines are routed through the BOB. Each line is monitored for logic 1 and logic 0 on both sides of the break-out switch. When starting to test an interface, the operator should close all the switches (right side down) and open the 2-3, 3-2 reversal switches (fig. U2-11).

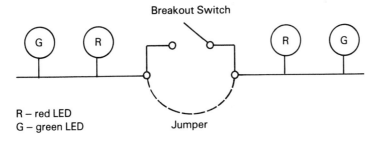

R – red LED
G – green LED

Figure U2-11   The Remaining 25 Switches

DEMONSTRATION

Cable Testing

The model 100 can be used to test a cable for continuity, for open circuits, and for bridging using the following sequence of operations:

1. Open all break-out switches.
2. Connect the cable being tested to each side of the BOB.
3. Using a jump strap, apply either a positive or negative test voltage to each pin post in sequence.

The results and their interpretation are tabulated in figure U2-12.

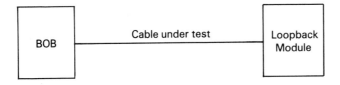

Result	Meaning
The appropriate LED lights on each side of BOB.	Continuity
Only one LED lights.	Open circuit
Two or more LEDs light on same side of BOB.	Bridging

Figure U2-12   Cable Testing

Unit

TERMINATIONS

OBJECTIVES

This unit deals with the use of microcomputers as terminals and relates directly to the discussion on terminal emulation in chapter 3. Any communications package has three major functions: 1) to make the microprocessor act like a variety of terminals, 2) to provide a simple way of specifying the communications parameters for operation with a particular remote host computer, and 3) to provide a simple mechanism for connection to a remote host. We will use ZSTEM, a commercially available communications package, to a) emulate a standard VT100 terminal, b) configure the terminal for communication with an IBM host, and c) sign on to the IBM host by striking one key. This will be accomplished in a laboratory.

BACKGROUND

Communications Functions

One of the most useful attributes of the microcomputer is its ability to emulate a wide variety of terminals by using communications software. As well as emulating the keyboard and screen parameters of a specific terminal, the communications package usually has menu-driven set-up procedures, file handling capability and softkey programming. Terminal emulation, configuration setting, and softkey programming will be discussed in this unit, file transfer is a subject for unit 5.

Terminal Emulation

To handle screen control and accept data and control codes from the keyboard, most packages use an interrupt-driven approach. For example, while the software is displaying information on the screen, the remote device can interrupt this process to send information to the terminal. The sequence of steps for an interrupt is:

1. suspend the program interrupted, noting the point of interruption and the contents of registers in use at the time;

2. transfer control to the interrupt service routine which is responsible for putting the received character in a buffer; and

3. restore the original program and continue processing.

The same general sequence holds for a keyboard interrupt or a printer interrupt. There are normally three internal buffers available with the communications package.

1. The remote communications buffer is used to store data received from the remote device.

2. The keyboard buffer is also a first-in-first-out buffer that ignores input characters when full, at which time it sounds a bell. This buffer is also used for storing control information received from the printer.

3. The disk buffer accepts characters from the remote buffer for writing to the disk and characters read from the disk.

The kernel of the terminal emulation program is the polling routine which removes characters from the buffers and directs them to the correct output device. If all the buffers are empty the polling routine continues looping. A typical polling routine is shown in figure U3-1.

Configuration Setting

Most communication packages have the facility to set baud rate, parity, and the number of stop bits. Many other parameters can also be set prior to executing the package (fig. U3-2). This menu includes terminal setting, printer setting, and wait command setting. The wait command is a feature of

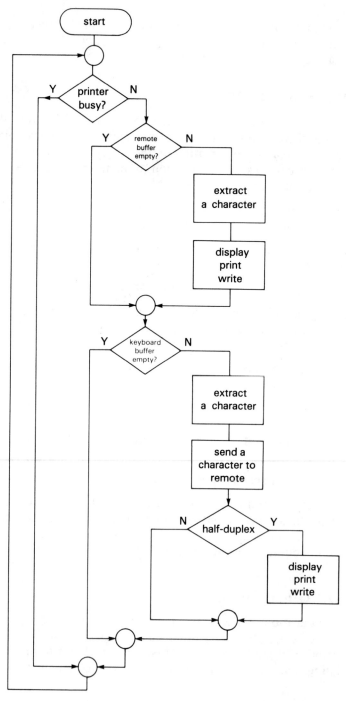

Figure U3-1   Polling Routine

```
                          ZSTEM Configuration

Remote Port (COM2)                  Serial Printer Port (COM1)
10. Baud rate:            1200       20. Baud rate:            1200
11. Data bits:               8       21. Data bits:               8
12. Stop bits:               1       22. Stop bits:               1
13. Parity: None Even Odd            23. Parity: None   Even   Odd
                                     24. Protocol: Xon/Xoff Hardware Etx/Ack
Printers                             25. Ready state: DTR1 DTR0 RTS1 RTS0
30. Parallel printer on:     N       26. Etx/Ack packet size:    32
31. Serial printer on:       N
                                     Terminal
Zstem                                50. Type: VT100 VT52
40. Softkey wait character  <NUL>    51. Half-duplex mode:        N
41. Softkey wait time:       1       52. Transparent mode:        N
42. Intercharacter delay:    0       53. Answerback softkey      7F
43. Cmnd mode delete char: <DEL>     54. Printer controller:      N
44. Local mode:              N       55. Smooth scroll delay:    20
45. Restore ports on exit:   N
46. Remote softkeys:         N       File transfer
47.*Optimize screen output:  Y       A.  ASCII
48. Strip escape codes:      N       K.  Kermit
49. Terminate on error:      N       X.  Xmodem

Select item?

*For the graphics version this question is:
47.  Switch modes on DOS call:  N
```

Figure U3-2 Configuration Menu

Source: Reproduced courtesy of KEA Systems Ltd.

soft key processing that permits a terminal to wait until it has received a specified character from the remote device, or to wait a specified time, before replying. For example, in signing on to a mainframe you might wait two seconds for a colon in the message

ENTER TERMINAL TYPE:

A typical selection for a terminal to mainframe remote port configuration might be

Baud rate:	1200
Data bits:	7
Stop bits:	1
Parity:	even

Softkey Programming

The use of softkey programming for setting keyboard control keys, both to match the remote device's expectations (for example, the IBM mainframe terminal CLEAR key sends the ASCII sequence <esc><.>) and to automate standard functions such as sign-on sequence, may be clarified by reference to a specific communication package and to specific examples.

ZSTEM

KEA Systems Ltd.'s ZSTEM is a terminal emulation package with two modes of operation.

1.   Emulation (or terminal) mode in which the microcomputer acts like a VT52 or VT100 terminal

2.   Command (or alternate) mode in which you can enter ZSTEM commands to modify the configuration, to program softkeys, or to initiate file transfers.

   The Alt key is used to enter the command mode; all other keys are available in emulation mode. By programming the softkeys, ZSTEM can be configured to invoke any command or output any character string with the press of any key, providing total transparency and single keystroke execution to the user. Figure U3-3 lists a few of the commands available in ZSTEM.

Specific Examples

DISPLAYING THE HELP MENU

It is usually necessary to type HELP in command mode to display the HELP menu. A softkey can be programmed to directly display the HELP menu in emulation mode (fig. U3-4).

PROGRAMMING A KEY TO DUMP THE SCREEN

In many applications the Shift-Prt-Sc key is used to dump the screen to the printer. This is not a feature pre-assigned by emulation programs, but it can be implemented using softkey programming (fig. U3-5).

CONFIGURE	used to set up port parameters, terminal parameters, and file transfer parameters
HELP	used to display ZSTEM's command summary
KERMIT	used for file transfer using Kermit
SAVE	used to save a configured, softkey-programmed version of ZSTEM
WAIT	used to set softkey wait character and its timeout value
XMODEM	used for file transfer with XMODEM
SCREEN	used to dump the contents of the screen to the printer

Figure U3-3   ZSTEM Commands

COMMAND	EXPLANATION
<ALT>	Enter command mode
ZSTEM? SO<SC>	Program a softkey
Select key . . . <PF1>	Choose PF1 as your softkey
Key XX = <listed below>	Key is programmed as listed in the following lines: –
<Alt>	enter command mode
HELP	execute the HELP command
<CR>	terminates HELP
<PF1>	terminates the text entry
<PF1>	
SA	saves the softkey program

NOTE: when displayed KEY XX = <Alt>HELP<CR> where XX is the hexadecimal value of the key chosen.

Figure U3-4   Displaying the HELP menu.

COMMAND	EXPLANATION
<Alt>	Enter command mode
ZSTEM? SO<CR>	Program a softkey
Select key . . . .shift-Prt Sc	Select a key
Key AB = <Listed below>	
<Alt>	Enter command mode
SC	Execute SCREEN command
<CR>	terminates screen command
Shift-Prt Sc	terminates softkey program
Shift-Prt SC	

Figure U3-5   Dumping the screen

LOGGING ON TO A MAINFRAME

It is possible to program a single key in ZSTEM to:

- — dial-up a remote computer,
- — enter a sign-on ID, and
- — enter a password.

ZSTEM will display any received characters from its remote port, detect the arrival of a specific character before each reply, or wait a specified time before each reply (fig. U3-6).

COMMAND	EXPLANATION
<Alt>	Enter command mode
ZSTEM? SO<CR>	Program a softkey
Select key . . . <PF2>	Select the PF2 key
Key 98 = <listed below>	
ENDP4718604<CR>	Causes modem to dial
<Alt>	Enter command mode
WA<CR>	Enter the WAIT command
:3	Wait 3 seconds for a colon
<CR>	Exit WAIT
<CR>	Exit command mode
CTRL @	Execute the wait
NAIT<CR>	Enter ID
<Alt>	Enter command mode
WA<Alt>	Enter WAIT command
D2<CR><CR>	Wait 2 sec and for a D and exit the WAIT command and the command mode.
CTRL @	Execute the WAIT
MYPASS <CR>	Enter the password and you're in.

Figure U3-6   Sign-On to a Remote System

LABORATORY

Softkey Programming

Objectives

After completing this lab you should be able to:

a) Configure a terminal emulation package to operate in conjunction with a mainframe computer.
b) Program a terminal emulation package, establish connection, and sign on to a mainframe by pressing one softkey.

Purpose

To gain an appreciation of and experience with the features of a typical terminal emulation package.

Procedure

a) Use the CONFIGURE command to set the following parameters:

    BAUD RATE   9600
    DATA BITS   7
    STOP BITS   1
    PARITY   EVEN

    for the remote port.

b) Use the SOFTKEY command to:
    i. Execute a carriage return to establish contact with the mainframe.
    ii. Detect the ':' in ENTER TERMINAL TYPE:
    iii. Enter VT100 <CR>
    iv. Enter <CR> to bring up log-on procedure
    v. Enter L <user ID><CR>
    vi. Detect D in PASSWORD
    vii. Enter <password><CR>
    viii. Print "YOU'RE IN THANKS TO ZSTEM AND ONE KEY"

Lab Requirement

The purpose of providing a single-key sign-on facility for microcomputers is to eliminate the need for users having to carry out multi-step procedures to make connection to remote hosts. This facility is useful for signing on to different hosts, each of which has a different sign-on procedure. Softkey programming is a powerful tool in creating user-friendly communications software.

Demonstrate the use of a single-key sign-on to your instructor.

Unit

JUNCTIONS AND CONNECTIONS

OBJECTIVES

This unit uses the concepts developed in chapters 4 and 5 to examine the alternate strategies used to optimize network connections and to consider the importance of response time to network performance. Exercises illustrate the strengths and weaknesses of point-to-point, multipoint, and multiplexed solutions to the same problem. They also compare the response times of microwave and satellite systems.

BACKGROUND

Configuration Choices

The design of a network depends on many different factors, some of which have alternatives (for example, routing) and some of which are fixed (for example, the location of an organization's branch offices). Factors that must be considered in the design of the network are:

— the distances between terminations,
— the rates charged by the telephone companies that the network uses,

258

— the number and speed of the computer channels,
— the equipment costs, and
— the application response demands.

Clearly this is a complex matter, but consideration of one of the sub-problems associated with the price and the performance of a network will illustrate the kinds of things network designers must consider. This problem raises two questions: 1) what is the best way of replacing a point-to-point system with a multipoint or multiplexer system? and 2) does the inclusion of multiport modems enhance the solution?

MULTIPOINT

The chief advantage of a multipoint over a point-to-point system is the cost, but the optimum configuration depends on distance. For example, what would be the best multipoint route for the point-to-point configuration shown in figure U4-1?

Note with the multipoint version the total line distance is much shorter since only one line is necessary to reach Alberta. At the same time, fewer computer ports and modems are required (fig. U4-2). Multipoint, therefore, is a cost-effective solution whether the remote sites are adjacent or not. All remote sites receive the same information from the host computer, but only one can communicate with the host at a time. Communication between remote sites must take place via the host.

MULTIPORT MODEMS

These are modems that contain either internal or external splitting mechanisms that permit several (typically three) terminals to be attached to the same modem. This is a low-cost option to the multipoint configuration for a single remote station (fig. U4-3). Note the decrease in communications hardware required if the remote terminals are close to each other.

MULTIPLEXER

The three main types of multiplexer can be distinguished in the following way:

FDM   is relatively slow, less expensive, older technology.
TDM   is faster, more expensive, and most effective when all input channels are in use.
STDM   is the most expensive, most intelligent, and most popular of the multiplexers that can adjust to varying load demands.

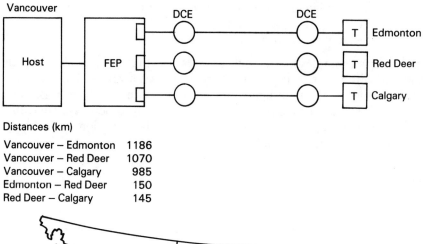

Distances (km)

Vancouver – Edmonton	1186
Vancouver – Red Deer	1070
Vancouver – Calgary	985
Edmonton – Red Deer	150
Red Deer – Calgary	145

Figure U4-1   A Point-to-Point Example

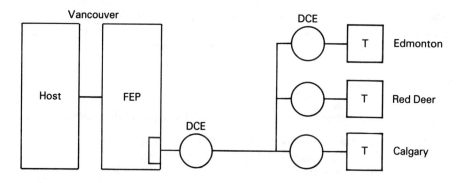

Figure U4-2   The Multipoint Version

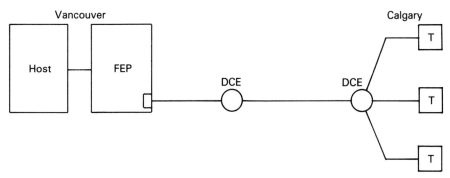

Figure U4-3   An Example of a Multiport Modem Configuration

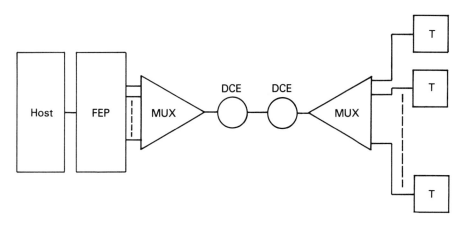

Figure U4-4   Typical Multiplexer Configuration

Figure U4-4 shows a typical configuration. A number of front-end-processor channels and a number of terminals share the same high-speed line. The remote multiplexer can be connected to different remote sites in the normal way. The need for a local multiplexer at the host depends on the capacity of the computer port.

Response Time Concepts

The response time of a polled network can be defined as the time taken by the first character, the last character, or the last needed character to arrive from a remote station. The response time is made up of

— data transmission time,
— propagation delay on the line, and
— modem delays.

DATA TRANSMISSION TIME

The data transmitted includes the control bits associated with each character in asynchronous transmission and the control characters mostly associated with synchronous transmission. The calculation of percentage overhead shows a major advantage of synchronous communication. Using a standard 7-bit ASCII code + start bit + stop bit + parity bit:

%overhead = $3/10 \times 100 = 30\%$

In synchronous communication, X.25 has three bytes of control information in a standard 256-byte packet:

%overhead = $3/259 \times 100 = 1\%$

There are other packets involved in this type of transmission that will increase the overhead but to nowhere near the asynchronous transmission figure. The data transmission time on synchronous systems can be approximated to:

time (ms) = (message length $\times$ 8 $\times$ 1000)/transmission rate.

PROPAGATION DELAY

The propagation delay is the delay caused by the electrical characters of the medium of transmission and it equals the time taken for a signal to travel the distance between stations (fig. U4-5).

Distance (km)	Medium	Delay (ms)
<320	local loop (twisted pair)	km/10
>320	local loop + microwave	12 + km/10
>320	local loop + satellite	312

Figure U4-5 Propogation Delay Table

MODEM DELAYS

There are two delays that can be incurred by the modem: transit delay and RTS/CTS delay.

1. Transit delay is the delay caused by modulating and demodulating the digital signal. The delay is related to the transmission speed of the modem (fig. U4-6).

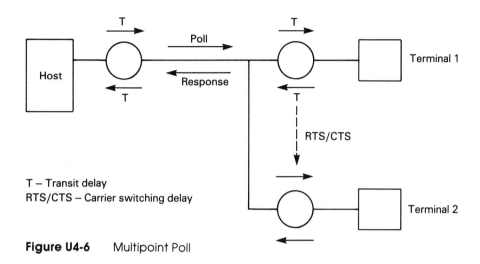

T – Transit delay
RTS/CTS – Carrier switching delay

Figure U4-6   Multipoint Poll

Transit Delay

Speed (bps)	Delay (ms)
2400	2.5
4800	4
9600	5.5

RTS/CTS Delay

Speed (bps)	Delay (ms)
2400	50
4800	130
9600	200

Figure U4-7   Modem Delay Figures

2. RTS/CTS delay is caused by switching the carriers among remote stations on a multipoint line. The host has permanent carrier, therefore no RTS/CTS delay is incurred at the host end. The delay is related to the transmission speed of the modem (fig. U4-6).

The modem delay figures in figure U4-7 were supplied by a modem manufacturer and can be used to provide an estimate of response time in a multipoint system (fig. U4-11). For example, the response time for the first character from the first remote station in a multipoint configuration would be:

$$
\begin{aligned}
\text{Response Time} = \ &\text{poll data transmission time} \\
&+ 2 \times \text{propagation delay} \\
&+ 4 \times \text{transit delay} \\
&+ 1 \times \text{RTS/CTS delay}
\end{aligned}
$$

EXERCISE

Optimizing Configurations

Given the point-to-point configuration in figure U4-8 and the geographical layout of figure U4-9, draw the optimum configuration for:

1. a multipoint solution,
2. a multipoint/multiport modem solution, and
3. a multiplexer solution.

Also complete the table in figure U4-10.

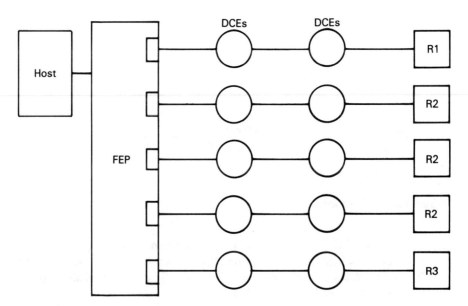

Figure U4-8   Point-to-Point

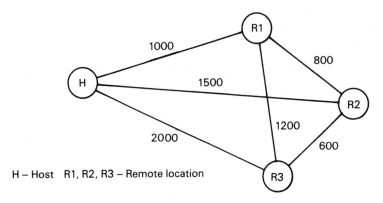

H – Host   R1, R2, R3 – Remote location

Figure U4-9   Geographical Layout

	CONFIGURATION			
Component	Point-to-Point	Multipoint	Multipoint/ Multiport Modem	MUX
Number of computer ports				
Line length				
Number of modems				

Figure U4-10   Comparison Table (configuration exercise)

EXERCISE

Response Time Comparison

Given the system shown in figure U4-11, calculate the time till the third terminal responds, assuming that terminals 1 and 2 responded with a single character (usually EOT) to indicate no communication requirement.

Data required:

   Medium microwave
   Transmission rate 9600
   Poll message 800 characters

Response from R1   1 char.
Response from R2   1 char.
Response from R3   400 char.

Assume response time is measured as the time till the last character is received. Repeat the exercise for satellite transmission.

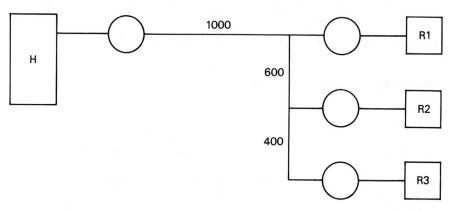

Figure U4-11   Response Time Exercise

Unit

PROTOCOL

OBJECTIVES

This unit closely parallels the material developed in chapter 6 of Section A on protocol. The exercise on HDLC provides insight into what has become the standard wide-area-network, full-duplex, synchronous protocol. By first dealing with it as though it were a half-duplex protocol we eliminate the confusion of simultaneous transfer in both directions. Kermit is a widely used asynchronous terminal-emulation and file-transfer package for micro/mainframe communication. The laboratory in this unit gives you a chance to move files in both directions and to analyze the construction of the Kermit packet. The datascope is a much more sophisticated device than the break-out-box. The demonstration allows you to capture the same information as the Kermit Log (all the control and data packets of a file transfer) as well as the timing relationships between packets being sent and received.

BACKGROUND

HDLC Protocol

The data link control level of the X.25 protocol is based on the ISO's HDLC frame structure (fig. U5-1). There are three types of frame used by X.25 (fig. U5-2) that describe the commands issued by the transmitting terminal and

F	FCS	D	C	A	F

F	Flag	1 byte
A	Address	1 byte
C	Control	1 byte
D	Data	1-256 bytes
FCS	Frame check sequence	2 bytes
F	Flag	1 byte

Figure U5-1   The HDLC Frame

Frame Type	Function	Code
Information	information transfer I frame acknowledge	I
Supervisory	acknowledges I frames when receiver has no information to transmit	RR Receive ready RNR Receive not ready REJ Reject
Unnumbered	link control	SARM Set asynchronous response mode DISC Disconnect UA Unnumbered acknowledge CMDR Command reject

Figure U5-2   Types of Frame

the responses or acknowledgments of the receiving terminal. The contents of these frames are summarized in figure U5-3. The DCE and DTE communicate with each other on a four-wire full-duplex line as follows.

INITIATION

The DTE issues a SARM frame that requires a UA frame from the DCE to confirm initiation in one direction. The DCE repeats this process to establish initiation in both directions (fig. U5-4).

DATA FLOW

When a station (DTE or DCE) has an information frame (I) to transmit, it places the current value of the send-sequence counter in the N(S) bits of the control field with the N(S) count one higher than the last information frame

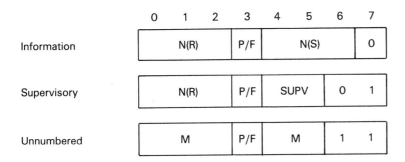

0	1	2	3	4	5	6	7

Information: | N(R) | P/F | N(S) | 0 |

Supervisory: | N(R) | P/F | SUPV | 0 | 1 |

Unnumbered: | M | P/F | M | 1 | 1 |

N(S)   – sequence number of this frame
N(R)   – sequence number of frame expected
P/F   – poll/final bit
SUPV – supervisory functions
M   – additional link control functions

Figure U5-3   Frame Control Byte

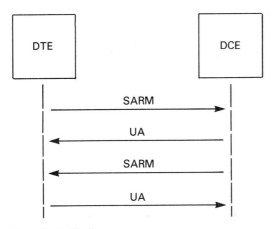

Figure U5-4   Transfer Initiation

transmitted. The transmitter also places the value of its receive-sequence counter into the N(R) bits of the control field. This receive-sequence count, N(R), is only incremented when an information frame with a valid frame check sequence (FCS) and the expected send-sequence count, N(S), are received from the other station. This means that the N(R) count in the transmitter information frame represents the send-sequence number of the next frame that the transmitter expects to receive (fig. U5-5).

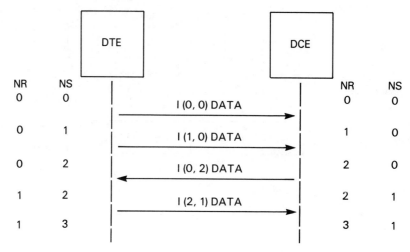

Figure U5-5   Data Flow

TERMINATION

Once the link is no longer required for information transfer, a disconnect command is used to terminate the link (fig. U5-6).

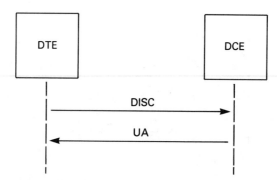

Figure U5-6   Link Termination

KERMIT Protocol

The Kermit protocol was designed at the Columbia University Center for Computing Activities (CUCCA) by Bill Catchings and Frank da Cruz. Its purpose is to transfer sequential files over ordinary serial telecommunication lines. Kermit is a terminal-oriented file transfer protocol that has been implemented on a wide variety of microcomputers and mainframes. Data is transferred in packets, the format of which is shown in figure U5-7.

Kermit can be used on a variety of systems by using a common subset of their features. Communication is half-duplex. A 96-character packet can be accommodated on most hosts without buffering problems. Packets are sent in alternate directions in a handshaking mode. A time-out facility allows transmission to resume after a packet is lost. The transmission code is ASCII and includes prefixing of ASCII control characters.

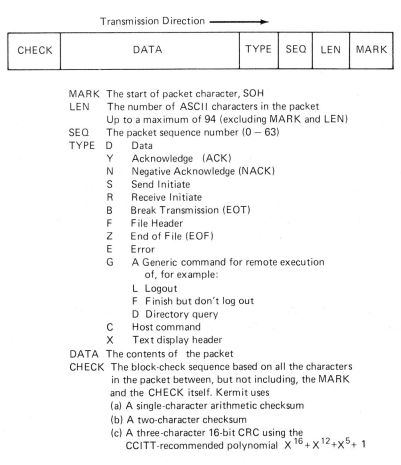

Transmission Direction ⟶

| CHECK | DATA | TYPE | SEQ | LEN | MARK |

MARK   The start of packet character, SOH
LEN   The number of ASCII characters in the packet
       Up to a maximum of 94 (excluding MARK and LEN)
SEQ   The packet sequence number (0 − 63)
TYPE   D   Data
       Y   Acknowledge (ACK)
       N   Negative Acknowledge (NACK)
       S   Send Initiate
       R   Receive Initiate
       B   Break Transmission (EOT)
       F   File Header
       Z   End of File (EOF)
       E   Error
       G   A Generic command for remote execution
            of, for example:
            L Logout
            F Finish but don't log out
            D Directory query
       C   Host command
       X   Text display header
DATA   The contents of the packet
CHECK The block-check sequence based on all the characters
       in the packet between, but not including, the MARK
       and the CHECK itself. Kermit uses
       (a) A single-character arithmetic checksum
       (b) A two-character checksum
       (c) A three-character 16-bit CRC using the
           CCITT-recommended polynomial $X^{16}+X^{12}+X^5+1$

Figure U5-7   The Kermit Packet

FILE TRANSFER

The simplicity of Kermit's file transfer protocol is based on the fact that each packet must be acknowledged. Figure U5-8 illustrates the sequence of communication for receiving files based on the packet types listed in figure U5-7. Although this flowchart indicates the packet sequence for receiving several files:

SFDDDDDDDDDFDDDZFDDDDDDDDZFDDDDDDDDDDDDDDZB

it does not include:

— the ACK packet, which acknowledges receipt of a valid packet;
— the NACK packet, which acknowledges receipt of a bad packet or that a time out has occurred; or
— the Error packet, which is sent by the side that encountered the error and that contains an error message.

The flowchart for sending files is very similar but begins with a Send Initiate packet (S) and incorporates Y,N, and E packets.

Kermit operates in such a way that during a particular transaction the sender is the master and the receiver is the slave. These roles can be reversed for the next transaction. The Kermit at either end of the line, therefore, can act as either a master or a slave. A simpler way to operate between a mainframe and a microcomputer is to make the mainframe a permanent slave or server. The mainframe Kermit then gets all its instructions from the microcomputer Kermit in the form of a special command packet. The server will even log itself out upon command from the microcomputer Kermit.

PACKET ANALYSIS

Kermit provides a valuable debugging aid which is also useful for understanding the packet protocol. This is the log facility which may be invoked locally using:

LOG [OPTION] [filespec]

where the options are:

TRANSACTIONS logs successful and unsuccessful file transfers;
SESSION   creates a transcript of a connect session when running a local Kermit connected to a remote system;
DEBUGGING   records debugging information in the specified file; and

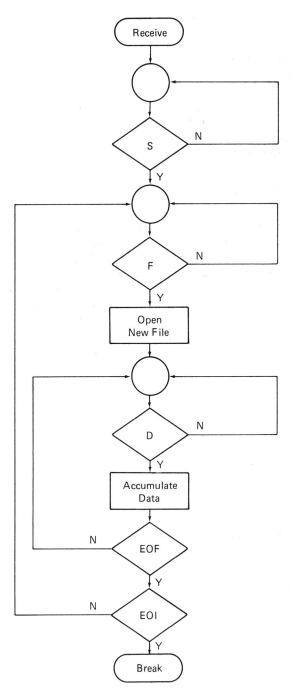

Figure U5-0   Kermit Packet Flow

PACKETS   records packets and all communications during file transfer.

Another option is to invoke the log facility in the remote Kermit using:

SET DEBUG ON

This keeps a journal of all packets sent and received in the file KER LOG Al when using the IBM VM/CMS Kermit at the remote end.

Once you've logged a file transfer, the next problem is to interpret the control characters in the packets and verify the error-checking mechanism.

CONTROL CHARACTERS

These lie in the ASCII range 0 to 31 and 127 (delete code). A printable ASCII character lies in the range 32 to 126. Kermit converts control characters to printable characters by adding 32 to the ASCII code so that null, which is ASCII(0), becomes space, which is ASCII(32). SOH which is ASCII(1) becomes exclamation mark which is ASCII(33) and so on. Screen control characters are preceded by the pound sign (#). For example, #M means carriage return and #J means line feed. Figure U5-9 shows how the packets are logged by VM/CMS Kermit during a send operation. All packets have a MARK, LEN, SEQ, and TYPE field. The data packet includes the checksum.

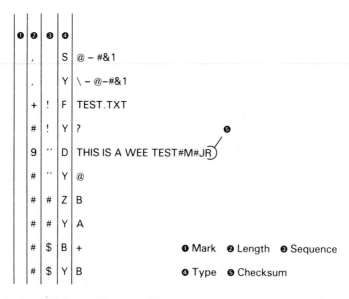

Figure U5-9   The Kermit Log

ERROR CHECKING

The check character in a data packet provides a block check on the characters between, but not including, the MARK and the CHECK character itself. The check for each packet is computed at both ends of the link and it must be the same at both ends for the packet to be accepted. The single-character arithmetic checksum of six bits is computed using:

$$CHECK = CHAR((S+((S \text{ AND } 192)/64)) \text{ AND } 63)$$

where S is the arithmetic sum of the ASCII characters and $CHAR(x) = x + 32$ (fig. U5-10).

```
1. 9 "THIS ⬧ IS ⬧ A ⬧ WEE ⬧ TEST #M #J = 632H

2. 632H AND C0H = 0

3. 0 ÷ 40H = 0

4. 0 + 632H = 632H

5. 632H AND 3FH = 32H

6. CHAR(X) = 32H + 20H = 52H = R
```

Figure U5-10   Checksum Calculation

A two-character checksum based on the low-order 12 bits of the arithmetic sum of the characters in the packet and a three-character 16-bit CRC error check are optionally available.

SAMPLE SESSION

Kermit is prompt oriented; that is, Kermit issues a prompt, the user types a command, Kermit executes the command and issues another prompt. A typical Kermit session in a microcomputer to mainframe connection consists of:

— invoking the microcomputer's Kermit,
— making the connection,
— signing on to the mainframe,
— invoking the remote Kermit and entering server mode,
— returning to the microcomputer's Kermit,
— transferring files,
— releasing the remote Kermit,
— signing off the mainframe, and
— exiting from Kermit.

Figure U5-11 shows a typical session between the CDC CYBER 170 and an IBM PC.

```
                    Turn on microcomputer and monitor

                    A > KERMIT
                    IBM - PC Kermit - MS  V2.26
                    Type ? for help
                    Kermit - MS > SET PARITY SPACE
                    Kermit - MS > SET BAUD 300
                    Kermit - MS > C
                    (Connecting to host, type CTRL right square bracket
                      to return to PC)
                    <Return>
                    <Return>
                    Normal CYBER log-in procedure
                    /ATTACH, KERMIT/UN = LIBRARY
                    /KERMIT
                    Kermit — 170 > SERVER
                    <CTRL> ] C
                    Kermit - MS > GET MYFILE

                                Filename:  MYFILE
                         Kbytes transferred:
                                 Receiving:
                         Number of packets:
                          Number of retries:
                                Last error:
                              Last warning:
                    Kermit - MS > FINISH
                    Kermit - MS > C
                    /BYE
                    <CTRL> ] C
                    Kermit - MS > QUIT
                    A>
```

Figure U5-11   A Typical Kermit Session (user input underlined)

Datascope Concepts

These devices resemble CRT terminals. Their primary application is in the debugging of new communications software, new transmission formats and newly-installed hardware rather than the routine diagnosis of telephone line or modem failure once a system is functioning properly. The datascope is used to monitor protocol and to simulate DTE and DCE operation. It can be used to solve timing and control signal problems.

MONITORING PROTOCOL

The datascope is attached to the data line at the digital modem interface (on the RS-232-C connector rather than the two- or four-wire modulated signal side which is sometimes referred to as the analog modem interface). It monitors both send and receive data and includes in the display an indication of when Carrier Detect, Request to Send, and Clear to Send come on in relation to the data. Underlining, reverse video, and dim and bright attributes are used to distinguish between send and receive modes, and between data and control characters. Datascopes contain buffer memories for off-line searches through stored data. Two features that reduce the need for storage are the idle character delete option and the programmable trigger. The idle character delete option is used to distinguish between the data and the spaces between data blocks so that the data can be stored and the spaces ignored. In many cases, there is more space than data occurring during transmission. This option can be useful on occasion to store and display idle characters to measure turnaround time in a multipoint system.

The programmable trigger starts storing data when a particular event or character sequence occurs, for example, when the carrier comes on, when a parity error occurs, or when a NAK is received. The feature can be set to preserve characters both before and after the event to observe both cause and effect.

The datascope can monitor asynchronous and synchronous data as well as set the block synchronization character to a particular code. The CRT displays characters as text or in hexadecimal form. Special patterns are used to display control codes.

SIMULATION

Simulation is used to mimic any terminal or computer format. It is important to be able to test a new terminal when computer time is not available and to test computer software before the terminal arrives. Simulation means being able to monitor and transmit using a keyboard. The keyboard is used to enter or program the parameters of a given protocol such as message format, polling interval, RTS/CTS delay, polling message, terminal response message, and X.25 requirements. To avoid re-entering data, the parameters are stored in the datascope memory and minor modifications are made on the keyboard. The datascope permits downloading from remote computers as well as bit error rate testing (BERT) and block error rate testing (BLERT).

THE INTERVIEW (FIG. U5-12)

This is a representative datascope with the following features:

1. Protocol Set-up

The protocol set-up menu provides a means of specifying the computer software protocol. For example, the parameter selection for a Kermit transmission between the IBM PC and an IBM mainframe is shown in figure U5-13.

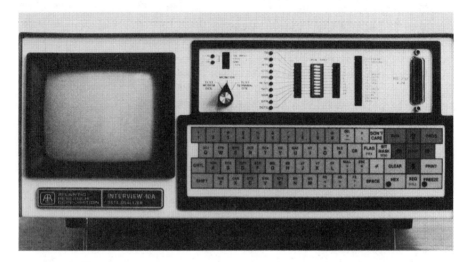

Figure U5-12 The Interview

2. Triggering

Trigger logic monitors both send and receive lines for such conditions as:

— specific character combinations,
— internal flags set by the datascope, and
— timeout conditions;

and takes such actions as:

— message display,
— sounding an alarm, and
— controlling a counter/timer for statistical measurement.

3. Printer Control

```
**PROTOCOL SETUP**

CODE: ASCII EBCDIC IPARS BAUDOT
   BITS: 8 7 6 5
   +PARITY: NONE ODD EVEN MRK SFC
FORMAT: SYNC BOP BOP/NRZI ASYNC
   SYNC CHARS: Sγ Sγ
   OUTSYNC: OFF ON  CHAR: Fε #:1
   IDLE DISPLAY: OFF ON
   AUTO SYNC: OFF ON
REC BCC: OFF ON

DATA: NORMAL INV REV INV/REV
I/F: EIA MIL
CLOCK: EXT INT
DISPLAY: SINGLE DUAL
   SUPPRESS: _____
   ENHANCE: _____
```

Figure U5-13   Protocol Set-up

Printer control facilitates printing any program menu or the entire data buffer.

4. Interactive Testing

By generating bit patterns the datascope can be used to analyse the response to those patterns and count the number of errors (BERT). Using BLERT the datascope can duplicate the operation of live traffic and thus provide a more comprehensive performance check.

5. Test Library

The Interview also stores a test library of basic protocol set-ups and fifty complete tests.

EXERCISE

Packet Flow

Diagram the HDLC flow for DTE/DCE communication in which the DTE sends a 90-byte enquiry to a remote location and receives via the DCE a 700-byte reply. The maximum packet size is 256 bytes of data. Assume the counters are initialized to zero.

The exercise is a simplification of the HDLC system in that the communication is half-duplex. One information frame arrives at the receiver before the receiver can transmit a frame. In reality, the communication is full-duplex so that each station must anticipate which frame it will receive as it transmits its own frames. This is what makes the N(R) parameter so useful and the protocol so efficient. Figure U5-14 illustrates this type of communication.

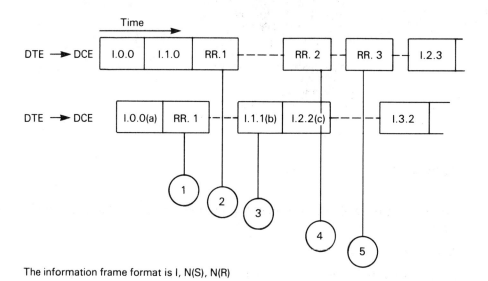

The information frame format is I, N(S), N(R)

At time =

1   The DTE has transmitted 2 frames, the DCE has received one.

2   The DTE has received the first DCE frame (a).

3   The DCE sends its second frame (b) and is waiting on the second DTE frame [I.1.1].

4   The DTE receives the second DCE frame and the DCE sends its third frame (c). The DCE has received the second DTE frame and is waiting on the third [I.2.2].

5   The DTE receives the third DCE frame.

Figure U5-14   Overlapping Transmission

DEMONSTRATION

Packet Transfer on the Datascope

The datascope can be used to demonstrate the packet characteristics in a typical micro-mainframe transfer and the transmit/acknowledge nature of half-duplex communication. When it is used to monitor a Kermit transfer between a microcomputer and a mainframe, the CRT of the datascope displays the same information as the Kermit log of figure U5-9. The main difference is that on the CRT there are separate traces (lines) for the transmit packets and the receive packets as well as a clocking trace (line). This is very useful for making accurate time measurements. The Kermit log simply provides a list of all the packets that have been transmitted in both directions. Notice that in figure U5-9 the list alternates between send and receive (or acknowledge) packets. The receive packets all have a type Y designation.

LABORATORY

Uploading and Downloading Files

Objectives

Upon completion of this lab you should be able to:

a) Use KERMIT to upload and download files in both normal and server modes.
b) Log a KERMIT file transfer, identify packet types, and control information associated with data packets.

Purpose

To use communication software to transfer files between a microcomputer and a mainframe computer.

Exercises

a) Upload a file in normal mode.
b) Download a file in normal mode.
c) Upload a file in server mode.
d) Download a file in server mode.

Lab requirements

a) Demonstrate any of the above exercises.

b)   Submit the Kermit log for the transfer of a short file annotated to identify:
- packet type,
- data packet length,
- sequence, and
- checksum.

6

LOCAL AREA NETWORKS

OBJECTIVES

The basic concepts, classifications and applications of local area networks were covered in chapter 8. This unit deals with the practical considerations of using a local area network. You will learn the commands and restrictions of the network as well as the effect of load on network performance.

BACKGROUND

LAN Features

Major user requirements include:

1. Network access and security incorporating ID, password, and file protection.

2. Network help facilities for handling errors, station/user monitoring, and capacity/load monitoring.

3. File sharing, protection and updating.

4. Printer spooling and queuing.

LAN Performance

The purpose of implementing LANs is to share expensive resources such as disk space, print facilities, and software among users who may also benefit from shared, current, and accurate data files. As the number of users increase, the performance of the LAN will decrease. The degree of performance degradation is a major concern for manufacturers, data processing staff, and users. The main concerns include the effect of LAN load on:

— signon time,
— file transfer,
— updating,
— print spooling, and
— software execution.

All these factors can be tested by coordinating the efforts of several users on a LAN as described in the sample laboratory following.

LABORATORY

LAN Workstation Interaction

Objectives

Upon completion of the lab the student should be able to:

a) Obtain information about the status of the network and about other users.
b) Manipulate file servers to avoid multiple access problems.
c) Suspend, hold, cancel, and restart print jobs.
d) Evaluate network loading.

Purpose

a) To become familiar with the features of a typical LAN.
b) To consider the effect of LAN loading on response time.

Exercises

Test the following features and include the appropriate command in the space provided.

a)   Check your station number.   _____

b)   Check if station 5 is on the network.   _____

c)   Check all the stations on the network.   _____

d)   Display network drive status.   _____

e)   Display network server status.   _____

f)   Display network user status.   _____

Working with another student test the following facilities.

a)   Create a short read-only file and attempt to change it. Convert it to read/write mode and attempt to change it.

b)   Reserve a file for updates and have your partner attempt to change it. Release the file and have your partner change it.

Create a short text file and perform the following operations on it. This exercise requires multiple users.

a)   Print three copies of the file.

b)   Display the spooler status.

c)   Suspend the printing of the file.

d)   Release the file for printing.

e)   Stop the file from printing in mid print and start printing from the beginning of the file.

f)   Cancel a print request.

Performance appraisal

With up to seven units on the LAN, measure response times to multiple simultaneous requests and produce the following graph.

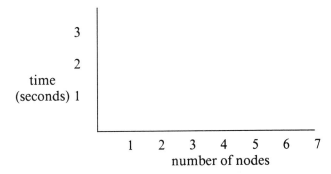

This should be completed by setting up the command on one machine then two, then three, and so on, and hitting the carriage return simultaneously on all the machines under test and measuring the response time.

Complete the graph for:

a)   DIR D:
b)   MSBASIC

Lab requirements

Submit the performance appraisal graph with a brief analysis of the results.

7

COMMUNICATIONS PROGRAMMING

OBJECTIVE

This unit broadly relates to all of the material in the rest of the book. Specifically, it refers to hardware (a specific USART), to terminal emulation, the micro/mainframe link, transferring files, and most particularly to programming. Although writing a short terminal emulation program cannot be compared with the time it takes to create the sophisticated network architectures referred to in chapter 12, the exercise still provides valuable insights into the major problems of data communications. These problems include establishing parity or baud rate, responding to remote devices, and operating in full- or half-duplex. Most importantly, this chapter provides practical reinforcement for all the basic concepts of data communication in a way that is familiar to most analysts and programmers and to many users, that is, through software.

The main themes of the chapter are:

— communications programming in BASIC,
— the characteristics of communications programs, and
— hardware programming.

BASIC is a useful language for explaining data communication concepts. Not only is it well known, but it also contains statements especially designed for communications, such as the OPEN COM statement. It also has a means of referencing memory addresses (PEEK and POKE). The first section of this unit deals with the BASIC commands for keyboard, screen, and communications buffer control.

The second section deals with analyzing simple, widely used communications programs, and suggestions for possible improvements are made.

The third section takes you to the very heart of the matter and deals with programming the USART to send and receive individual characters. These routines are central to all communications software.

BACKGROUND

Communications Programming in BASIC

All terminal emulation programs perform three functions:

1. They monitor the keyboard and send input from the keyboard to the remote device via the USART.

2. They monitor the USART for incoming data from the remote device.

3. They process the incoming data in one of three ways:
   a) display it on the screen,
   b) direct it to the printer, or
   c) store it on disk.

Before considering a program to perform all these functions and their inter-relationships we must deal with each of the functions separately.

The Keyboard

The most useful BASIC instructions are:

1. INKEY$ — to read a character from the keyboard.

2. FRE — collects and compresses all the useful data in string buffer and frees up unused areas so that the program may continue.

3. INPUT — to read a string of characters from the keyboard.

4. KEY — to program the function keys to produce an executable string. For example PF3 displays LOAD" on the screen. This feature is included in many versions of BASIC.

Keyboard Concerns for Communication

It can be demonstrated, using the INKEY$ function, that some keystrokes entered on the keyboard result in the production of two characters in the BASIC buffer. The left-most character is always 0 (or null) and may be ignored. The right-most character uniquely identifies the key struck.

The INKEY$ function allows you to detect a keystroke and decide what to do with it before the keystroke is displayed. This allows you to discard keystrokes, transform them, for example, from lower to upper case, or accept them as they are. INKEY$ returns an extended code for keys or key combinations not represented in standard ASCII. A null character (ASCII code 0) will be returned as the first character of a two-character string. A table of second characters is listed in figure U7-1.

Most of the keyboard is typamatic. Holding a key down sends the character to the keyboard buffer till the buffer is full.

When creating, modifying, and deleting strings in BASIC the string buffer area may be fragmented with strings scattered through it, or separated by short empty areas which have been deleted. When this happens, BASIC halts processing till the string buffer is cleaned up. The time for this may be unacceptable during a communication transfer. The solution is to execute the FRE statement on a regular basis thus minimizing the time taken at any particular point in the process.

The INPUT function is useful for string creation but causes BASIC to pause. This could result in a loss of incoming data during a communications transfer.

The KEY statement may be used for three purposes in a communications program.

a) To set the function keys to produce specific strings when pressed. The format for setting the function keys is:
    KEY n, X$ where
            n is the function key number
            X$ is the string.
    The default in BASIC is: LOAD", RUN, LIST, etc.

b) To turn the display of these function keys on or off on the 25th line of the screen use:
    KEY ON
    KEY OFF

c) The contents of the function keys may be displayed using
    KEY list

Note: The contents of a softkey are erased by setting it to null.
    KEY 1, ""

SECOND CODE	MEANING
3	(null character) NUL
15	(shift tab) - - < + +
16-25	Alt- Q, W, E, R, T, Y, U, I, O, P
30-38	Alt-A, S, D, F, G, H, J, K, L
44-50	Alt- Z, X, C, V, B, N, M
59-68	Function keys F1 through F10 (when disabled as soft keys)
71	Home
72	Cursor Up
73	Pg Up
75	Cursor Left
77	Cursor Right
79	End
80	Cursor Down
81	Pg Dn
82	Ins
83	Del
84-93	F11-F20 (Shift- F1 through F10)
94-103	F21-F30 (Ctrl- F1 through F10)
104-113	F31-F40 (Alt- F1 through F10)
114	Ctrl-Prtsc
115	Ctrl-Cursor Left (Previous Word)
116	Ctrl-Cursor Right (Next Word)
117	Ctrl-End
118	Ctrl-Pg Dn
119	Ctrl-Home
120-131	Alt- 1,2,3,4,5,6,7,8,9,0,-,=
132	Ctrl-Pg Up

Note: The extended code consists of a null character (ASCII Code 000) and a second code which is usually the scan code of the primary key.

Figure U7-1   Extended Codes

DISPLAY

The most useful BASIC instructions are:

CLS — clears the screen.

COLOR — selects foreground and background colors and may be used with monochrome display for reverse video, underlining and highlighting.

CSRLIN — returns the current line (row) position of the cursor.

POS(0) — returns the current column location of the cursor. 0 is a dummy argument.

LOCATE — moves the cursor to the specified location on the screen. It can also be used to turn the cursor on and off and change its size.
PRINT — displays data on the screen.
SCREEN — used to set the screen attributes for graphics monitors.

Display Concerns for Communication

Printing data on the screen affects the position of the cursor on the screen. During communication sessions the remote system must know where the cursor is before and after a data transfer. Terminating a print statement without a semicolon, to keep the cursor at the end of the data displayed, may confuse the remote device.

The CSRLIN and POS(0) statements may be used to remember where the cursor is before moving to another part of the screen to print a message so that you can return to the original position and continue.

The LOCATE is used to move the cursor from one area of the screen to another during split screen operation. The cursor may not be moved to the 25th line if the function keys are displayed there, whether they are disabled or not. To use the 25th line like any other line you must execute:

KEY OFF

Screen layout is an essential design consideration of communication software so that rigid control of cursor movement may be retained.

The color statement can be used on a monochrome display to distinguish information sources, for example transmitted and received data. A color adapter can be used to transform a monochrome monitor into multiple independent screens. An 80-column screen line will have four independent screens in text mode. You can switch among the screens using the SCREEN command.

COMMUNICATIONS

Communications Considerations

The BASIC communications buffer has a default size of 256 characters. It can be set in DOS using

GWBASIC/C: <m> where m is a binary multiple

The buffer operates in a first-in-first-out mode. When a character arrives, it is placed in the buffer. When the program requests data, it is supplied in the sequence in which it arrived. BASIC passes all the characters it can as a string variable and erases them from the buffer. The other waiting characters, if any, move to the front of the buffer.

Communication Control Characters

EOT CHR$(4)	communication will be terminated shortly.
XON CHR$(17)	remote system is ready for transmission.
XOFF CHR$(19)	indicates remote system is busy and does not want you to transmit to it.
ESC CHR$(27)	used in multiple-character control characters.
CHR$(27) + "A"	cursor up.
CHR$(27) + "B"	cursor down.
CHR$(27) + "C"	cursor right.
CHR$(27) + "D"	cursor left.

Communication Programming

Opening a communication file:

> OPEN <COM.filename> AS [ ] <file number>

allocates a communication buffer for input from the remote device and output to the screen, the printer, or to disk. It is valid only with the USART operating as an asynchronous communication adapter.

> <COM.filename>= "<dev>:<speed>,<parity>,<data>,
> <stop>[,RS]
> [,CS<n>][,CS<n>][,CD<n>]

The OPEN COM statement specifies:

<dev>	COM1,COM2 two asynchronous ports
<speed>	baud rate (300-9600)
<parity>	ODD, EVEN, MARK, SPACE, NONE
<data>	no. of transmit/receive bits
<stop>	no. of stop bits 1,1.5,2
RS	suppresses RTS
CS<n>	specifies no. of milliseconds wait for CS n=0 ignores the CS line

DS<n>   specifies no. of milliseconds wait for DS
           n=0 ignores the DS line

CD<n>   specifies no. of milliseconds wait for CD
           n=0 ignores the CD line

The RS, CS, DS and CD parameters are useful for DTE to DTE connection where the modem signals are not available.

Input

The INPUT$ function is preferable to INPUT # and LINE INPUT # for reading communication files since all ASCII characters may be significant in communications. INPUT # stops for a comma or a carriage return, LINE INPUT # stops for a carriage return. INPUT$ allows all characters read to be assigned to a string. The form of INPUT$ most useful for communications is:

    INPUT$(<num chars>,#<file number>)

where <num chars> is the number of characters read; #<file number> is the communications buffer

Flow Control

At rates of 1200 baud or higher it may be necessary to suspend character transmission from the remote device till the data can be "processed." This is achieved by sending XOFF (CHR$(19)) to the remote device and XON (CHR$(17)) when you are ready to resume. This is a common convention but not universal. The remote device protocol must be checked before implementing this form of flow control. The EOF function is used to check whether any unprocessed communication data is waiting in the communication buffer.

The LOC function returns the number of characters waiting in the communication buffer to be read and may be used in conjunction with INPUT$ to read the complete contents of the buffer for processing. It is also useful for anticipating overflow of the buffer, for example:

    IF LOC(1)>128 THEN PRINT #1, XOFF$

checks to see if the buffer is more than half full (assuming a buffer size of 256 characters) and if so sends XOFF to the remote device to halt transmission of data.

Note: GET and PUT permit fixed length I/O for COM files, for example:

    GET #1, 256 means load the file buffer with a record
    PUT #2, 256 means send the record to the remote device.

Because of the low performance associated with the telephone line, GET and PUT are not used without error checking mechanisms.

COMMUNICATIONS PROGRAMS

The TTY Program

The full-duplex communication program provided by the Microsoft Corporation in their GWBASIC manual provides insight into full-duplex programming. The TTY program is listed in fig. U7-2 and can best be understood by breaking it up into a number of modules and studying the flowchart of each module.

THE TTY PROGRAM

(An exercise in Communication I/O.)

```
10    SCREEN 0,0:WIDTH 80
15    KEY OFF:CLS:CLOSE
20    DEFINT A-Z
25    LOCATE 25,1
30    PRINT STRING$(60," ")
40    FALSE=0:TRUE=NOT FALSE
50    MENU=5 'Value of MENU key (ctrl-E)
60    XOFF$=CHR$(19):XON$=CHR$(17)

100   LOCATE 25,1:PRINT "Async TTY Program";
110   LOCATE 1,1:LINE INPUT "Speed?"; SPEED$
120   COMFIL$="COM1:"+SPEED$+",E,7"
130   OPEN COMFIL$ AS #1
140   OPEN "SCRN:" FOR OUTPUT AS #2

200   PAUSE=FALSE
210   A$=INKEY$: IF A$= " " THEN 230
220   IF ASC (A$)=MENU THEN 300 ELSE PRINT #1,A$;
230   IF EOF(1) THEN 210
240   IF LOC(1)>128 THEN PAUSE = TRUE: PRINT #1,XOFF$;
250   A$=INPUT$(LOC(1),#1)
260   PRINT #2,A$;:IF LOC (1)>0 THEN 240
270   IF PAUSE THEN PAUSE=FALSE:PRINT #1,XON$;
280   GOTO 210

300   LOCATE 1,1:PRINT STRING$(30," "):LOCATE 1,1
310   LINE INPUT"File?"; DSKFIL$

400   LOCATE 1,1:PRINT STRING$(30," "):LOCATE 1,1
410   LINE INPUT" (T)ransmit or (R)eceive?";TXRX$
420   IF TXRX$="T" THEN OPEN DSKFIL$ FOR INPUT AS
         #2:GOTO 1000
430   OPEN DSKFIL$ FOR OUTPUT AS #2
```

```
440   PRINT #1,CHR$(13);

500   IF EOF(1) THEN GOSUB 600
510   IF LOC(1)>128 THEN PAUSE=TRUE: PRINT #1,XOFF$;
520   A$=INPUT$(LOC(1),#1)
530   PRINT #2,A$;:IF LOC (1)>0 THEN 510
540   IF PAUSE THEN PAUSE=FALSE:PRINT #1,XON$;
550   GOTO 500

600   FOR I=1 to 5000
610   IF NOT EOF(1)THEN I=9999
620   NEXT I
630   IF I>9999 THEN RETURN
640   CLOSE #2:CLS:LOCATE 25,10:PRINT "* Download
      complete *";
650   GOTO 200

1000   WHILE NOT EOF(2)
1010   A$=INPUT$(1,#2)
1020   PRINT #1,A$;
1030   WEND
1040   PRINT #1,CHR$(26); 'CTRL-Z to make close file.
1050   CLOSE #2:CLS:LOCATE 25,10:PRINT "** Upload
       complete **";
1060   GOTO 200

9999   CLOSE:KEY OFF
```

Figure U7-2 The TTY Program

Source: Reproduced courtesy of Victor Technologies Inc.

Terminal Emulation (fig. U7-3)

After initialization and setting the PAUSE flag FALSE, the program checks the keyboard for:

1. No character entered—NULL
2. A special key signifying a file transfer requirement—CTRL-E
3. Any other character, which is transmitted to the remote host.

The communication buffer is checked, and if it is empty, the keyboard scan routine is repeated. If the buffer is more than half-full, this is used to signal a halt to the transmission of data from the remote device by sending an XOFF character. The communication buffer is then read and printed on the screen. The buffer is checked again to see if it is empty. The string variable A$ has a maximum capacity of 256 characters, but the buffer may be much larger. In that case it will take several reads to empty the buffer. Another reason for checking the buffer again is that more characters may have arrived while the

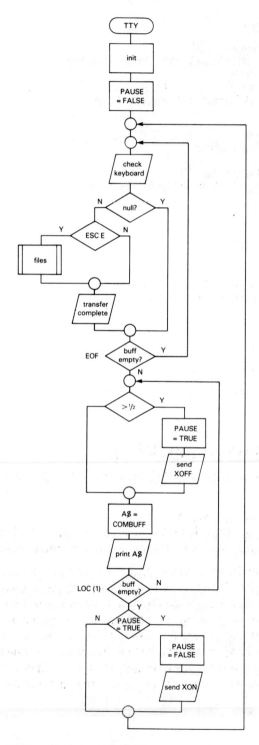

Figure U7-3   Terminal Emulation

print process was going on. If the buffer is not empty, the process is repeated from the half-full check; otherwise, if the PAUSE flag was set TRUE, it is set FALSE and an XON signal is sent to the remote device to restart the transmission. The whole sequence is then repeated starting at the keyboard check.

File Transfer Menu (fig. U7-4)

The short menu program asks whether you want to transmit or receive a file.

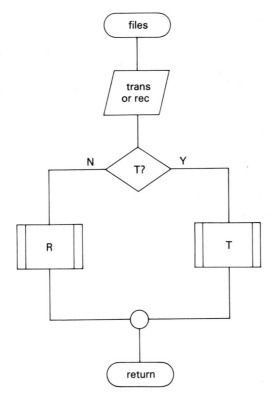

Figure U7-4   File Transfer Menu

File Transmit Routine (fig. U7-5)

After opening a file for input, a DO/WHILE loop, consisting of read-a-character and transmit-a-character statements, is executed until the end of the file is reached, at which time a file terminating character (CTRL-Z) is sent, the files closed, and a successful completion message displayed.

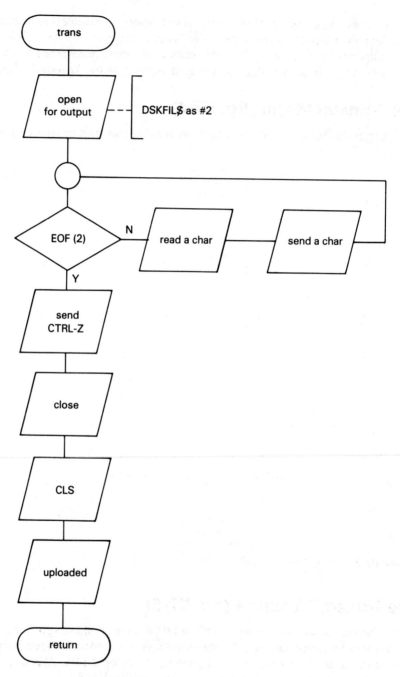

Figure U7-5   File Transmit Routine

File Receive Routine (fig. U7-6)

The file to receive the data is opened for output. A carriage return character is sent to the remote device to initiate the transfer. (This is a common device for initiation which assumes that the remote device is poised and ready for transmission.)

When the transfer is complete and the buffer is empty, a TIMEOUT routine is invoked to account for possible delays and to make a final decision on whether the transfer is in fact complete. The rest of the receive routine is identical to the major portion of the terminal emulation program (fig. U7-3) and consists of:

- checking to see if transmission is too fast, in which case it halts it by sending XOFF;
- transferring the contents of the communication buffer to the file designated to receive the information from the remote host; and
- rechecking the communication buffer and restarting the transfer with XON if the buffer is empty.

The Timeout Routine (fig. U7-7)

The timeout routine is the least structured portion of the code and consists of a wait loop during which the communication buffer is continuously checked. If the buffer stays empty for around 20 seconds, this is taken to mean transmission is complete and the files are closed, the screen cleared, and the successful completion message displayed. If a character arrives during the wait, the whole transfer process continues at the check-if-buffer-is-half-full point (fig. U7-6).

Note: Although the flowchart is based on the program listed in figure U7-2, it does not accurately represent it. I have introduced a measure of structure not present in the original code to provide a clearer understanding of the sequence of operations.

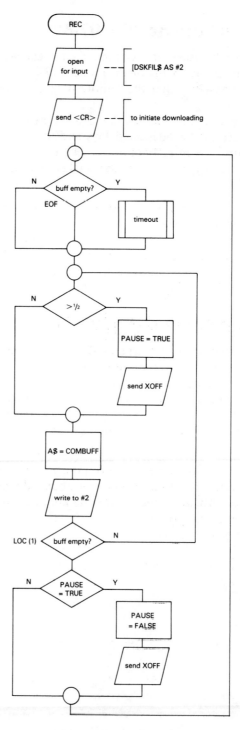

Figure U7-6   File Receive Routine

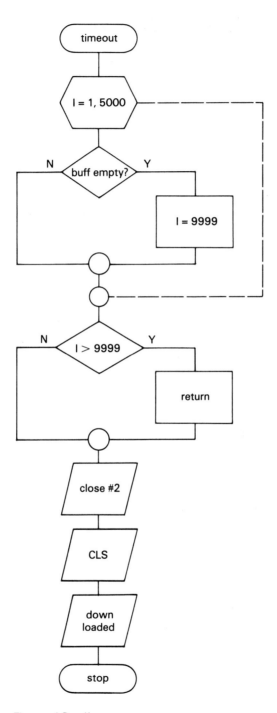

Figure U7-7 Timeout Routine

THE COMM.BAS PROGRAM (fig. U7-8)

COMM.BAS is a communications program provided by IBM as part of the supplementary programs which accompany PC-DOS (fig. U7-8). The program provides a means of communicating with:

> Dow Jones/News Retrieval
> IBM Personal Computer
> Series 1
> The Source
> Other services

```
1 REM The IBM Personal Computer Comm

2 REM Version 1.10 (C)Copyright IBM Corp 1981, 1982

3 REM Licensed Material - Program Property of IBM

4 REM Author - M. C. Rojas

10 KEY OFF: SCREEN 0,0: WIDTH 40: COLOR 7,0: CLS:POKE 106,0

11 FOR I=1 TO 10:KEY I,"":NEXT

12 CLOSE: DEFINT A-Z: FALSE=0: TRUE=NOT FALSE: XOFF$=CHR$(19):
XON$=CHR$(17):ON ERROR GOTO 460:T=0:ECH$=""

15 DEF SEG=0: IF (PEEK(&H410) AND &H30)=&H30 THEN WIDTH 80:T=20:
MODE$="b":DEF SEG:GOTO 30

16 FOR I=1 TO 10:KEY I,"":NEXT

17 LOCATE 25,10+T/2:PRINT"F1 = 40 COLUMN        F2 = 80 COLUMN"

18 DEF SEG

30 WIDTH "com1:",255:DEF SEG

40 LOCATE 2: PRINT TAB(10+T) "COMMUNICATIONS MENU"

50 LOCATE 6,3+T: PRINT "Choose one of the following:"

60 LOCATE 9,10+T: PRINT "1 Description of program"

70 PRINT TAB(10+T) "2 Dow Jones/News Retrieval"

80 PRINT TAB(10+T) "3 IBM Personal Computer"

90 PRINT TAB(10+T) "4 Series/1"

100 PRINT TAB(10+T) "5 THE SOURCE"
```

(Continued)

Figure U7-8   COMM.BAS Listing

```
110 PRINT TAB(10+T) "6 Other service"
115 PRINT TAB(10+T) "7 End program"
120 LOCATE 18: PRINT SPACE$(40+T): LOCATE 18,3+T,1:PRINT "choice";
122 A$=INKEY$ A$="" THEN 122
123 IF LEN(A$)=1 THEN LT=VAL(A$):GOTO 130
124 IF MODE$="b" THEN LT=0:GOTO 130
125 B$=MID$(A$,2,1)
126 IF ASC(B$)=59 THEN WIDTH 40:T=0:CLS:GOTO 17 ELSE IF ASC(B$)=60
THEN WIDTH 80:T=20:CLS:GOTO 17 ELSE LT=0:GOTO 130
12/ GOTO 122
130 IF LT=7 THEN CLS: PRINT TAB(10+T) "- COMMUNICATION ENDED -": END
ELSE IF (LT=2 OR LT=4 OR LT=5) THEN 230 ELSE IF LT=1 THEN GOSUB 530:
GOTO 10:ELSE IF (LT<1 OR LT>7) THEN FL=1: PRINT:
PRINT TAB(3+T) "Invalid choice, try again"
140 IF FL=1 THEN FOR I=1 TO 2,00: NEXT: LOCATE 19:
PRINT SPACE$(40+T):FL=0: GOTO 120
145 CLS: LOCATE 1,10+T: PRINT "USER DEFINED LINK":
IF LT=3 THEN LOCATE ,3+T: PRINT "TO ANOTHER IBM PERSONAL COMPUTER"
150 LOCATE 4,3+T,1:PRINT "BAUD RATE ";:GOSUB 465: SPEED$=B$
160 LOCATE 5,3+T,1:PRINT "PARITY ";:GOSUB 465: PARITY$=B$
170 LOCATE 6,3+T,1:PRINT "NUMBER OF BITS PER CHARACTER ";:
GOSUB 465:BITS$=B$
180 LOCATE 7,3+T,1:PRINT "NUMBER OF STOP BITS ";:GOSUB 465: STP$=B$
185 LOCATE 8,3+T,1:PRINT "CHARACTERS ECHOED TO SCREEN (Y/N) ";:
GOSUB 465: ECH$=B$
190 LOCATE 10,3+T,1: PRINT "Data entered correctly (Y/N) ";:
GOSUB 465:CR$=B$
200 IF CR$="N" OR CR$="n" THEN 145 ELSE GOSUB 480
210 LOCATE 21,3:COMFIL$="COM1:"+SPEED$+","+PARITY$+","+BITS$+","+STP$
220 OPEN COMFIL$ AS #1
230 IF LT=4 THEN NM$="Series/1":GOSUB 470:OPEN "com1:300,e,7,2" AS 1
240 IF LT=2 THEN NM$="Dow Jones News/Retrieval":GOSUB 470:
OPEN "com1:300,e,7" AS 1
```

(Continued)

```
250 IF LT=5 THEN NM$="THE SOURCE":GOSUB 470:OPEN "com1:300,e,7" AS 1
260 OPEN "SCRN:" FOR OUTPUT AS #2
270 LOCATE ,,1
280 PAUSE=FALSE:ON ERROR GOTO 460
290 B$=INKEY$ B$="" THEN 320
300 IF LEN(B$)>1 THEN IF ASC(MID$(B$,2,1))=68 THEN 450 ELSE 320 ELSE
IF B$=CHR$(8) THEN LOCATE ,POS(0)-1,1:PRINT " ";:LOCATE ,POS(0)-1,1
310 PRINT #1,B$;: IF ECH$="Y" OR ECH$="y" THEN PRINT#2,B$;
320 IF EOF(1) THEN 290
330 IF LOC(1)>128 THEN PAUSE=TRUE:PRINT#1,XOFF$;
340 A$=INPUT$(LOC(1),#1)
360 FOR I=1 TO LEN(A$)
370 IF (ASC(MID$(A$,I,1))<31 AND MID$(A$,I,1)<>CHR$(13)) OR
MID$(A$,I,1)=CHR$(127) THEN 410
380 IF MID$(A$,I,1)=CHR$(10) THEN MID$(A$,I,1)=" "
400 PRINT MID$(A$,I,1);
410 NEXT I
420 IF LOC(1)>0 THEN 290
430 IF PAUSE THEN PAUSE=FALSE:PRINT#1,XON$;
440 GOTO 290
450 POKE 106,0: CLOSE: ON ERROR GOTO 0: GOTO 10
460 IF ERR=68 THEN CLS:LOCATE 12,8+T:PRINT "THIS PROGRAM REQUIRES THE":
PRINT TAB(3+T) "ASYNCHRONOUS COMMUNICATIONS ADAPTER.": END
461 IF ERR=24 THEN CLS:
LOCATE 12,,1:PRINT "A DEVICE TIMEOUT ERROR HAS OCCURRED.":
PRINT "MAKE SURE THE HARDWARE IS CORRECTLY":
PRINT "SET UP, THEN PRESS ENTER.";:GOSUB 465: CLS:RESUME
462 RESUME
465 A$="":B$="":CR$="": WHILE A$<>CHR$(13)
466 A$=INKEY$: IF A$="" THEN 466 ELSE IF LEN(A$)>1 THEN
IF ASC(MID$(A$,2,1))=68 THEN 450 ELSE 466: ELSE IF A$<>CHR$(8) THEN
PRINT A$;: ELSE LOCATE ,POS(0)-1,1:PRINT " ";:LOCATE ,POS(0)-1,1:
B$=MID$(B$,1,LEN(B$)-1)
```

(Continued)

```
467 IF A$<>CHR$(13) AND A$<>CHR$(8) THEN B$=B$+A$
468 WEND:RETURN
470 CLS: LOCATE 1,12+T: PRINT NM$:PRINT
480 PRINT:PRINT:PRINT TAB(3+T) "- Place your call, and insert the"
490 PRINT TAB(3+T) " phone receiver into the modem, or"
495 PRINT TAB(3+T) " switch your data set from talk to"
500 PRINT TAB(3+T) " data. Then press ENTER to begin.   ": PRINT: PRINT
510 PRINT TAB(3+T) "-PRESS F10 TO GO TO MENU":PRINT
512 GOSUB 465
515 RETURN
530 CLS: LOCATE 1,15+T: PRINT "DESCRIPTION"
540 LOCATE 4,3+T: PRINT "An asynchronous communication link"
550 PRINT TAB(3+T) "will be established between the"
560 PRINT TAB(3+T) "selected service and the"
570 PRINT TAB(3+T) "IBM PERSONAL COMPUTER, as follows:"
580 LOCATE 9,3+T: PRINT "Baud rate";TAB(13+T)"300"
590 PRINT TAB(3+T) "Parity";TAB(14+T)"E"
600 PRINT TAB(3+T) "Data bits";TAB(14+T);"7
610 PRINT TAB(3+T) "Stop bits";TAB(14+T);"1  Dow Jones, THE SOURCE"
620 PRINT TAB(14+T) "2  Series/1"
630 LOCATE 15,3+T: PRINT "Options 3 and 6 allow for the above"
640 PRINT TAB(3+T) "characteristics to be supplied by"
650 PRINT TAB(3+T) "the user to define a communication"
660 PRINT TAB(3+T) "link to other services or computers."
661 IF MODE$="b" THEN 670
665 LOCATE 20,3+T: PRINT "You can select 40 column display or"
666 PRINT TAB(3+T) "80 column display by pressing F1 or"
667 PRINT TAB(3+T) "F2 before selecting menu choice."
670 LOCATE 24,3+T: PRINT "PRESS ANY KEY TO GO TO MENU";
671 CR$=INKEY$ CR$="" THEN 671 ELSE RETURN
```

Components

The design of the communications handling code appears to be based on the simple TTY program discussed previously. It can be divided into the following units.

Line No. From To	Purpose
1—200	Initialization and Option selection
210—280	OPEN statements
290—310	Keyboard Routine (fig. U7-9a)
320—440	Communication Buffer Routine (fig. U7-9b,c)
450—462	Termination and error handling
465—468	Building COMFIL$ for OPEN
480—510	Connection instructions
530—671	Program documentation

Improvements

The COMM.BAS program is more sophisticated and complex than the TTY program. Its improvements include:

- — menu driven selection of standard remote connections;
- — collection of OPEN statement parameters on-line;
  - baud rate,
  - parity,
  - number of bits,
  - number of stop bits,
  - echo requirements;
- — error handling routines; and
- — program documentation.

In the terminal emulation part of the program, improvements include:

- — checking for PF10 as a way of terminating the program,
- — creating a destructive backspace if backspace character is entered,
- — ignoring carriage returns and deletes sent by the remote station, and
- — converting line feeds sent by remote station into blanks.

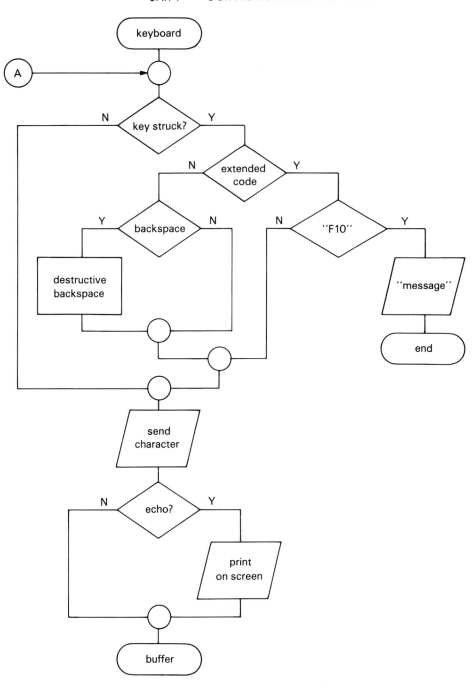

Figure U7-9a   Keyboard Routine (COMM.BAS)

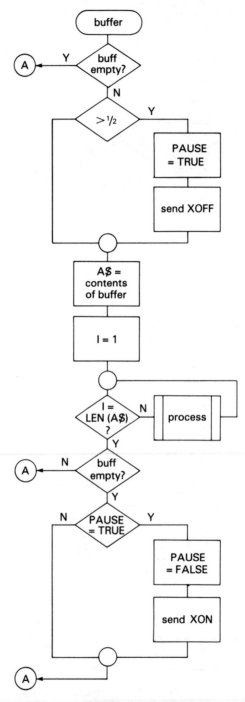

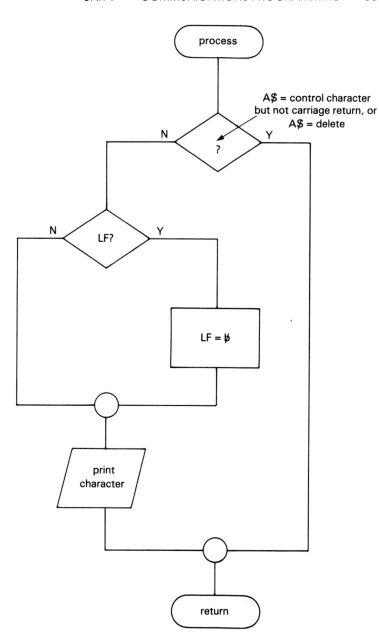

Figure U7-9c   Communication Buffer Routine Process (COMM.BAS)

Problems

The program still has problems from a communication-handling perspective:

— the program is limited to 300 bps transfer because it is so slow;
— the program cannot be compiled because of line 450 (POKE 106,0);
— the backspace technique does not always work, for example, right after a carriage return; and
— each character received from the remote is printed individually. This contributes to the low speed performance.

FULL-DUPLEX COMMUNICATION PROGRAM (IMPROVED)

The full-duplex program can be improved in three areas: user friendliness, flexibility, and speed. Speed can be improved by concentrating on the central portion of the code, which contains keyboard servicing and communication buffer servicing and which makes this code more efficient. The flexibility and user friendliness can best be implemented by means of parameter choice, progress information, and information clean-up.

Parameter Choices

The program starts with a title printed on the screen followed by a data collection routine to establish:

Speed (bps),
Number of bits per character,
Parity (O, E, M, S, N),
Number of stop bits, and
Communication port (1 or 2).

This data is used in the OPEN statement. As soon as the OPEN statement is executed, the size of the communication buffer can be measured using LOF.

Progress Information

Although the default size of the communication buffer is 256 it can be useful in some situations, particularly at higher speeds, to expand this to 1024 or 2048 characters. Since the INPUT$ command used to extract information from the buffer transfers its contents to a variable and the variable size limit is 256, it is necessary to define the following variables to monitor the communication buffer.

BEFORE%=the space available in the buffer before the INPUT$ is executed.

AFTER%=space available in the buffer after the INPUT$ is executed.

BUFF%=size of the buffer established during GWBASIC initialization.

HALF%=BUFF% /2 to test whether to send XOFF or not.

An opportune time to display these variables occurs when the number of characters in the buffer is checked. If the buffer is greater than half-full (warranting the sending of XOFF) the progress information can be displayed.

Information Clean-up

The following characters should be extracted from the input string:

   SOH, LF, XON, XOFF, RS, and DEL

The backspace character that causes problems in BASIC should be replaced by a cursor-left character.

   A two-character code, signifying termination, may be tested for in the input routine. The sample terminal emulation lab on p. 000 provides an opportunity to incorporate these ideas into a full-duplex communication program using GWBASIC.

HALF-DUPLEX COMMUNICATION PROGRAM

Half-duplex programming normally refers to the use of a half-duplex protocol on a full-duplex line (a four-wire line or modem capability for full-duplex on two wires). The major distinction between full- and half-duplex operation is that only transmission or reception can occur at any instant in time for half-duplex communication. A major preoccupation is the transfer of control between the terminal and the remote device and this is accomplished by means of a turnaround character which is not necessarily the same for both devices. The turnaround character transmitted is called the outbound turnaround character; the turnaround character received is called the inbound turnaround character.

   The half-duplex program has two modes, transmit and receive. When in the transmit mode, there is no information flow from the remote device until the terminal gives up control of the line by sending the outbound turnaround character. Conversely, in the receive mode, keyboard input will not be transmitted until reception of the inbound turnaround character

Communications Handling

The inbound and outbound characters are defined. The receive flag is set and the receive sub-routine called. On return from the receive routine, the receive flag is RESET and the transmit (keyboard) routine called. This process is repeated (fig. U7-10).

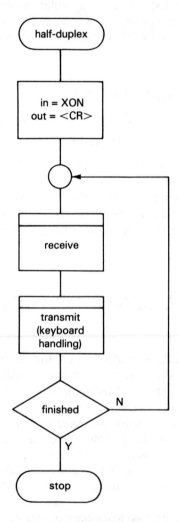

Figure U7-10   Outline Flowchart for Half-Duplex Program

INTERRUPTS

The previously described programs are completely devoted to data communication. There are often requirements for programs that perform other functions, for example, problem solving while handling the data communication chores.

There are two fundamental ways in which a computer operates in a multi-service environment. One is by polling, that is, the computer checks with each device in turn to see whether that device requires servicing, for example, the multipoint configuration of distance networks, the star configuration of local area networks. The two previous communication programs, TTY and COMM both operate this way (fig. U7-11).

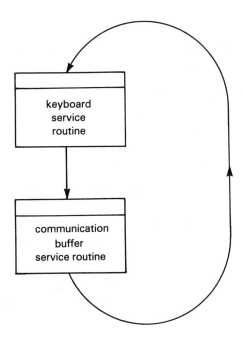

Figure U7-11   Polling

Another way to approach the problem is by using interrupt-driven software. When a remote device requires service, it takes the initiative and sends an interrupt to the computer, which can either service that interrupt immediately or, in more complex systems, apply a rating or priority to the particular interrupt to distinguish it from all other interrupts. For example, peripheral devices such as disk storage, terminals, and the operator's console are interrupt-driven in a mainframe installation.

In the bus LAN configuration a work station "grabs" the bus to communicate with another work station. It cannot interrupt another work station, but it does take the initiative. It is not polled.

GWBASIC provides statements that allow communications programs to interrupt other program functions so that they need only be invoked when information is being received from a remote device. The statements that provide this capability are:

1. COMM(<n>) ON   To enable or disable trapping
    COMM(<n>) OFF   of communication activity to
    COMM(<n>) STOP   a serial port.

ON—allows trapping *
  *Every time GWBASIC starts a new statement it checks to see if any characters have come into the specified port n (usually 1 or 2).

OFF—inhibits trapping and forgets if it does take place.

STOP—inhibits trapping but remembers it for use when an ON occurs. (Prevents nested interrupts).

2. ON COMM(<n>) GOSUB <line number>

Sets up a line number for GWBASIC to trap to when there is information coming into the buffer.

A COM STOP is automatically issued immediately before entering an event trapping routine. A COM ON is automatically executed on exiting an event trapping routine (if there is no COM OFF in the program in effect).

These instructions permit GWBASIC to process an application in the "foreground" and monitor the reception of data from a remote device in the "background" (fig. U7-12).

```
10   'A BASIC PROGRAM FOR UPDATING
20   'AN INVENTORY CONTROL SYSTEM
30   'WHILE ACCEPTING INFORMATION
40   'FOR NEWDATA file from a
50   'REMOTE TERMINAL
60   COM ON
70   ON COM GOSUB 1000
80   'INVENTORY SYSTEM
```

```
          ''
          ''
          ''
          ''
          ''
 900   END
1000   'SERVICE ROUTINE FOR COMMUNICATION
1010   'INTERRUPTS TO TRANSFER DATA
1020   'TO FILE NEWDATA'
1030
          ''
          ''
          ''
          ''
          ''
1200   RETURN.
```

Figure U7-12   Foreground/Background Program

HARDWARE PROGRAMMING

Although terminal emulation and file transfer programs written in BASIC may be complex, they are not difficult to write. The addition of routines to make the program more friendly, by inputting such communication parameters as speed and parity, increases the amount of code. The complexity of the software is increased by defining functions and special keys that:

— transmit a hardware break signal to the remote device,
— display arriving data,
— write all received data to a file,
— print received data, and
— use line 25 on the screen for progress monitoring.

Nevertheless, at the heart of the matter is a relatively simple routine which monitors the keyboard and the communication buffer and displays/prints/stores information. The next step to a fuller understanding of communication software is to study the USART (used for asynchronous transmission in this context), the way it connects the computer to the outside world, and how to program it.

USART Hardware

The USART is typically a 40-pin integrated circuit chip. It therefore has 40 possible signals going to or coming from it. The USART contains gates which perform the same logic functions that programmers use, for example, AND,

OR, NOT. The only difference is that these functions are implemented by circuitry. In fact, of course, the programmer's logical statements are eventually converted into signals and the results achieved by using the same switching circuits. The other major component within the USART is the storage device. This is familiar to the assembly language programmer using registers to index or accumulate or temporarily store information. The USART holds data, control information and status information in these registers. It is programmed by setting values into these registers that select from options to enable the USART to perform in a certain way.

The NEC MPD7201

The Multiprotocol Serial Communications Controller (MPSCC) is typical of the USARTs used in standard 16-bit microcomputers. The MPSCC receiver reverses the process performed by the transmitter. It converts the serial data from the remote device to parallel data for the microcomputer. The processor interface comes between the transmitter/receiver sections and the microcomputer bus (the main information highway for the microcomputer). It performs four functions:

1. Bus control logic determines the source, destination, and direction of data and control transfers between the MPSCC and the microcomputer bus.

2. The interrupt control logic determines whether to accept an interrupt and, if so, issues an interrupt signal to the microcomputer. It contains all the logic necessary for *two* complete full-duplex serial communication channels (fig. U7-13). Each channel consists of a transmitter section and a receiver section. A common processor interface section connects the MPSCC to the microcomputer.

   The MPSCC transmitter performs all the functions necessary to convert parallel data to the appropriate serial bit streams (dependent on the protocol requirements). Data flows through the transmitter from the internal bus, to a buffer register and finally to the shift register used for sending the data to the remote device (least significant bit first).

3. The DMA control logic is used to avoid interrupting the processor to make a data transfer. The data is moved directly from the MPSCC to the microcomputer memory, or vice versa.

4. The clock and reset logic controls the timing in the MPSCC and is usually connected to the microcomputer clock. The reset function is used to reset the MPSCC to its initial state, for example at power-up time.

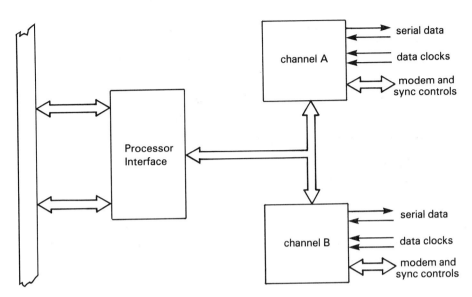

Figure U7-13 USART Block Diagram

Programming the USART

Prior to developing complete programs for the USART we need to consider some specific problems:

1. memory-mapped input/output,
2. the control and status registers,
3. programming the clock, and
4. programming the status register.

MEMORY-MAPPED INPUT/OUTPUT

The microprocessor (the heart of the microcomputer) usually communicates with the USART by means of memory-mapped input/output (I/0) programming. This refers to the concept of providing physical memory locations to represent the USART data, status, and control registers. For example the hexadecimal address E0040 in the computer's main memory is the location that is used to program the data register for channel A in the MPSCC. By writing a value to that memory address we effectively send that data to the remote device. When we read the contents of that memory address we are reading the contents of the data register for channel A in the MPSCC. In other words we are reading the data sent by the remote device. When we should be storing (transmitting) and when we should be reading (receiving) depends on how we've programmed the USART.

The BASIC statement to write a byte to a memory location is:

> POKE n,m where
> n   must be between 0 and 65535, and
> m   is the data to be written to that location.

The BASIC statement to read a byte from a memory location is:

> PEEK(n)
> n   must be between 0 and 65535

Since the range of values of n will not extend to the range of memory locations in a typical microcomputer, n is referred to as the relative address. The address represented by n is relative to a segment pointer that establishes which segment in memory you are dealing with. The segment pointer is programmed using:

> DEF SEG = <address>

So, for example, to send an ASCII code of x (58 hexadecimal) to the remote device we would execute the following:

> DEF SEG = &HE004   'initialize the segment pointer
> POKE 0, &H58   'write an X in E0040 which means
>   send it to the remote device.

In another example, if the data port for channel B is E0041, read the value sent by the remote device:

> DEF SEG = &HE004   'initialize segment pointer
> PEEK (1)   'read the contents of E0041.

CONTROL AND STATUS REGISTERS

There are seven control registers and three status registers for each channel in the MPSCC (fig. U7-14). We are primarily interested in Control Register

> 0   for register pointer control
> 3   for receiver control
> 4   for mode control
> 5   for transmitter control

and Status Register

> 0   for monitoring transmit and receive status.

CONTROL REGISTER	FUNCTION
0	FREQUENTLY USED COMMANDS AND REGISTER POINTER CONTROL
1	INTERRUPT CONTROL
2	PROCESSOR/BUS INTERFACE CONTROL
3	RECEIVER CONTROL
4	MODE CONTROL
5	TRANSMITTER CONTROL
6	SYNC/ADDRESS CHARACTER
7	SYNC CHARACTER

STATUS REGISTER	FUNCTION
0	BUFFER AND "EXTERNAL/STATUS" STATUS
1	RECEIVED CHARACTER ERROR AND SPECIAL CONDITION STATUS
2 (CHANNEL B ONLY)	INTERRUPT VECTOR

Figure U7-14 Control and Status Registers

Interrupt Control (Register 1), Processor/Bus Interface Control (Register 2), Synchronous Control (Register 6 and 7), Error Conditions and Interrupt Vectors (Status Register 1 and 2) are beyond the scope of this text. The addresses used for the data, control, and status registers for the MPSCC are listed in figure U7-15.

The rotating file is the manual equivalent of programming the control and status registers. In the days before computers, a manual filing system would be placed in the center of an office with desks ringing the filing system (fig.U7-16). To obtain a particular client's file, the desk clerk would spin the rotating file till the appropriate slot appeared and extract the desired file. The rotating file would then return to its initial position.

Control Register 0 is used to select another control register as if you were dialing another slot in the rotating file, for example, to program the mode control register (Register 4) we must first obtain Control Register O.

DEF SEG = &HE004   'Set up the segment pointer for the control and status registers of channel A.

Location	Function
E0040	Data Port for channel A
E0041	Data Port for channel B
E0042	Control/Status port for channel A
E0043	Control/Status port for channel B
E0023	Baud Rate Clock control
	– use value 36h for channel A
	– use value 76h for channel B

Figure U7-15   MPSCC Addresses

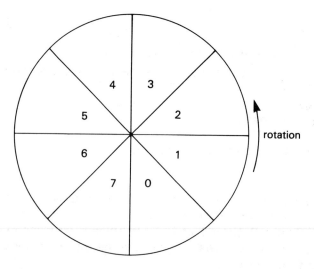

Figure U7-16   The Rotating File

POKE 2,4   'Set register pointer in control register 0 to 4.
POKE 2,value   'write value to control register 4.

This intermediate step must be performed prior to accessing any of the control registers (1-7) and any of the status registers (1-2) (fig. U7-17).

TRANSMITTER CONTROL AND STATUS REGISTERS

CONTROL REGISTER	D_7	D_6	D_5	D_4	D_3	D_2	D_1	D_0
0	CRC CONTROL		COMMAND			REGISTER POINTER		
1							Trans. Int Enable	Ext/Status Int Enable
4	Clock Mode		Sync Format Select		Sync/Async Mode Select		0-ODD 1-EVEN	PARITY ENABLE
5	DTR	Bits/Char		Send Break	Transmitter Enable	CRC Type	RTS	CRC Enable
6	SYNC 1							
7	SYNC 2							
3	NO. OF BITS/ CHARACTER		Auto Enables					RECEIVE ENABLE

STATUS REGISTER	D_7	D_6	D_5	D_4	D_3	D_2	D_1	D_0
0		Trans Underrun/ EOM	CTS			Trans Buffer Empty		REC CHAR AVAIL
1								All Async Characters Sent

RECEIVE

D_7	D_6	BITS/CHARACTER
0	0	5
0	1	7
1	0	6
1	1	8

TRANSMIT

D_6	D_5	BITS/CHARACTER
0	0	5 OR LESS (SEE BELOW)
0	1	7
1	0	6
1	1	8

CLOCK

D_7	D_6	CLOCK RATE
0	0	CLOCK RATE = 1× DATA RATE
0	1	CLOCK RATE = 16× DATA RATE
1	0	CLOCK RATE = 32× DATA RATE
1	1	CLOCK RATE = 64× DATA RATE

STOP BITS

D_3	D_2	MODE
0	0	SYNCHRONOUS MODES
0	1	ASYNCHRONOUS 1 BIT TIME (1 STOP BIT)
1	0	ASYNCHRONOUS 1 1/2 BIT TIMES (1 1/2 STOP BITS)
1	1	ASYNCHRONOUS 2 BIT TIMES (2 STOP BITS)

Figure U7-17 Control and Status Register Functions

PROGRAMMING THE CLOCK

The baud rate is programmed by inserting a 16-bit (2-byte) number into location E0020. The two bytes are entered sequentially, first the high byte, then the low byte (fig.U7-18).

Prior to programming the baud rate the appropriate clock for either channel A or channel B must be selected by setting E0023 to 36 hexadecimal for channel A, or 76 hexadecimal for Channel B. To program channel A for 1200 baud we use the following code:

```
DEF SEG = &HE002          'initialize the pointer
POKE 3, &H36              'select channel A
POKE 0,40                 'load the high byte
POKE 0,0                  'load the low byte
```

Rate	MSB	LSB
300	0	1
600	80	0
1200	40	0
2400	20	0
4800	10	0
9600	8	0
19200	4	0

Figure U7-18   Baud Rate Table

PROGRAMMING THE STATUS REGISTER

Since the microcomputer and the remote device are operating independently of each other, it is important to be able to establish when the USART is ready to transmit (Transmitter Buffer Empty signal equals a 1, Bit 2 in Status Register 0) and when the USART has received a character which is available for the processor to read (Received Character Available signal equals a 1, Bit 0 in status register 0). These bits may be checked using a mask and the AND function, for example:

```
TRANS = TRANS AND 4
IF TRANS THEN
    POKE DATAPORT, ASC(X$)
```

transmits a character if bit 2 of the status register (TRANS) is set to "1".

BASIC EXERCISE

1. What three functions are performed by a terminal emulation program?

2. Write the statement to program the PF5 key to LAB5<CR>

3. a) Write the statement to print out the number of bytes in BASIC's data space that are not being used.
   b) What other important function does this statement perform?

4. Write a program to accept a keystroke, identify the number of characters in the keystroke, and print the results of the keystroke in the form *<keystroke>*

5. Write a program to clear the screen, move the cursor to the center of the screen and print in reverse video the message.

   "THIS IS THE CENTRE OF THE SCREEN"

   "THE CURSOR IS NOW IN POSITION X, Y"

   "WHERE X IS THE ROW POSITION"

   "Y IS THE COLUMN POSITION"

6. Write a program to print a character string and then delete it.

7. Write the command line to run a MENU.BAS program in GWBASIC to access 5 files with a maximum record length for random files of 80 bytes and a communications buffer of 4096 bytes.

8. Write the statement that transfers the contents of the communications buffer to a variable X$ (up to a maximum of 256 characters). Assume the communications buffer has been designated file 1.

USART EXERCISE

1. Using the USART reference material, write the code to program the USART control registers for channel A as follows:

   a) set register 3 to receive 5 bits per character;

   b) set register 4 for a clock rate of 32x, with 1½ stop bits and odd parity; and

   c) set register 5 to transmit 5 bits.

2. Modify the program supplied in figure U1-9b to print the decimal code, the hexadecimal code, and the symbolic representation of each character transmitted.

LABORATORY

TERMINAL EMULATION

Objective

Upon completion of this lab you should be able to:
• Write a full-duplex emulator.

Purpose

To reinforce the concepts of terminal emulation by providing practical experience in writing a full-duplex emulator in BASIC.

Processing

1. The program must handle full-duplex communication.

2. It must allow for selection of communication speed, parity, and communication port. Speeds can range from 300 to 9600 bps with a default of 1200 bps. Parity can be space, odd, mark, even, or no parity with a default of even. The port can be either 1 or 2, with a default of 1.

3. Received data may contain extra non-display characters that must be removed or modified. Eliminate all SOH, XON, XOFF, RS and DEL characters. Replace all backspace characters with cursor left characters.

4. Because BASIC has problems in a communications environment with displaying information, the Print Received Data routine is supplied. It handles the correct positioning of the data to be displayed, which is complicated by extra or missing LF and CR characters and by lines that overflow the physical line limits.

5. The program must monitor the keyboard and transmit keyboard input to the remote device.

6. A flag must be maintained that indicates whether the remote device should transmit or not. The flag is set when the communications buffer is more than half full and reset when the buffer is empty. An appropriate XON or XOFF must be transmitted in conjunction with the setting of this flag.

7. A good time to clean up memory on a regular basis would be upon input of a CR from the keyboard.

8. Use TYPETERM as the terminal type when connecting to the mainframe.

9. Figure U7-19 is an outline flowchart.

10. Figure U7-20 is a listing of a print-received data routine.

Lab Requirement

1. Demo to instructor.
   Starting with a switched off microcomputer, the student must:

   a) bring the system up,
   b) activate the modem,
   c) run the terminal emulation program,
   d) sign on to the mainframe computer using personal ID and password, and
   e) demonstrate full working of the program by listing his/her mainframe files.

2. Documentation.

   a) the supplied lab specification,
   b) a listing of the program including comments, and
   c) a discussion that identifies problems that occurred and their solution as well as any distinctive features of the solution.

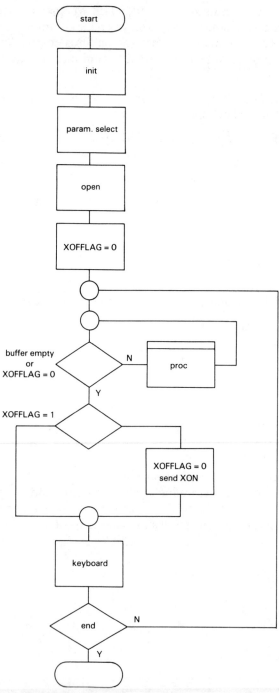

Figure U7-19 Outline Flowchart for Full-Duplex Program (sample terminal emulation lab)

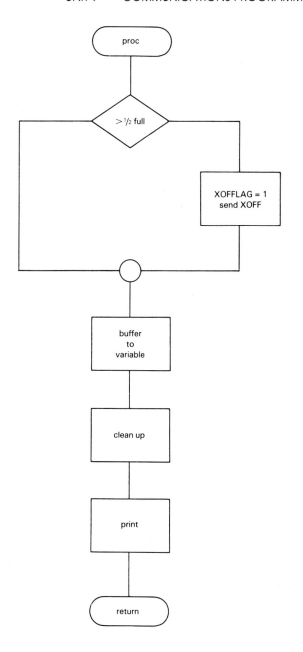

Figure U7-19 (cont.)

INITIALIZATION AT BEGINNING OF PROGRAM

1000 RT$=CHR$(13):CR%=−1

PRINT-RECEIVED DATA ROUTINE

```
2000    C%=POS(0):L%=LEN(C$)
2010    IF (CR%=0 AND LEFT$(C$,1)=RT$) THEN C$=RIGHT$(C$,L%−1)
2020    CR%=−1
2030    IF (C%+L%)<=81 THEN 2090
2040       I%=81−C%:L$=LEFT$(C$,I%):PRINT L$;
2050       C$=RIGHT$(C$,L%−I%):CR%=INSTR(1,L$,RT$)
2060       IF (CR%=0 AND LEFT$(C$,1)=RT$) THEN C$=RIGHT$(C$,L%−1)
2070       CR%=−1
2080       C%=POS(0):L%=LEN(C$):GOTO 2030
2090    PRINT C$;:IF (C%+L%)=81 THEN CR%=INSTR(1,C$,RT$)
2100    RETURN
```

EXPLANATION OF PRINT-RECEIVED DATA ROUTINE

C$ is the string of characters that has been received from the communications buffer.

IF a return has been printed AND
  first character of C$ is a return, THEN
    strip off the return
Set flag to indicate a return hasn't been printed
WHILE (cursor position + length of C$) > 81
  calculate I (number of characters that will fit from current
    position to end)
  print the leftmost I characters of C$
  set C$ = remaining characters that haven't been printed
  IF a return has been printed AND
    1st character of C$ is a return, THEN
      strip off the return
  Set flag to indicate a return hasn't been printed
WEND
print C$
IF (cursor position + length of C$) = 81 THEN
  set flag to indicate whether or not a return has been printed.

Figure U7-20   Print-received Data Routine (terminal emulation lab)

LABORATORY

THE USART

Objectives

Upon completion of this lab, you should be able to:
• demonstrate an understanding of hardware programming;

- gain exposure to the simplest form of data transmission: byte transfer;
- code a USART initialize routine; and
- code a program in BASIC that will perform simple data transmission without protocol. Use the PEEK/POKE/INKEY$/AND commands of BASIC.

Purpose

To provide insight into the communications process at its lowest level. The USART converts one character at a time from parallel to serial form for transmission and converts the incoming serial pulses to characters. The USART routines are central to all communications software.

Processing

Code the supplied flowchart (fig. U7-21). The use and purpose of each sub-routine is as follows:

a) Initialize—use this routine to set the USART as follows:

- 8 data bits per word,
- no parity,
- set the baud rate to 1200 baud.

b) Transmit—this subroutine is called to wait until the USART is ready to transmit a character, then to transmit it.
   —the character to be sent should be stored in a variable named SEND$.

c) Receive—this routine is called to check if a character has been received. If a character is waiting, it is printed.
   —the received character should be stored in a variable named RECEIVE$.

Lab Requirement

To test your send/receive program use two microcomputers that are connected by an RS-232-C cable.

a) Run your program on one computer, and ASYNC in the terminal mode at 1200 baud on the other. Type characters on the keyboard of the computer running your program and see that they appear on the screen of

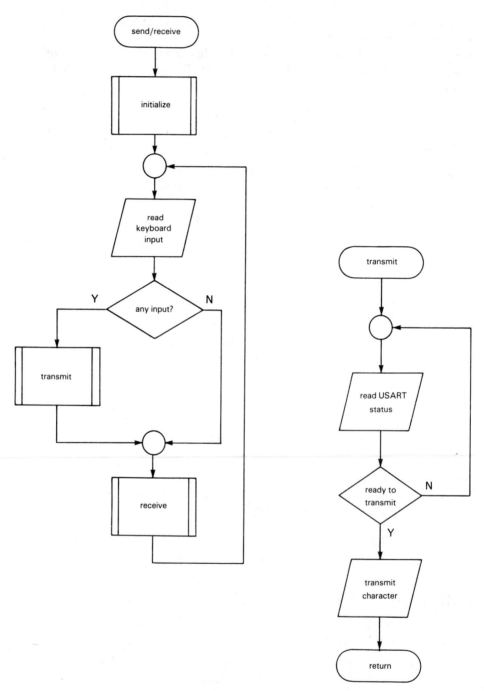

Figure U7-21   Mainline, Transmit, and Receive Routines (USART lab)

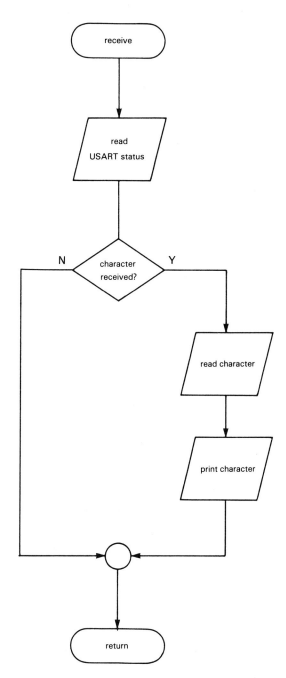

Figure U7-21   (cont.)

the other. Now try the reverse, type on the computer running ASYNC and ensure that they appear on the screen of the computer running your program.

b) Run your program on both machines.

c) Demonstrate the running program to your instructor.

LABORATORY

FILE TRANSMISSION

Objectives

Upon completion of this lab, you should be able to:
- demonstrate an understanding of data communications concepts by coding a file transmission program using a simple protocol.
- gain exposure to error detection and recovery.
- construct a transmission packet and apply a simple checksum to it.

Purpose

To provide insight into the features of the file transfer process by dividing a file into packets and using the routines developed in the USART lab to send each packet, one character at a time.

Processing

1. Given the code for the INITIALIZE, WAIT, SEND, and RECEIVE routines (fig. U7-22), code the supplied flowchart (fig. U7-23) for the file transmission lab. The use and purpose of each of these routines is as follows:

a) INITIALIZE (entry line 20)   —used to initialize USART baud rate, number of bits per word, and no parity.

b) WAIT: (entry line 190)   —used to *wait* for a character from the receiving computer. If a character is received within the specified time it is returned in RECEIVE$, otherwise RECEIVE$ is null.

   —the only parameter passed to the routine is WAITSECONDS which is set to the maximum number of decimal seconds to WAIT.

```
10     GOTO 240
20     CONTROL=2
30     DATAPORT=0
40     DEF SEG = &HE002
50     POKE 3, &H36
60     POKE 0, 0
70     POKE 0, 1
80     DEF SEG = &HE004
90     POKE CONTROL, &H3
100    POKE CONTROL, &HC1
110    GOSUB 130
120    RETURN
130    STATUS=PEEK (CONTROL):STATUS=STATUS AND 1
140    IF STATUS
       THEN
         RECEIVE$=CHR$(PEEK(DATAPORT))
       ELSE
         RECEIVE$="  "
150    RETURN
160    STATUS=PEEK(CONTROL):STATUS=STATUS AND 4
170    IF STATUS
       THEN
         POKE DATAPORT, ASC(SEND$)
       ELSE
         GOTO 160
180    RETURN
190    FOR I=1 TO WAITSECONDS*50
200       GOSUB 130
210       IF LEN(RECEIVE$)>0
          THEN
            I=WAITSECONDS*51
220    NEXT I
230    RETURN
240       Your Code Begins Here On Line 240
```

Figure U7-22   Initialize, Wait, Send, and Receive Routines.

c) SEND: (entry line 160)   — the purpose of this routine is to send the single ASCII character contained in SEND$ to the receiving computer.
— when called, SEND$ should contain one character.

d) RECEIVE: (entry line 130)   — this routine is called to check whether a character has been sent from the receiving computer.
— if present, the character is placed in variable RECEIVE$, otherwise RECEIVE$ is null.

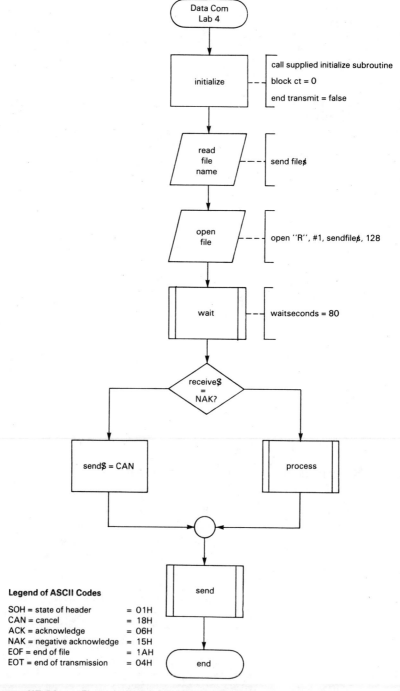

Legend of ASCII Codes

SOH = state of header = 01H
CAN = cancel = 18H
ACK = acknowledge = 06H
NAK = negative acknowledge = 15H
EOF = end of file = 1AH
EOT = end of transmission = 04H

Figure U7-23   Flowchart for Transmission Lab

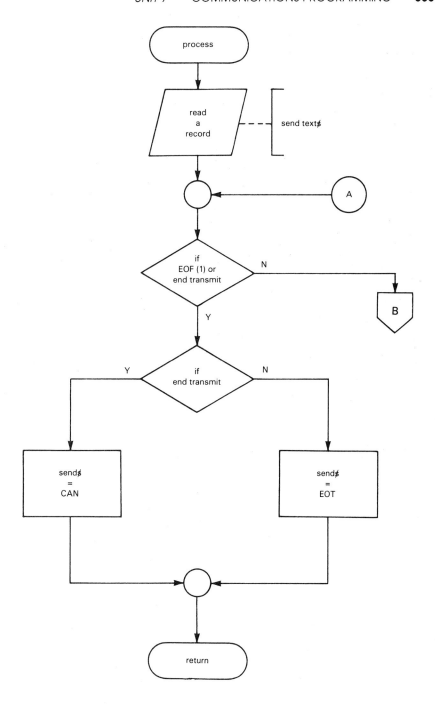

Figure U7-23   (cont.)

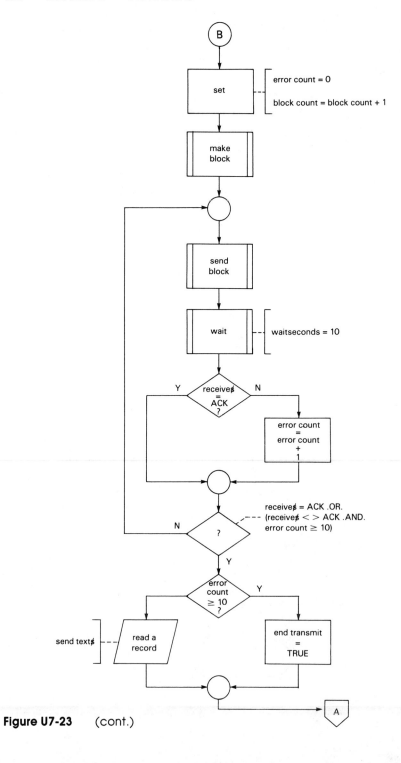

Figure U7-23   (cont.)

2. You are to flowchart, code, and supply the following two routines:

a) MAKE BLOCK
   —all blocks transmitted are a fixed length of 133 characters as follows:

SOH	BLOCK NO.	255— BLOCK NO.	TEXT	CHECK SUM	NAK

   —The purpose of this routine is to create the 133 Byte Block.

   The sum of these two numbers will always be 255

CHECKSUM is a one-byte value obtained by summing the ASCII values of the text and performing modulo arithmetic on the sum using 256 as the divisor.

b) SEND BLOCK

   The send block is called to transmit the block created by MAKE BLOCK. To accomplish this you must repeatedly call the supplied routine, SEND, with each successive character in the send block using a loop from 1 to the length of the string.

Lab Requirement

1. Use your transmit program to send a textual file to another microcomputer that is using ASYNC without CRC-16 error checking. Use TYPE to view the integrity of the transmitted file.
2. Introduce errors into the transmission by unplugging the cable between the two computers to ensure that the block resend feature works.
3. Send another file, this time the BASIC program that is the file transmit program. Run it on the receiving computer.
4. Demonstrate the transmit program to your instructor.

Note: The initialized subroutine should be executed on the receiving computer prior to running ASYNC, thus ensuring proper set-up for the USART.

338 SECTION C PRACTICAL

SECTION C: CONCLUSION

Section C provided you with the opportunity to test your understanding of the material in Section A. The sequencing of Section C was, for the most part, parallel to that of Section A. Deviations occurred at times to introduce new but related material, for example, electrical noise. The new material in Section C was added for the most part to support the laboratories, exercises, and demonstrations.

Other possibilities exist for practical learning experiences. A visit to a central office in your area will help to demystify the workings of the telephone system, particularly if the office still uses the older switching systems.

Our emphasis on communications software is important not only because software controls the hardware, but also because most analysts, programmers, and network users have more affinity with software. Just as in programming, we use languages that allow us to focus on the problem to be solved, so too, in data communication, it is more important to understand how the software controls the relationships between the components of a network than to grasp the details of how each component works.

The important conclusion to draw from using communications software and writing terminal emulation programs is that the software is no more obscure or difficult to understand than, for example, COBOL business programs.

Theoretically and from a didactic point of view, BASIC is a useful language for writing communication programs because it is well known and contains commands specifically designed for communications programming. In practice, however, and even in its compiled form, it is not used for this purpose because it is not fast enough. Most programs in the field of communications are actually written in assembly language or C.

APPENDIX A: ACRONYMS

ACF	advanced communication function
ACK	acknowledge
ACK0	acknowledge even blocks
ACK1	acknowledge odd blocks
APPC	advanced-program-to-program communication
ASCII	American standard code for information interchange
ATDM	asynchronous time division multiplexing
AT&T	American Telephone and Telegraph Company
BEP	back-end processor
BERT	bit error rate testing
BCC	block check character
BCD	binary coded decimal
BISYNC	binary synchronous communications protocol
BIT	binary digit
BLERT	block error rate testing
BOC	Bell Operating Company
BPS	bits per second
BSC	*see* BISYNC
CC	communication control characters
CCITT	Consultative Committee for International Telephony and Telegraphy
CICS	customer information control system
CODEC	coder/decoder
CNCP	Canadian National Canadian Pacific
CRC	cyclic redundancy check
CRF	central retransmission facility
CRT	cathode ray tube
CRTC	Canadian Radio Television and Telecommunication Commission
CSMA/CD	carrier sense multiple access/collision detection
CTS	clear to send
DAS	Datapac access software
DCD	data carrier detect
DCE	data communication equipment
DDB	distributed data base
DDBMS	distributed database management system
DDCMP	digital data communication message protocol
DELNI	digital ethernet local network interconnect
DEMPR	digital ethernet multiport repeater

DISC	disconnect
DLE	data link escape
DMA	direct memory access
DNA	Digital Network Architecture
DSA	Dataroute serving areas
DSP	display systems protocol
DTE	data terminal equipment
EBCDIC	extended binary-coded decimal interchange code
ECMA	European Computer Manufacturers' Association
EEPROM	electronically eraseable programmable read only memory
EIA	Electronic Industries Association
EOT	end of transmission
EP	emulation program
ENQ	enquiry
ETB	end of text block
ETX	end of text
FCC	Federal Communicatons Commission (USA)
FCS	frame check sequence
FDM	frequency division multiplexer
FE	format effector
FEP	front-end processor
HDLC	high level data link control
IRC	International Record Carriers
IS	information separators
ISDN	integrated services digital network
ISO	International Standards Organization
LAN	local area network
LCI	logical channel identifier
LDM	limited distance modem
LED	light emitting diode (a visual indicator)
LRC	longitudinal redundancy check
LU	logical unit
MAN	metropolitan area network
MAU	multistation access unit
MODEM	modulator/demodulator
MPSCC	multiprotocol serial communications controller
MSNF	multi-system network facility
NAK	negative acknowledge
NAU	network addressable unit
NCC	network control center
NCP	network control program
NMCC	network management control center

NPSI	NCP packet switching interface for X.25
NTO	network terminal option
OSI	open systems interconnection
PAD	packet assembly/disassembly
PAM	pulse amplitude modulation
PBX	private branch exchange
PCM	pulse code modulation
PDN	public data network
PEP	partitioned emulation program
PIU	path information unit
PSDN	packet switched data network
PSS	packet switch stream
PU	physical unit
QAM	quadrature amplitude modulation
RAPID	remote access protocol interface device
RH	request/response header
RTS	request to send
RU	request/response unit
SARM	set asynchronous response mode
SDLC	synchronous data link control
SHF	super high frequency
SOH	start of header
SNA	Systems Network Architecture
SP-1	stored program one
SSCP	system services control point
STDM	statistical time division multiplexing
STX	start of text
SYN	synchronization character
TCAM	telecommunication access method
TDM	time division multiplexer
TH	transmission header
TSO	time sharing option
TTY	teletype
T1	terrestrial digital circuit class one
UA	unnumbered acknowledge
USART	universal synchronous/asynchronous receiver/transmitter
VAN	value added network
VDT	video display terminal
VRC	vertical redundancy check
VTAM	virtual telecommunications access method
WAN	wide area network
WATS	wide area telecommunications access service

XOFF	transmit off
XON	transmit on
X.21	level one standard for X.25
X.25	an international standard packet-switching protocol
X.28	asynchronous terminal interface standard

NUMERICS (for IBM devices)

3174	subsystem control unit
3270	display terminal
3274	cluster control
3276	an integrated control and display unit
3278	monochrome display
3279	color graphics display
3299	terminal multiplexer
3705	communications controller
3725	communications controller

APPENDIX B: GLOSSARY

amplitude   (of a signal) the size of the signal, used to define the signal if it is known at all times.

amplitude modulation   a method of transmitting information by modulating it on the basis of size.

analog signal   a continuously changing signal which conveys information.

asynchronous   occurring without a regular or predictable time rate (refers to the lack of synchronization between characters transmitted).

bandwidth   the range of frequencies present in a signal or the capacity of a channel to transmit signals.

baseband transmission   transmitting a signal without modulation.

baud   the number of signal events per second.

baudot code   a five-bit code.

bit rate   the rate at which bits are transmitted over a channel.

break-out-box   a device which allows enabling, jumpering, crossing over, and bussing of interface signals.

broadband transmission   the modulation of several signals for simultaneous transmission over a channel.

byte   eight bits.

carrier   a sine wave whose attributes (amplitude, frequency, phase) are altered to facilitate analog transmission.

centralization   (of a database) one copy of the data resides at a central node.

central office   a telephone company switching center for subscriber line switching.

channel   a data communication path.

character   a member of a group of symbols used for the control and representation of data, for example, an ASCII character.

circuit switching   the establishment of the route between two DTEs using one or more physical switching centers.

coaxial cable (coax)   a communications medium consisting of a central insulated wire surrounded by a fine copper mesh and an outer insulated shield.

concentrator   an intelligent multiplexer.

Conference 600   Telecom Canada's colour video service.

contention   a protocol in which LAN nodes compete for control of the line on a first-come, first-served basis.

control node   a network node responsible for line control.

crosstalk   the unwanted transfer of a signal on one line to another line.

data communications   the transmission of computerized information between nodes in a data communications network.

data communications network   a collection of computers, terminals, and related devices connected by communications facilities.

data processing   the conversion of raw data to useful information, primarily in a business context.

data switch   a simplified version of a many-to-many concentrator.

data transmission   the production, movement, and delivery of computerized information over a transmission medium.

Datalink   Telecom Canada's digital circuit switching network.

Datapac   Telecom Canada's digital packet switching network.

Dataroute   Telecom Canada's dedicated digital data network.

datascope   a device for monitoring and displaying data transmission signals in character form, including control signals and timing relationships in full-duplex mode.

debugging   the art of diagnosing and correcting problems in a computer program.

directory routing   network routing based on routing tables maintained at Network Control Centers.

distributed database   a logical collection of data physically located in different nodes.

DMS-100   a digital switching system used as a Central Office (manufactured by Northern Telecom).

emulate   the ability of a terminal to imitate another terminal or the ability of a PC to imitate a terminal.

Envoy 100   Telecom Canada's electronic message service.

Ethernet   A Local Area Network using CSMA/CD protocol and coaxial cable for baseband communication.

fiber optics   a technology that uses light as a digital information carrier.

flooding   a routing method employing the transmission of multiple copies of the same packet.

fourth generation language   a productivity tool used to speed up applications development, reduce maintenance, and provide a user-friendly environment for end-user programming.

frequency   (of a repetitious signal) is the number of complete waveforms or cycles of that signal per unit of time.

frequency modulation   a method of transmitting a signal by modulating it on the basis of carrier frequencies.

front-end processor   a communications node designed to handle the communications functions for a mainframe or minicomputer.

full-duplex circuit   a circuit capable of transmitting in both directions at the same time.

full-duplex protocol   a protocol that permits data transmission between two nodes to occur in both directions at the same time.

gateway   a device for connecting two networks that use different protocol.

half-duplex circuit a circuit capable of transmitting in either direction but in only one direction at a time.

half-duplex protocol a protocol that allows data transmission between two nodes to occur in one direction at a time.

heterogeneous DDBMS consists of at least two different DBMSs.

homogeneous DDBMS consists of the same DBMS at each site.

hot standby a backup computer in an immediate state of readiness.

iNET 2000 Telecom Canada's database access network.

Infodata CNCP's dedicated digital data network

Infoexchange CNCP's digital circuit switching network.

Infoswitch CNCP's digital packet switching network.

interrupt-driven a process in which stations request service from a central node.

jumpering the direct interconnection of two or more communications lines.

junction a network node which connects at least two other nodes to the network. Junctions may be modems or control nodes.

local area network a network which is restricted to a building or contiguous buildings.

Mach III CNCP's integrated network.

medium the physical path between nodes of a network.

metropolitan area network a group of Local Area Networks connected together by gateways.

modem a network junction used to transmit data over the telephone system.

modulation the process of converting an information signal into a form suitable for analog transmission.

multiplexer a device that combines inputs from terminals, computer ports or other multiplexers for transmission over a single high speed line.

multipoint a communications line to which three or more nodes are connected.

multiport modem a modem which allows multiple terminal connection.

network a group of nodes connected by media.

network control center a computer that monitors and controls network operation.

node a connection point in a network which may be a termination (user node) or a junction (network node).

noise a random signal which tends to affect the performance of a network detrimentally.

null modem a cable which connects two DTEs together without the use of a modem.

optical fiber a communications medium made of plastic or glass used for the transmission of light signals.

packet   a sequence of bits including data, control, and error-checking information, arranged in a specific format.

packet switching   a technique that breaks a message up into packets that are individually addressed and that may be transmitted through a network via different routes.

partitioning   (of a database) division of a database into parts which are allocated geographically or functionally to specific nodes.

period   (of a repetitious signal) a measure of the time taken to generate one cycle.

phase angle   the displacement between two sine waves of equal amplitude and equal frequency.

phase modulation   a method of transmitting information by modulating on the basis of carrier phases.

polling   a process in which a central node, using a predefined sequence, invites termination nodes to transmit.

protocol converter   a device which converts a terminal's protocol to a mainframe's protocol (and vice-versa) and acts as a concentrator.

replication   (of a database) a process of providing copies of key data files at each site.

self-reconfiguring   the ability of a terminal to emulate other terminals.

signal   the form that information takes when it is produced, moved, and delivered in a network.

simplex   a circuit capable of transmitting in one direction only.

sine wave   a repetitious signal commonly generated by electronic equipment whose magnitude varies in exactly the same way as the geometric function sine.

SP-1   an analog switching system used as a Central Office (manufactured by Northern Telecom).

telecommunications   the process of sending and receiving information electronically.

termination   a user network node such as a terminal, personal computer, minicomputer or mainframe computer.

token passing   the process of circulating a token, in a LAN, which grants access to each node in turn.

topology   the physical description of a network.

Transpac   the French public packet switching network.

transparency   a transmission mode which causes control codes imbedded in data to be ignored.

twisted pair   a communication medium consisting of two insulated wires wound round each other.

Tymstar   Tymnet's digital satellite network.

Venus-P   the Japanese international packet switching network.

virtual circuit   a logical bidirectional association between two DTEs.

volume shadowing   a security feature which automatically writes multiple copies of a record to multiple disks.

wide area network   a network which uses the telephone system to communicate over long distances.

APPENDIX C: ANSWER KEY

PRETEST

a-7   b-3   c-4   d-10   e-8   f-9   g-14   h-16
i-5   j-6   k-1   l-19   m-2   n-13   o-12   p-15
q-17   r-20   s-11   t-18

SECTION A

Chapter 1: answers to odd-numbered questions

1. no. of characters = $10 \times 50 \times 10 \times 6 = 30\,000$
   no. of bits = $30\,000 \times 8 = 240\,000$
   no. of seconds = $240\,000/4800 = 50$ secs

3. no. of unique codes = $2 \times (32 - 2) = 60$

5. communications control, format effector, information separator

7. half-duplex circuit

9. advantages of synchronous communication:
         higher speeds
         lower transmission overhead
         mainframe-to-mainframe communication

   advantages of asynchronous communication:
         lower cost
         simpler implementation
         micro-to-mainframe communication

11. permits transmission over larger distances with less signal degradation

Chapter 2: answers to odd-numbered questions

1. telephone system: dial-up and leased line analog transmission

   Message switching   electronic mail

   Special carriers   satellite systems

   PSDNs   packet switching

3. local loop is a two-wire connection
   trunk line is a four-wire connection

5. Medium   Advantage   Disadvantage

    twisted pair   inexpensive   susceptible
                        easy to install   to noise

    coax   voice video & data   single channel (baseband) re-
                                                 quires tuning (broadband)

    fiber optics   bandwidth   system modification

7. radio transmission requires repeaters every 50 km and is dependent on
    physical geography.
    satellite transmission operates over 1000 km with broad bandwidth and
    is subject to substantial delays.

Chapter 3: answers to odd-numbered questions

1. a-4   b-5   c-1   d-2   e-3

3. a) WY-75
    b) WY-75, VC4604
    c) CIT-101e
    d) CIT-101e, VC4604
    e) WY-75

Chapter 4: answers to odd-numbered questions

1. multiplexer   — frequency
    FEP   — communications controller
    NCC   — monitor
    modem   — DCE
    concentrator   — contention management
    protocol converter   — ASCII to BISYNC
    intelligent switch   — traffic cop

3.   300 — frequency
     1200 — phase
     9600 — QAM

5. monitoring
    alternate routing
    standby
    network statistics

Chapter 5: answers to odd-numbered questions

1.

connection	advantage	disadvantage
point-to-point	no polling or switching overhead	cost
multipoint	cost	underuse of terminals
circuit switching	cost	physical switching
message switching	logical switching	variable length data
packet switching	efficiency	not economical for low volume data

3. (a) star   (b) ring   (c) irregular mesh or point-to-point

5. ring — none
   star —table lookup
   bus —none
   tree —none
   loop — table lookup in control node

Chapter 6: answers to odd-numbered questions

1. a-2   b-5   c-2   d-2   e-1   f-6   g-2   h-1   i-4   j-6   k-3
   l-3   m-5   n-1   o-7

3. BISYNC — VRC/LRC
   DDCMP — CRC
   X.25 — CRC

5. a) sliding windows
   b) stop and wait
   c) sliding windows
   d) stop and wait

7. retry counter, timeout mechanism, ACK0/1

9. transparency

11. increased line utilization

13. source address, destination address, error handling

15. inject a second character with an F zone immediately following the data character. (all numeric characters contain a hexadecimal F in the zone portion of the EBCDIC code.)

17. a) clear request packet
    b) clear indication packet
    c) DCE clear confirmation

Chapter 7: answers to odd-numbered questions

1. dial-up and permanent lines.

3. for low volume of data, transmitted intermittently, circuit switching using dial-up on the telephone system is most efficient.

5. using repeater circuits to reshape the signal.

Chapter 8: answers to odd-numbered questions

1. the irregular topology of wide area networks versus the simple, symmetrical topologies of LANs.

3. failsafeness — the network will continue to operate when one node is down.

5. it temporarily restricts file access by other stations.

SECTION B

Chapter 9: answers to odd-numbered questions

1. decentralization and technological developments

3. simple concept / complex implementation

5. response, end-user control, flexibility, cost

Chapter 10: answers to odd-numbered questions

1. physical distribution, logical correlation

3. the user's ignorance of remote access

5. horizontal, vertical

Chapter 11: answers to odd-numbered questions

1. terminal emulation, asynchronous packages, asynchronous/synchronous conversion, electronic mail

3. async/sync protocol conversion
   ASCII/EBCDIC conversion
   keyboard differences
   video control

5. to store a softkey program

Chapter 12: answers to odd-numbered questions

1. functional distribution under central control

3. uses addresses and routing tables to connect nodes and control flow

5. a) Internets   b) Packetnets

7. Ethernet, X.25, SNA

SECTION C

Unit 7: Basic Worksheet, answers to odd-numbered questions

1. keyboard handling, remote device handling, display/print/store

3. a) PRINT FRE(0)   b) housecleaning

5.
```
10 CLS
20 LOCATE 12,30
30 PRINT "THIS IS THE CENTRE OF THE SCREEN";
40 LOCATE 13, 30
50 PRINT "THE CURSOR IS NOW IN POSITION";
60 ROW = CSRLIN
70 COL = POS(0)
80 PRINT ROW;", "COL;
90 LOCATE 14,30
100 PRINT "WHERE ROW IS THE ROW POSITION";
110 LOCATE 15,30
120 PRINT "AND COL IS THE COLUMN POSITION";
130 END
```

7. INPUT$ (LOC(1),#1)

INDEX